A CISO Guide to Cyber Resilience

A how-to guide for every CISO to build a
resilient security program

Debra Baker

A CISO Guide to Cyber Resilience

Group Product Manager: Pavan Ramchandani
Publishing Product Manager: Prachi Sawant
Book Project Manager: Ashwin Kharwa
Senior Editor: Divya Vijayan
Technical Editor: Arjun Varma
Copy Editor: Safis Editing
Proofreader: Divya Vijayan
Indexer: Tejal Daruwale Soni
Production Designer: Prafulla Nikalje
Senior DevRel Marketing Executive: Linda Pearlson
DevRel Marketing Coordinator: Marylou De Mello

First published: April 2024
Production reference: 1050424

Published by Packt Publishing Ltd.
Grosvenor House
11 St Paul's Square
Birmingham
B3 1RB, UK.

ISBN 978-1-83546-692-6
www.packtpub.com

To my parents, who always kept me on the right path and taught me the value of hard work and ethics. To my husband, Bill – I would not have been able to write this book without his love and support. To my children, who are always cheering me on.

– Debra Baker

Foreword

While CEO of RedSeal, Inc. in San Jose, California, I had the privilege of working with Debra Baker. RedSeal, a cyber security analytics company, had a robust business assessing the network risks of enterprises. Our many customers included large Fortune 500 companies as well as many US Government civilian agencies, branches of the armed services, and the IC. During this time, in the late 201X's, ransomware evolved to be the #1 attack on companies. It seems the bad guys had indeed found where the money was, and that was in ransoming data. Debra came to RedSeal with a mission in mind, and that mission was to secure the nation.

Debra has a wealth of knowledge, practical real-world experience, much hearty advice, and most importantly, a great way of communicating all that to me, to RedSeal, and to our customers. She rocks when it comes to certifications, of which there are too many to list. She was a sought-after expert in the RedSeal world. Ultimately, Debra was selected as one of the 10 Most Eminent Women Leaders in Security (2021), successfully completed several management programs with an emphasis on cybersecurity, and was eventually named among the "Top 100 Women in Cybersecurity." She, simply put, is one to be reckoned with if you are a cyber bad guy.

Cyber is ever-changing. Attacks are increasing in number and complexity. Their success rate is enough to still make the news. And the skills required to defend an organization remain scarce. To be able to discuss, understand, and ask the right questions in order to trust your cyber team and leadership is essential. Debra brings all that home in a way we all can understand. So, it was no surprise when she reached out to me about her book, *A CISO Guide to Cyber Resilience*. It made perfect sense that she, of all people, should share her experiences with us all through the printed word. If I had to commission someone to write such a book, Debra would be my first call.

A CISO Guide to Cyber Resilience is both a strategy and a tactics knowledge set. A former CISO herself, she gets the power of a policy and the intricacies of implementing it. She lays out in plain management English how to think about the data in your organization and how to protect it. She talks clearly about unencrypted data, phishing, malware, third-party vendor compromise, software vulnerabilities, unintended misconfigurations, and the many other things that contribute to an organization's vulnerability.

Cyber vulnerability is here to stay. Therefore, Debra's book, *A CISO Guide to Cyber Resilience*, is an invaluable resource for you, tattered corners and all. I highly recommend it to all managers of any organization.

Ray Rothrock
Former CEO, RedSeal
Author, Digital Resilience (2018)
Feb 7, 2024

Contributors

About the author

Debra Baker is a cybersecurity expert with over 30 years of experience. She began her career in the U.S. Air Force and has worked at IBM, Cisco, and Entrust DataCard. As President of TrustedCISO, she specializes in strategic cybersecurity, risk management, and compliance advisory services, helping clients navigate complex frameworks such as NIST, SOC2, ISO27001, FedRAMP, and StateRAMP. A CISSP and CCSP holder, Debra has a provisional patent for an AI-driven vendor assessment tool and founded Crypto Done Right. She's recognized as one of the top 100 Women in Cybersecurity.

About the reviewer

Jean-Luc Dupont is a seasoned Chief Information Security Officer with a proven track record in strengthening global corporations, especially in highly regulated industries. With over 25 years of experience in cybersecurity, he has served as a CISO for companies such as Kestra, American Credit Acceptance, IDEMIA, and Oberthur. He holds a Bachelor of Science in applied computing from Newcastle Polytechnic (UK) and a Master of Science from EPITA (France). His passion for cybersecurity extends beyond his professional duties to side projects such as Security Rabbits, a daily security digest, and his book *Secur-What?! Learning Cybersecurity from Mistakes*, Independently published.

Alex Bazay is the CISO of Align, a leading provider of cloud-based IT solutions for the financial industry. He oversees the security strategy, operations, and governance of the company's global network and data. Alex boasts over 25 years of experience in designing, implementing, and managing intricate IT infrastructures and security systems for hedge funds and asset managers, with multiple certifications in information systems auditing and security.

Alex excels in insider threat detection, network security, risk management, data center, and vulnerability management. He is passionate about protecting the integrity, confidentiality, and availability of his clients' data and assets and ensuring compliance with industry standards and regulations. Collaborating with a skilled and diverse team of security professionals, he partners with internal and external stakeholders to deliver innovative and effective solutions that address the evolving needs and challenges of the financial sector.

Table of Contents

Preface   xiii

Part 1: Attack on BigCo

1

The Attack on BigCo   3

BigCo – the attack	3	BigCo – the anatomy of an attack	9
BigCo – cross-team co-ordination	4	Summary	13
BigCo – recovery	8		

Part 2: Security Resilience: Getting the Basics Down

2

Identity and Access Management   17

Two-factor authentication and why you need it	17	Application security	23
Something you know	18	Password manager	25
Something you are	20	Quick reference	26
Something you have	21	Summary	27
Password complexity and NIST 800-63-3B	22		

3

Security Policies   29

Where are your policies,
and are they being used?   29

Compliance begins with laws
and regulations   32

Nortel hack   34

Importance of Due diligence   35

Summary   37

4

Security and Risk Management   39

What is risk management?   39

Identifying risks   40

Risk assessment   41

Monitoring your controls   47

Key performance indicators (KPIs)   48

Quick reference   49

Summary   50

5

Securing Your Endpoints   51

Antivirus/anti-malware   51

Virtual private network (VPN)   53

What is phishing?   53

Moving to remote work   55

LastPass hack   55

Testing your home firewall   56

Network access control (NAC)
and Zero Trust   56

Application firewall   57

Mirai botnet   57

Securing your browser   58

Turning on your application firewall   58

Okta hack   58

Quick reference for endpoint security   61

Summary   63

6

Data Safeguarding   65

Offline backups	65	Succession planning	73
Testing your backups	68	AWS DDOS attack	73
Cryptographic hashing	69	**Disaster recovery**	**74**
Availability in the cloud	71	Redundancy in architecture	75
Business continuity	71	Disaster recovery roles and responsibilities	75
Recovery time objective (RTO)	72	Testing disaster recovery	76
Recovery point objective (RPO)	72	**Summary**	**76**
Maximum tolerable downtime (MTD)	72		

7

Security Awareness Culture   77

Security awareness training is foundational	77	Governance and management	86
		Third-party involvement	86
Security is everyone's responsibility	84	**Security awareness training is mandatory and tracked**	**86**
Materiality assessment	85		
Disclosure requirements	85		

8

Vulnerability Management   89

What are software vulnerabilities?	89	CVE, CWE, and KEV	93
Common Vulnerabilities and Exposures	90	What we're up against	93
What is the NIST definition of software vulnerabilities?	90	**Prioritizing your remediations**	**94**
CVSS	91	CISA's KEV Catalog	94
Common Weakness Enumeration	92	CVSS metric – Attack Vector	95
Known Exploited Vulnerabilities	93	CVSS metric – Attack Complexity	97

CVSS metric – Privileges Required   97
CVE priority   98
Starting with vulnerability scans   98
Making it fun   98
In the cloud   98

Securing your code   **99**

IaC   99
SAST   99
DAST   100
IAST   100
Software composition analysis   101
OWASP   101

Summary   **104**

9

Asset Inventory   105

Asset inventory   **105**
Identifying your assets   106
What is the NIST definition of
asset inventory?   106
Automating your asset inventory   107

Change management   **107**
NIST security-focused change management   108
Phase 1 – Planning   108

Phase 2 – Identifying and
implementing configurations   109
Phase 3 – Controlling configuration changes   110
Phase 4 – Monitoring   111

Mobile device management (MDM)   **111**
Knowing your network   **112**
Quick reference for asset management   112

Summary   **114**

10

Data Protection   115

Encrypt your data!   **115**
Introduction to encryption   116
History of encryption   116
Encryption basics   116
Encrypted data means there is no breach!   117

What is PII? It depends…   **118**
NIST's definition of PII   119

Third-party risk management   **123**
SolarWinds attack   124

Vendor management policy   124
Vendor management contract clauses   124
Critical vendors   125
Train your staff   126
Vendor risk rating   126
Data loss protection   126
Insider threats – the hidden danger   127
Quick reference for data protection   127

Summary   **130**

Part 3: Security Resilience: Taking Your Security Program to the Next Level

11

Taking Your Endpoint Security to the Next Level   133

Endpoint detection and response (EDR) – Focusing on the "R"   133

Managed detection and response (MDR)   134

Extended detection and response (XDR)   135

SOAR   135

Cloud security posture management (CSPM)/Cloud-native application protection program (CNAPP)   136

What is CSPM/CNAPP?   136

Zero trust vs. software-defined perimeter   138

How a typical TLS session works   139

What is mutual authentication?   140

DNS protection   146

What do DNS protections provide?   146

Quick reference for zero trust   146

Summary   155

12

Secure Configuration Baseline   157

Security baseline   157

What compliance does your company have to meet?   158

System and Organizational Controls (SOC) 2   160

International Standard Organization (ISO) 27001   161

North American Electric Reliability Corporation Critical Infrastructure Protection (NERC-CIP)   161

Cybersecurity Maturity Model Certification (CMMC)   162

NIST 800-171 vs. CMMC   164

SOC 1   164

Sarbanes-Oxley Act (SOX)   164

Payment Card Industry Data Security Standard (PCI-DSS)   165

Health Insurance Portability and Accountability Act (HIPAA)   165

Health Information Technology for Economic and Clinical Health (HITECH)   166

HITRUST   166

NIST 800-53 – One framework to rule them all   167

Creating your security baseline   167

Quick reference for creating a security baseline   168

Summary   172

13

Classify Your Data and Assets   173

Start with your data	173	**Subnetting**	179
Shared Responsibility Model	176	**Segmentation**	179
Classifying your assets	177	Sony hack	180
Monitoring	178	Quick reference for securing critical assets	183
		Summary	186

14

Cyber Resilience in the Age of Artificial Intelligence (AI)   187

ChatGPT	188	**AI and cybersecurity – The good, the bad, and the ugly**	195
Securing ChatGPT	188		
What can go wrong with ChatGPT?	188	The good	195
Artificial intelligence (AI)	189	The bad	196
Machine learning (ML)	190	The ugly	197
Natural language processing (NLP)	190	**AI bias**	197
Deep learning (DL)	190	Systematic bias	198
Generative AI (Gen AI)	190	Statistical bias	198
What is responsible AI?	191	Human bias	199
EU AI Act	192	**NIST AI RMF**	199
Secure AI framework (SAIF)	193	**Summary**	202

Index   203

Other Books You May Enjoy   214

Preface

Greetings, fellow cybersecurity enthusiasts! Welcome to the world of cyber resilience, where the goal is to build a security program that enables your organization to not only withstand cyber-attacks but also to recover swiftly. As the United States Department of Homeland Security aptly defines it, cyber resiliency is the "*ability to resist, absorb, recover from or successfully adapt to adversity or a change in conditions.*"[1] It's not just a process; it's an ultimate state of readiness. An organization achieves resilience when it can bounce back from any disruption, be it a ransomware attack or any other cyber threat, without major disruptions.

In today's landscape, cyber-attacks are becoming increasingly sophisticated and prevalent. In the book *Big Breaches*[2], it is highlighted that the root causes of nearly every data breach can be traced to six key factors:

- Unencrypted data
- Phishing attacks
- Malware
- Third-party vendor compromise
- Software vulnerabilities
- Unintended misconfigurations

In this book, we will explore practical safeguards that you can implement immediately to defend against these root causes of data breaches. These safeguards will not only enhance your information security program but also make it cyber-resilient, ready to face the latest threats. We'll delve into some of the most significant cyber-attacks in recent history and discuss what could have been done to prevent or mitigate their impact. Most importantly, this book will guide you on how to transform your network into a cyber-resilient fortress, ensuring your organization's ability to recover swiftly from any cyber-attack.

This book takes you on a journey, partly fictional, where you'll witness a catastrophic cyber attack on BigCo and see how Megan, the **Chief Information Security Officer (CISO)**, responds decisively. Megan's actions will stop the attack, initiate responses, and put measures in place to prevent future attacks. As the saying goes, it's not a matter of *if* your company will be cyber-attacked, but *when*. *Chapters 1* to *10* will provide you with foundational tools to prepare for and respond to cyber-attacks.

---

1   (Schwien and Jamison)

2   (Daswani, 15)

Chapters 11 to *14* will elevate your company's IT security program to the next level of cyber resilience. You'll find step-by-step guidance on implementing the necessary safeguards in your security program, whether your organization is small, medium, or large. Each chapter focuses on a specific safeguard, and the good news is that the steps you'll learn here not only form the foundation of cyber defense but also assist your organization in meeting various compliance frameworks, standards, and laws while becoming cyber-resilient.

Who this book is for

This book is for CISOs, directors of information security, aspiring CISOs, and cybersecurity professionals at all levels who want to learn how to build a resilient security program. Cybersecurity professionals will uncover valuable insights for enhancing their strategic and operational roles. This book is crafted to serve the following key personas in the cybersecurity field:

- **Cybersecurity leaders and CISOs**: As a leader in cybersecurity, you are continuously navigating the evolving threat landscape. You have to balance organizational needs with the budget while defending from the latest threats. This book provides strategies to elevate your leadership by developing and implementing a comprehensive cyber-resilient information security program.

- **Cybersecurity practitioners**: Whether you are delving into the cybersecurity arena or looking to deepen your existing expertise, this guide offers a wealth of practical knowledge. From important safeguards to effective risk management techniques, you will gain skills to understand a more holistic view of cybersecurity as well as fortify your role and progress in your career trajectory.

- **IT professionals and support staff**: Often the first line of defense in an organization, your role is crucial in maintaining cyber hygiene and resilience. This book equips you with an understanding of common and emerging threats, as well as best practices in response and recovery procedures. Enhance your capabilities in supporting cybersecurity initiatives and excel in roles focused on maintaining organizational cybersecurity.

Each chapter of the *CISO Guide to Cyber Resilience* includes real-world examples, actionable recommendations, and distilled wisdom from my extensive experience in the field. This book is more than a guide; it's a companion in your journey toward mastering cyber resilience.

What this book covers

Chapter 1, The Attack on BigCo, explains a ransomware attack on a fictional company, what worked to limit the damage, and how they recovered. It explains what ransomware is, how it can bring down a network, and how to recover.

Chapter 2, Identity and Access Management, explains that 99.99% of account attacks can be prevented by using **two-factor authentication** (**2FA**). It also includes a discussion on methods to use for 2FA and password managers, as well as how NIST 160-3 can be successfully utilized.

Chapter 3, Security Policies, explains that security policies are foundational to guide your organization's security program. It covers how your security policies meet laws and regulations, and the importance of due diligence.

Chapter 4, Security and Risk Management, explains that security and risk management is the process of balancing cyber risks, the controls to thwart attacks, and the budget. Business is about making money. Security and risk management is the process of choosing the controls that work for your company's budget. Your company can't be 100% secure, nor can there be 0% risk. Security is a balance of what is most important, what can wait, and what risks are acceptable to your business.

Chapter 5, Secure Your Endpoints, talks about securing your endpoints. At a very basic level, you need an antivirus. Endpoint security has evolved. For getting the basics down, we'll talk about antivirus and anti-malware. In addition, we will discuss testing your home firewall to ensure it is configured properly.

Chapter 6, Data Safeguarding, explains that good backups are critical. More importantly, ensuring *offline* backups is paramount to secure your company's data. We will be discussing the importance of testing backups, leveraging the cloud, and business continuity.

Chapter 7, Security Awareness Culture, explains the importance of developing a security awareness culture. No matter what tools and security controls you have deployed, you still need security awareness training for everyone in your company.

Chapter 8, Vulnerability Management, explains the importance of vulnerability scanning and patching security vulnerabilities. If you stay up to date with the latest threats, you will understand that it's not easy to keep up with patching all those thousands of vulnerabilities. We'll be discussing practical strategies to prioritize vulnerability patching, as well as ensuring your source code is secure.

Chapter 9, Asset Inventory, explains the importance of creating an asset inventory. To know what to protect, you have to understand what assets you have, whether they are software, hardware, or ephemeral. An asset inventory is foundational in a cyber-resilient organization. We'll also discuss mobile device management and knowing your network.

Chapter 10, Data Protection, explains the importance of encrypting your company's data, whether in transit or at rest. The reason is that if an attacker can gain access to your network or even steal an employee's laptop, if the data is encrypted, then the data is protected. The most amazing part is that there is no breach if the data stolen is encrypted.

Chapter 11, Taking Your Endpoint Security to the Next Level, explains the importance of moving past the basics and into more advanced safeguards. The latest antivirus is called **Endpoint Detection and Response (EDR)**. It takes the traditional antivirus to the next level. Some even include 24/7 helpdesk support, also known as **Managed Detection Response (MDR)**. We'll also demystify **Extended Detection Response (XDR)**, **Cloud Security Posture Management (CSPM)**, and the **Cloud Native Application Protection Program (CNAPP)**.

Chapter 12, Secure Configuration Baseline, explains the importance of creating a security baseline. Essentially, this is a configuration that is applied across devices, hosts, and the cloud. For the commercial space, the **Center for Internet Security (CIS)** is typically used, whereas for the federal government, it's STIGS.

Chapter 13, Classify Your Data and Assets, explains the importance of classifying your data and assets. A fully developed, mature, advanced information security program has an asset inventory and has classified those specific assets with sensitive data as critical.

Chapter 14, Cyber Resilience in the Age of Artificial Intelligence (AI), explains the importance of cyber resilience in the age of AI. With the rush to use and deploy AI, there are new cybersecurity concerns such as data leakage, use of AI by hackers, and bias in AI. This chapter will discuss responsible AI and measures to take to ensure your company deploys AI in a safe manner.

To get the most out of this book

It is good to have a basic understanding of information security and the cloud before reading this book. I will explain each concept and each chapter builds on the previous, providing a roadmap of how to build a resilient cybersecurity program.

Download templates and the roadmap to cyber resilience

You can download the following templates and my roadmap to cyber resilience from my TrustedCISO website (`https://trustedciso.com/e-landing-page/ciso-guide-to-cyber-resilience/`):

- *CISO Guide to Cyber Resilience*
- Software evaluation template
- Encryption template

Conventions used

There are a number of text conventions used throughout this book.

Bold: Indicates an important word(s), command, topic, or title. For example, words that need to be taken into consideration such as this example: ">**nslookup google.com**"

Italics: emphasizing an important word or topic. An example is "This is a big caution. I can't recommend *not* using a complex password."

> **Tips or important notes**
> Appear like this.

Get in touch

Feedback from our readers is always welcome.

General feedback: If you have questions about any aspect of this book, mention the book title in the subject of your message and email us at customercare@packtpub.com.

Errata: Although we have taken every care to ensure the accuracy of our content, mistakes do happen. If you have found a mistake in this book, we would be grateful if you would report this to us. Please visit www.packtpub.com/support/errata, select your book, click on the Errata Submission Form link, and enter the details.

Piracy: If you come across any illegal copies of our works in any form on the Internet, we would be grateful if you would provide us with the location address or website name. Please contact us at copyright@packt.com with a link to the material.

If you are interested in becoming an author: If there is a topic that you have expertise in and you are interested in either writing or contributing to a book, please visit authors.packtpub.com.

Reviews

Please leave a review. Once you have read and used this book, why not leave a review on the site that you purchased it from? Potential readers can then see and use your unbiased opinion to make purchase decisions, we at Packt can understand what you think about our products, and our authors can see your feedback on their book. Thank you!

For more information about Packt, please visit packtpub.com.

Share Your Thoughts

Once you've read *A CISO Guide to Cyber Resilience*, we'd love to hear your thoughts! Scan the QR code below to go straight to the Amazon review page for this book and share your feedback.

https://packt.link/r/1835466923

Your review is important to us and the tech community and will help us make sure we're delivering excellent quality content.

Download a free PDF copy of this book

Thanks for purchasing this book!

Do you like to read on the go but are unable to carry your print books everywhere?

Is your e-book purchase not compatible with the device of your choice?

Don't worry!, Now with every Packt book, you get a DRM-free PDF version of that book at no cost.

Read anywhere, any place, on any device. Search, copy, and paste code from your favorite technical books directly into your application.

The perks don't stop there, you can get exclusive access to discounts, newsletters, and great free content in your inbox daily

Follow these simple steps to get the benefits:

1. Scan the QR code or visit the following link:

https://packt.link/free-ebook/9781835466926

2. Submit your proof of purchase.
3. That's it! We'll send your free PDF and other benefits to your email directly.

Part 1:
Attack on BigCo

In this part, you will follow a fictional company called *BigCo* as it undergoes a ransomware attack. You'll get to see firsthand how Megan, BigCo's CISO, leads the company through the attack and how it recovers. You'll learn how to limit the damage caused by these kinds of attacks, mastering what ransomware is and how it can take down a network. Most importantly, you'll see how to prepare for and recover from a ransomware attack.

This section contains the following chapter:

- *Chapter 1, The Attack on BigCo*

1
The Attack on BigCo

This chapter is fictional and based on a horrendous cyber-attack on BigCo and how Megan, the **Chief Information Security Officer** (**CISO**), responds. Megan will decisively stop, respond, and put measures into place that will help prevent another attack. As the saying goes, it's not if your company will be cyber-attacked; it's when. By the end of this chapter, you will understand how the hackers gained access to BigCo's network, how the ransomware was deployed, and the measures that were taken in order to make the network resilient.

In this chapter, we're going to cover the following main topics:

- BigCo – the attack
- BigCo – cross-team co-ordination
- BigCo – recovery
- BigCo – the anatomy of a ransomware attack

BigCo – the attack

Megan, the **Chief Information Security Officer** (**CISO**) of a multi-national corporation, gets the call at 3:00 AM about major sections of her company BigCo's network being down. The CISO is responsible for the cybersecurity of the company, ensuring compliance, risk management, and sufficient defenses are in place. It's the highest-level position in cybersecurity. It can be at the Director level, Vice President, or directly under the CEO, depending on the importance of cybersecurity within an organization. Megan is a Director of Information Security at BigCo with the title of CISO, and she reports to the **Chief Information Officer** (**CIO**). Typically, the CIO will exist over the information technology and information security departments. In this case, Megan reports to the CIO, Mark.

Megan knows getting a call at 3:00 AM means this outage must be bad because she typically wouldn't be called in the middle of the night for a typical network outage. First, she quietly gets up so as not to wake her partner. She goes to her home office and calls Mark, the CIO of BigCo. Megan says, "Mark, hi. What happened?" Mark replies, "Well, from what we can tell, it wasn't a bogus email link like last time." "The new security awareness program you introduced is working as well as the email phishing campaign and email filtering tool we deployed. Honestly, we aren't exactly sure how the attackers got in yet. Headquarters and three of five major data centers are down. Our human resources data and much of our critical **personally identifiable information (PII)** data, which includes sensitive details such as names, addresses, and social security numbers of both employees and customers, for both employee and customer data have been encrypted."

Megan replies with, "Ugh." She takes a deep breath in for 1, 2, 3, and holds for 3, and then breathes out for 1, 2, 3, 4, and 5. She says, "Okay, it sounds like a ransomware attack. Well, we have good backups, right? What have we lost 6 hours or…" Mark interrupts, "Well some of the backup servers were encrypted also. We have them set up as online backups and the problem with this ransomware is that it encrypts all attached USB drives and mapped drives." Megan replies, "Sh**. We must immediately isolate the subnets affected so that the ransomware is unable to propagate through the network. Also, unplug any affected devices, so they can't propagate to unaffected devices. It can take hours for ransomware to propagate, so we may be able to halt some of the damage. Quick! Call the IT department director and let them know." Mark replies, "Sure, I'm on it." Megan replies, "Okay."

Megan says, "Let's call an emergency meeting with all of the department heads from InfoSec, IT, and SecOps first thing in the morning so we can get aligned. We need to know where we are and what steps to take next. Oh man, I wish we had gotten the **endpoint detection response (EDR)** deployment completed." Mark replies, "Actually, we were alerted by some hosts where the new EDR had been deployed. Yeah, the subnets where it was deployed were not affected." Megan replies, "Well, that's some good news, I guess. It also shows due diligence; we were working on the deployment. Oh, and we just signed a cyber-insurance policy." She lets out a deep breath. Mark replies, "Yes!" Megan continues, "We'll probably be hearing from the attackers soon. Some more advanced ransomware attackers will steal your data prior to launching the attack to ensure a payout." Mark replies, "What? Really, this is not what we need right now. Now we are looking at potential lawsuits and fines." Megan replies, "Yep! Let's get Legal involved and activate our incident response retainer. We'll also need to co-ordinate with our insurance company to check on our cyber insurance coverage. Mark replies, "I'm on it."

BigCo – cross-team co-ordination

Mark begins, "Thanks to all the leaders from the networking, infosec, and security ops teams for being able to make it to this meeting. You've probably already heard that BigCo is the victim of a ransomware attack. Currently, headquarters and three of the five major data centers are down. Our human resources data and much of our critical PII data for both employees and customers have been encrypted. We do have mostly good backups and, of course, we have backups at our disaster recovery site in case any online backups have been encrypted. There were also some online backups that were encrypted. To avoid this from happening, backups need to be offline or done intermittently since online mapped drives will also be encrypted by ransomware. Whether it is a USB drive or a cloud drive, any online connected drives will be encrypted by ransomware." Megan says, "I'm glad we invested in that disaster recovery as a service last year." Mark continues, "The network teams have been shutting down routers so that infected workstations can't self-propagate the ransomware to other subnets. The teams responsible for maintaining the hosts and servers have been working through the night trying to either turn off infected hosts and servers or begin restoring from backup." The Network Manager, Dave Brown, asks, "With COVID-19, most of our employees are working from home, so how have they been affected?" Mark replies, "Luckily, because they are on separate subnets on their home networks, they have been largely unaffected. The way they have been affected is that a server they might be trying to access may be down. A few remote employees' computers were infected when they tried to go to a shared resource using NetBios, which has been infected. The other good news is that since we are running Office 365 in the Azure cloud, email and other documents stored in Azure are unaffected. Kudos to Megan for getting the endpoint protection software deployed. We were mid deployment, but the good news is where had deployed it; these hosts and servers were protected. We discovered the ransomware infection from an alert from one of these EDR protected endpoints."

Megan begins, "I received a call from a ransomware group that wants us to pay a USD 10 million ransom in Bitcoin. This is typical for ransomware gangs now. They will steal your PII data before they launch the ransomware attack. By doing this, they ensure that the ransom is paid even if you have good backups. I have contacted the FBI to help us to deal with this situation. I'm also talking to a company that specializes in incident response and am negotiating with ransomware groups. In general, law enforcement does not want us to pay the ransom. But, in some circumstances, it makes sense. In many cases the ransom can be negotiated down to a lower price. I remember with the Colonial Pipeline ransomware attack a few years ago, the FBI was able to hack and get the ransom that was paid back from the ransomware gang. We are definitely following law enforcement's lead regarding the next steps and we are dealing with the ransomware gang. Now, since we have good offline backups, we'll continue to restore the hosts and servers from backup. The ransomware gang is threatening to dump the stolen PII data onto the dark web. This will cause not only privacy and security concerns for our employees and customers but will be damaging for BigCo's reputation. This is another reason we brought in the FBI and are talking to a specialized incident response firm experienced in dealing with ransom attacks and these gangs. Although law enforcement, in general, advises not to pay the ransom, sometimes, it makes sense. The reason is that it ensures the safety and security of our customer and employee data." Nate, the Director of IT, interjects, "But what if they don't have our PII data? What if they are bluffing?" Megan responds, "Yes, you are correct; there is a chance that they did not steal our PII data. We should be able to ask for proof that they have the data. We can ask for a sample of the data they claim they have. Let us see how the FBI wants us to respond. Now, the downside is if you pay the ransom, there is a tendency for these ransomware groups to come back and hit the same company." Nate injects, "You mean the ransomware gangs hit the same company multiple times to get the ransomware payment"? Megan replies, "Yes, the same company will get attacked by the same ransomware gang multiple times. I have a meeting set up with the FBI and the incident response firm right after this meeting. Unless you have something urgent where you can't attend this afternoon's call, please be available. Of course, responding to this ransomware attack and dealing with the ransomware gang is everyone's highest priority."

Figure 1.1 illustrates the more sophisticated ransomware attack, where the attackers gain access to the corporate network and maneuver their way around to find high-value data such as human resources PII on all employee data. Hackers are typically looking for databases with source code, intellectual property, and PII data. Essentially, any data that your company would pay to get back and not want sold on the dark web.

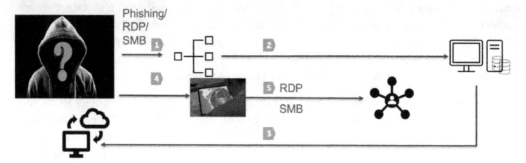

Figure 1.1 – Ransomware attack

Step 1 is how most hackers gain access to a corporate network: email phishing, RDP, or SMB. Phishing is where an attacker crafts an email with either malware attached or a link to a server that will download malware. **Remote desktop (RDP)** is commonly used to remotely access another desktop. It uses TCP port 3389. When you configure it, you need to use two-factor authentication (X.509 certificate, Microsoft Authenticator, or Google Authenticator) along with a complex 14-character password. Ensure RDP is disabled and only enabled for specific users as needed. Moreover, privileged accounts should never be able to RDP directly to a server. They should use a jump station. Ideally, add VPN access to avoid direct access to RDP from the internet. **Server message block (SMB)** is used to access shared resources such as printers, files, and serial ports on the network. SMB (ports 139, 445) should be secured by the following:

- Blocking ports 139 and 445 on perimeter firewalls
- Use a VPN
- Implement filtered VLANs to isolate internal network traffic
- Use Mac address filtering

Steps 2 and *3* illustrate that hackers have found the sensitive data they want to steal and have exfiltrated it offsite (*Step 3*).

Step 4 illustrates the deployment of ransomware onto the network.

Step 5 shows the ransomware self-propagating over RDP and SMB, infecting other computers on the network.

Megan begins the meeting by introducing FBI Agent Smith. Megan says, "Thank you everyone for making this meeting. Agent Smith is our assigned FBI Agent who is experienced in dealing with ransomware gangs and negotiations. Agent Smith, over to you." Agent Smith replies, "Thank you Megan. I am so glad BigCo reached out to the FBI. Dealing with these international ransomware gangs is tricky. You need our help in this. There is a trend where the attackers will find an entry point into your network using insecure RDP, SMB, or email phishing attempts. Once the attackers gain access to your network, they will quietly traverse through it. I say quietly because if their movements on your network are not carried out in such a way, then your **IDS, IPS, and SIEM** will alert you that something is wrong. In doing this, the hacker will search for the PII data on your network. This can be human resources data or customer data. Typically, they are looking for databases that can be compromised. The more sensitive and important the data that are exfiltrated are, then the more likely BigCo will pay the ransom to ensure that it is not leaked onto the dark web. Once the hackers find that database with the PII data, they will compromise it, gain administrator privileges, and then export the data. Again, very quietly, they will exfiltrate the data offsite to a server controlled by the hacker. Once they have secured copies of your data, they will deploy the ransomware. This way, even if you have good offline backups, you still must pay the ransom." Agent Smith continues, "The ransomware gangs know that once the data are released on the dark web, it opens the company up to more fines such as the EU **General Data Protection Regulation** (**GDPR**). GDPR fines can go up to 4% of the company's annual revenue, with a maximum of EUR 20 million, and these ransomware gangs know it. Also, we have to notify the EU about the breach within 72 hours. Recently we saw this with the CyrusOne breach, where the ransomware gang REvil posted on a dark web forum that they had gained access to the CyrusOne network and would sell their data to their competitors or post it on the dark web. The REvil gang even mentioned GDPR fines."

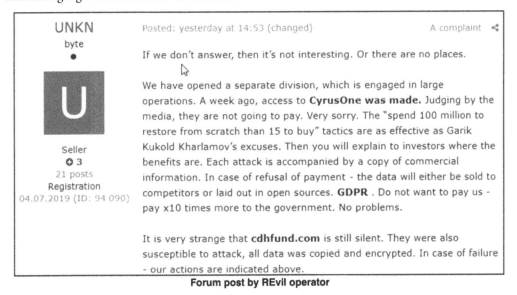

Forum post by REvil operator

Figure 1.2 – REvil dark web post on CyrusOne[1]

---

1   Courtesy of BleepingComputer: https://www.bleepingcomputer.com/news/security/another-ransomware-will-now-publish-victims-data-if-not-paid/

Agent Smith continues, "Law enforcement recommends not to pay the ransom. In some situations, we will recommend the company pay the ransom to get the systems up quickly and avoid sensitive data from being released. You must understand that most companies only get 61% of their data decrypted even if they pay the ransom.[2] I worked on the Colonial Pipeline hack, and the FBI was fortunate enough to be able to recover USD 2.3 million of the bitcoin that was paid to the ransomware gang.[3] Do you remember that time in 2021 when there were long gas lines and it ended up being related to the Colonial Pipeline ransomware attack? It was all over the news. With the supply chain shortages, most people have heard of it. The breach was so bad that Colonial had to take the pipeline offline. The day Colonial realized their network had been breached, they paid the ransom which was USD 4.4 million in bitcoin. The pipeline was offline for 6 days. The only bright side was that the FBI recovered 52% of the ransom."

Megan asks, "In BigCo's case, what do you suggest? Should we pay the ransom?" Agent Smith responds, "In BigCo's case, I think we should negotiate the ransom down. The original ransom was much higher for Colonial Pipeline, and we negotiated it down the ransom down considerably." Megan replies, "Okay, sounds good. What are our next steps?" Agent Smith continues, "At this point, I'll work with the ransomware incident response firm you are contracted with to begin negotiations with the REvil ransomware group. I'll be in constant contact; well, as much as I can be from here on out. I'll provide you with hourly updates as to our progress. Many times, it takes 12 hours to get a response from a ransomware gang. They want you to sweat and be ready to pay once they respond."

BigCo – recovery

Later in the day, Megan gives Mark, the BigCo CIO, a call. Mark answers the phone. "Hello Megan, how are you?" Megan replies, "Hi, Mark. Well, I'm a lot better knowing that we finally got all the affected systems recovered or restored from backup. Mark replies, "Yes, that was a tough few days, but we did it. Finally, the network is back up and operational. When the ransomware was propagating, we shut down the routers on the affected subnets so that the ransomware could not self-propagate." Megan says, "I think we were very fortunate to have been able to recover 100% of our data between paying the ransom and our good backups. Mark replies, "Yes, and the **endpoint protection** (**EPP**) software deployment has been escalated so that it will be rolled out to all datacenters and employee laptops by the end of the month." Megan replies, "We've completed our proof of concept of a segmentation solution and are now focused on getting it installed, deployed, and up and running. We've co-ordinated with the network and security teams to work closely on the deployment. Mark says, "Patching, operational

2   *The State of Ransomware 2022* - Assets.Sophos.Com., Sophos.Com, Sophos, 27 Apr. 2022, https://assets.sophos.com/X24WTUEQ/at/4zpw59pnkpxxnhfhgj9bxgj9/sophos-state-of-ransomware-2022-wp.pdf?hss_channel=lis-d8nusYzng6.

3   Kerner, Sean Michael. *Colonial Pipeline Hack Explained: Everything You Need to Know*. WhatIs.Com, TechTarget, 26 Apr. 2022, www.techtarget.com/whatis/feature/Colonial-Pipeline-hack-explained-Everything-you-need-to-know.

system maintenance, and the segmentation of the network are critical to ensure ransomware can't automatically propagate on the network. With a segmentation product, we can segment those subnets with critical assets as well as ones that have old machines and operating systems that can't be patched. By segmenting the network, ransomware can't propagate as easily. An unsegmented network is also called a flat network. The ransomware can easily self-propagate over RDP and SMB."

Megan says, "Back to the Basics, as I like to say. We will review our network inventory to ensure any old operating systems, especially pre-Windows 10, have been upgraded to ensure that SMB 3.0 is in use. Making sure SMB 1.0 is disabled is imperative to ensure the self-propagation can't occur." Megan continues, "For the cloud, we are deploying a **cloud-native application-protection program** (**CNAPP**) that will map our cloud environment and monitor the configurations and workloads. In this way, we can stay in compliance on a continual basis. This will help us maintain **PCI** compliance and stay compliant with other standards, such as SOC2 Type 2 and ISO 27001. Now, about that segmentation product I've been talking about. We have to get our high-value data secured on separate segmented subnets and monitored so that if a network change is made that allows access to one of these high-value subnets, we receive an alert. We must step up our company's cyber defenses." Marks says, "Yes, more than ever since these ransomware gangs like to attack the same companies again."

BigCo – the anatomy of an attack

In BigCo's case, it was determined that the ransomware gang found an unsecured RDP port 3389 open to the internet, which is how they gained access to the BigCo network. In the years prior to 2020, email phishing was the number one attack vector hackers used to gain access to a customer network. Email phishing is when you get a bogus email that either has a malware-infected file or image attached or includes a hyperlink to a website controlled by the hacker. Once you click on the link, your computer goes to the hacker's website and pulls down an infected file or malware. Companies have been vigilant in deploying email filtering solutions, so hackers have changed their tactics. By 2020, the number one attack vector was exploiting hosts with unsecured RDP port 3389s that were externally visible to the internet. How do attackers find these devices? Well, they use publicly available information from sites such as Shodan or Censys.io. In *Figure 1.3*, you can see a Censys.io search for RDP:

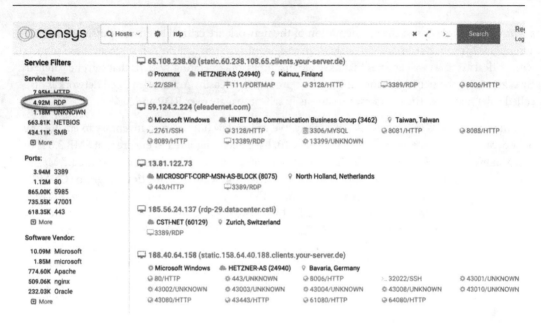

Figure 1.3 – Censys.io search for RDP open to the internet

You need to have an asset inventory and monitor the external devices on your internet. Hackers are targeting companies based on revenue and will leverage these publicly available assets. Ransomware will self-propagate to infect other computers on the same subnet by using SMB (ports 139 and 445) and RDP (port 3389).

Censys.io allows for several free searches for researchers each month. You can go out and query the domain of your company, such as www.cisco.com, and see what open ports exist, as well as the certificates, hosts, and devices on your company's domain that are externally visible to the internet. The great thing about Censys.io is that it queries the entire internet. When you query Censys.io, it just carries out a database query and not a real-time scan of your network. You don't have to be concerned about the sensors on your network going off. Censys.io has a free tool with which you can query your home network, and it will tell you if it is secure.

To find out what servers have an RDP port 3389 externally visible on the internet, a simple search on Censys.io of port 3389 can be done. I ran the query and found 3.8 million devices on the internet with port 3389 on the internet. Now, just having the ports externally visible doesn't mean that the server is at risk. If two-factor authentication and a strong password of 12 characters or more have been configured to secure RDP, then the risk is lowered. Ideally, a jump server with VPN access to hide RDP is recommended. In addition, as part of two-factor authentication, a certificate can be configured. See the chapter on *Authentication and Authorization* for more detailed information on passwords.

> **Important note**
>
> For each recommendation in this book, I will tell you what **basic** security means when you are first building out your security program, and you should consider this. **Moderate** means that as you build your security program, the next step is to provide more security. **Advanced** provides the highest level of security. For example, a startup would not want to use an advanced security product. For each suggested product, there are always two other choices. Do a search on the product type and Gartner magic quadrant. If a market for a product is rather new, then there may not be a magic quadrant yet; then, go to G2 to review customer ratings of similar products. Ideally, you should research two or more products. Include your team in the discussion of what products will be used. Ask your team if they have specific products that they have experience with and conduct proof of concept on at least one product. It's important to include your team in discussions so that they feel a part of the process. They will embrace the new product and process if they are involved.

You can use RDP if it's secured by using one or more of the following methods:

- Use **two-factor authentication** (**2FA**) with strong passwords

  - Software-based authentication token, i.e., Google Authenticator [**Basic**]

  - Okta provides single sign-on with 2FA [**Moderate**]

  - X.509 certificates [**Moderate**]

  - Smartcard (Yubikey, RSA) [**Advanced**]

- Limit privileged accounts that can log in remotely [**Basic**]

  - By default, on Windows machines, all Admins have RDP turned on

  - Turn off RDP for all administrators

  - Only assign RDP access to the specific, privileged accounts that need it

  - Use a jump station [**Moderate**]

  - Use a privileged access management solution [**Advanced**]

Now, the pendulum has swung back to where email phishing is again the top method of compromise. Even so, every company needs to review its external perimeter for open ports that can be exploited. Both email phishing and RDP should be addressed. To ensure your company has protected itself against email phishing, the following should be adhered to:

- Google Email Workspace includes email scanning and does a great job (included in subscription) [**Basic**]

- Email scanner

- Windows Defender for O365 (check the license because the basic level doesn't include email scanning) [**Basic**]

- Mimecast email scanner [**Moderate**]

- ProofPoint email scanner [**Advanced**]

- Cisco Email Scanning Agent (ESA) [**Advanced**]

- Abnormal Security [**Advanced**] utilizes artificial intelligence to identify malicious emails that other email security systems overlook.

- Security awareness training [**Basic**]

  - KnowBe4

  - SecurityNinja

- Email phishing campaign simulator [**Moderate**]

  - KnowBe4

  - SecurityNinja

As part of the security awareness training, you want to ensure you run phishing campaigns quarterly.

Other items to check to ensure your perimeter is secured:

- Review your firewall rules [**Basic**]

  - Have an official pen test at least annually
  - Review your firewall rules, especially those that are internet-connected

- Prioritized vulnerability management [**Moderate**]

  - Ensure critical devices are patched
  - Ensure internet-visible hosts are patched

- Run a scan on Censys.io of your perimeter [**Moderate**]

  - Identify any systems at risk
  - Identify any systems that are not documented
  - Reduce your internet footprint and remove systems that do not have to be internet-facing

Summary

Ransomware isn't going away anytime soon because the ransomware gangs are making so much money. In this chapter, we learned how attackers can gain access to your network and quietly move around in order to find the PII data on your network. It's imperative to ensure you have RDP and SMB secured. You need to deploy an email scanner to prevent phishing attempts. It's imperative to know the assets on your network and understand the assets with interfaces on the internet since hackers can easily search these open ports on sites such as Censys.io.

In the next chapter, we will be covering the importance of identification and authentication. When building out a security program, securing your passwords is paramount. We'll be covering how to prevent 99% of account attacks in the following chapter.

Part 2:
Security Resilience:
Getting the Basics Down

In this part, you will learn the fundamental policies and controls that need to be in place to secure your business. You will learn that multi-factor authentication can prevent 99% of account attacks. In addition, you'll learn the importance of security policies, due diligence, and security awareness, from the latest endpoint protection systems through to data protection. Through it all, you'll learn that security and risk management is the process of balancing cyber risks, the controls used to thwart attacks, and the budget. Your company can't be 100% secure nor can there ever be 0% risk. Security is about finding a balance of what is most important, what can wait, and what risks are acceptable to your business.

This section contains the following chapters:

- *Chapter 2, Identity and Access Management*
- *Chapter 3, Security Policies*
- *Chapter 4, Security and Risk Management*
- *Chapter 5, Secure Your Endpoints*
- *Chapter 6, Data Safeguarding*
- *Chapter 7, Security Awareness Culture*
- *Chapter 8, Vulnerability Management*
- *Chapter 9, Asset Inventory*
- *Chapter 10, Data Protection*

2
Identity and Access Management

This chapter is about identity and authentication. We will be discussing the importance of multi-factor authentication and why you need it. We'll cover NIST's new password requirements and why they have changed. Finally, we'll discuss how to ensure your passwords are secured using a password manager and are securely stored.

In this chapter, we're going to cover the following main topics:

- Two-factor authentication and why you need it
- Password complexity and NIST 800-63-3B
- Password manager

Two-factor authentication and why you need it

The importance of multi-factor authentication cannot be overstated. The CEO of True Digital Security, Rory Sanchez, stated that, "*Almost every phishing attack that we've seen could have been prevented with multifactor authentication.*"[1] If you are a data-driven person like myself, maybe this will convince you; Microsoft says that "*MFA can block over 99.9 percent of account compromise attacks.*"[2]

Typically, you log in with a username and password for most applications and websites. The best defense against account attacks is to use multi-factor authentication, also known as **two-factor authentication**

---

1   https://www.channelpronetwork.com/article/making-work-home-security-work

2   https://www.microsoft.com/security/blog/2019/08/20/one-simple-action-you-can-take-to-prevent-99-9-percent-of-account-attacks/

(**2FA**). Two-factor authentication means that in addition to the first form of authentication, a password, you use another form of authentication. This additional form of authentication may include the following:

- Something you know (a password or PIN code)
- Something you are (fingerprint, iris scan, face scan, or palm scan)
- Something you have (X.509 certificate, digital token, passkey, smart card, or mobile device)

The industry is moving away from passwords, referred to as passwordless, but this still is another form of multi-factor authentication. At the CyberCon 24 people were getting bent out of shape saying the industry is moving away from passwords which is true but passwordless using passkeys is still another form of MFA. Even when you setup passwordless, you still have a password.

Something you know

Passwords are typically used to secure your applications and websites. A password can be comprised of upper and lower case letters (A-Z), numbers (0–9), and special characters (!*#&). Did you know that a complex eight-character password can now be hacked in five minutes? Hive Systems does annual testing and reports on cracking passwords and the time it takes. In *Figure 2.1*, you can see that an eight-character password only using letters can be cracked instantly:

TIME IT TAKES A HACKER TO BRUTE FORCE YOUR PASSWORD IN 2023

Number of Characters	Numbers Only	Lowercase Letters	Upper and Lowercase Letters	Numbers, Upper and Lowercase Letters	Numbers, Upper and Lowercase Letters, Symbols
4	Instantly	Instantly	Instantly	Instantly	Instantly
5	Instantly	Instantly	Instantly	Instantly	Instantly
6	Instantly	Instantly	Instantly	Instantly	Instantly
7	Instantly	Instantly	1 sec	2 secs	4 secs
8	Instantly	Instantly	28 secs	2 mins	5 mins
9	Instantly	3 secs	24 mins	2 hours	6 hours
10	Instantly	1 min	21 hours	5 days	2 weeks
11	Instantly	32 mins	1 month	10 months	3 years
12	1 sec	14 hours	6 years	53 years	226 years
13	5 secs	2 weeks	332 years	3k years	15k years
14	52 secs	1 year	17k years	202k years	1m years
15	9 mins	27 years	898k years	12m years	77m years
16	1 hour	713 years	46m years	779m years	5bn years
17	14 hours	18k years	2bn years	48bn years	380bn years
18	6 days	481k years	126bn years	2tn years	26tn years

HIVE SYSTEMS   › Learn how we made this table at **hivesystems.io/password**

Figure 2.1 – Hive Systems password cracking

Source: Hive Systems – `https://www.hivesystems.io/password-table`.

If the attacker uses ChatGPT, then the times are even faster. For the first time, Hive Systems used ChatGPT to crack passwords. The password cracking times are significantly faster when using ChatGPT. The cracking of an eight-character password with upper and lower characters, numbers, and special characters can happen in one second versus five minutes. This means there is a need now more than ever for good password hygiene, such as long, complex passwords and using unique passwords for different applications and websites with multi-factor authentication:

USING CHATGPT HARDWARE TO BRUTE FORCE YOUR PASSWORD IN 2023

Number of Characters	Numbers Only	Lowercase Letters	Upper and Lowercase Letters	Numbers, Upper and Lowercase Letters	Numbers, Upper and Lowercase Letters, Symbols
4	Instantly	Instantly	Instantly	Instantly	Instantly
5	Instantly	Instantly	Instantly	Instantly	Instantly
6	Instantly	Instantly	Instantly	Instantly	Instantly
7	Instantly	Instantly	Instantly	Instantly	Instantly
8	Instantly	Instantly	Instantly	Instantly	1 secs
9	Instantly	Instantly	4 secs	21 secs	1 mins
10	Instantly	Instantly	4 mins	22 mins	1 hours
11	Instantly	6 secs	3 hours	22 hours	4 days
12	Instantly	2 mins	7 days	2 months	8 months
13	Instantly	1 hours	12 months	10 years	47 years
14	Instantly	1 days	52 years	608 years	3k years
15	2 secs	4 weeks	2k years	37k years	232k years
16	15 secs	2 years	140k years	2m years	16m years
17	3 mins	56 years	7m years	144m years	1bn years
18	26 mins	1k years	378m years	8bn years	79bn years

> Learn how we made this table at hivesystems.io/password

Figure 2.2 – ChatGPT password cracking

I recommend using a minimum of a 14-character password with upper and lower case letters plus one number and special character since it takes 3,000 years to crack even when using ChatGPT. For administrator and banking applications, I recommend using a minimum of 14 characters with upper and lower case letters, one number, and special characters since it takes 232,000 years to crack.

Something you are

"Something you are" refers to biometric characteristics unique to an individual. These are intrinsic attributes such as fingerprints, facial recognition, iris scans, palm scans, and voice recognition. I've only seen the iris scan in the movies. The fingerprint and face scan were originally introduced by Apple and are a great extra step in security for your phone and laptop. Biometric authentication leverages distinct physical or behavioral traits to verify an individual's identity. Due to the inherent uniqueness of these attributes, biometric systems offer a heightened level of security. However, it's crucial to handle biometric data with utmost care because, unlike passwords, biometrics cannot be changed if they are compromised. With advancements in technology, biometric authentication methods are becoming increasingly prevalent, particularly in devices such as smartphones and in high-security settings.

Artificial intelligence and biometrics

Biometrics have been made both more and less secure by **artificial intelligence** (**AI**). Let me explain: The security and accuracy of fingerprints, facial recognition, and voice recognition have been improved using machine learning. Using AI with facial recognition will create more accurate authentication methods.[3] AI can learn the depths, variations, and textures in order to make the biometric scan truly unique. AI can learn over time as a person's face changes. Maybe the person has lost or gained weight, or their face has changed with age. AI can recognize these subtle changes and adapt. AI can cross-reference a user's fingerprint with their face scan in order to reduce false positives and negatives. In addition, using AI with facial recognition will create more accurate authentication methods.[4]

While AI introduces significant advancements in biometric security, it also presents potential vulnerabilities. AI-powered biometric systems rely on machine learning models that, if not properly trained or secured, can be susceptible to adversarial attacks. Skilled adversaries can design input data, termed as adversarial examples, to deceive AI models. For instance, subtle, carefully crafted perturbations to a facial image, often imperceptible to the human eye, can cause an AI-driven facial recognition system to misclassify or falsely authenticate. Additionally, the vast amount of data required to train AI models introduces concerns regarding data privacy and the potential for unintentional biases. If training data are not diverse or representative, the biometric system could exhibit skewed accuracy rates across different demographic groups.

---

3   Joshi, Naveen. *Biometrics Is Smart, but AI Is Smarter. Here's Why: Artificial Intelligence AdvancedTech on Demand*, 1 Apr. 2019, http://www.allerin.com/blog/biometrics-is-smart-but-ai-is-smarter-heres-why.

4   Joshi, Naveen. *Biometrics Is Smart, but AI Is Smarter. Here's Why: Artificial Intelligence AdvancedTech on Demand*, 1 Apr. 2019, http://www.allerin.com/blog/biometrics-is-smart-but-ai-is-smarter-heres-why.

With the advent of Deepfakes, replicating biometrics is becoming more at risk. An example is Deepfakes being able to closely mimic voices and people's faces. The problem with it is that now, with social media and artificial intelligence, your voice and face can potentially be compromised. There are ways to secure the biometric data in a secure manner: "*We can use encryption, mask the replication keys and other methods. But we need to build algorithms with security in mind—ones that are hardened and protected, in a container that can't be accessed or compromised.*"[5]

Something you have

"Something you have" pertains to an object or device in a user's possession used for authentication purposes. This could range from a physical hardware token that generates **time-based one-time passwords** (**TOTPs**) to a smart card that contains an individual's cryptographic credentials, such as an X.509 certificate. Today, even smartphones can act as a "something you have" component, where they receive a one-time code via SMS or use an authenticator application to generate a code. This authentication method is especially protective because it requires an attacker to not only know a user's password but also to physically possess a specific device or object, thus adding a robust layer of security to the authentication process.

SMS is being used to share two-factor authentication, and OTP is not considered to be a secure method. Having said that, using SMS is better than not using it as a second factor. In 2021, Krebs on security wrote a great article titled *Can We Stop Pretending SMS Is Secure Now?*[6] In the article, Brian Krebs explains how a security researcher was able to pay a dark web service USD 16 in order to get all the texts of a particular person. Brian says it was "*sickeningly simple*". Another tactic is for the hacker to call up your cell phone carrier and trick the employee at the phone company to switch the SIM number so that the attacker gets all of your texts. SMS is still used primarily as an authentication method for many applications and websites. Ideally, you should use an authentication application such as Google Authenticator, Authy, or Microsoft Authenticator. Additionally, be careful with the OTP sign-on links you get sent to your phones and computers to authorize a login. Hackers are sending these, and people are quickly approving the login even if it wasn't them logging in. This can allow the hacker to gain control over their account by changing their password.

Passwordless is the new buzzword in authentication. Essentially, a unique public/ private key pair is generated, and the private key is stored on your device locally, ideally within a third-party password manager (Bitwarden, LastPass, or 1Password). The public key is stored on the website's key store. A password manager is a secure store for your passwords and will also generate a strong and unique password for each site. Google and Apple are offering passkeys, also known as Universal Authentication

5   O'Mara, Debra. *Deepfakes: New Path to Biometric Hacking?* Electrical Contractor Magazine. *Electrical Contractor*, 15 June 2019, http://www.ecmag.com/magazine/articles/article-detail/integrated-systems-deepfakes-new-path-biometric-hacking.

6   Krebs, Brian. *Can We Stop Pretending SMS Is Secure Now? Krebs on Security*, 16 Mar. 2021, krebsonsecurity.com/2021/03/can-we-stop-pretending-sms-is-secure-now/.

Framework (UAF)[7], as an alternative for logins. Once set up, your password manager will automatically launch and present signed data by the private key to the website that has the public key for login. You don't have to use a password in this case. I don't see passwords going away any time soon, but passwordless login is definitely a better alternative.

Password complexity and NIST 800-63-3B

You may have heard about the "new" NIST 800-63-3B password requirements and guidelines. I will cover the highlights of the new guidance for authenticators, where they got it right, and where to be cautious. It is important to highlight the major changes that have taken place and what they mean for individuals and businesses that use passwords to secure their data.

The NIST 800-63-3B guidelines for password management are the most recent version of password security standards from NIST. NIST 800-63-3B is a complete turnaround to what we typically think of as a secure password. You'll still hear people say the guidance is new, but it was released in June 2017. The IT Industry has been rather slow in implementing the new guidance into their products and applications. The guidelines provide more flexibility to users while maintaining security standards.

Traditionally, the longer and more complex a password, the harder it is to break. Looking at data on password cracking, you can see that complex passwords (meaning passwords with upper and lower case, special symbols, numbers, and letters are harder to crack, as can be seen in *Figures 2.1* and *2.2*. Complex passwords using upper and lower cases, numbers, and special characters with increasing length will be more difficult to crack. The problem is when you require users to create passwords that adhere to defined password complexity rules; the users typically create weaker passwords. The reason they create weaker passwords is that trying to remember a password made up of symbols, numbers, and upper and lower cases is difficult. When users are forced to create passwords that comply with these password complexity rules, they are more likely to create more easily breakable passwords. For example, take a dictionary word and simply replace the letter "O" with a number zero, the letter "L" with a number 1, or begin a word with a capital letter and end it with an exclamation point. The password cracking programs have known, breached passwords and dictionary words with common substitutions such as capitalized first letter and exclamations at the end. Forced password resets also contribute to users creating weak passwords.

The new NIST 800-63-3B guidelines emphasize the importance of **not** using complex passwords but focusing on using long passphrases instead. A passphrase is a sentence or several words strung together instead of a word. Since remembering complex passwords with upper and lower cases, numbers, and special characters can be difficult to recall, NIST is recommending using longer all-character passphrases in sentence form. If you think back to the *Something You Know* section, there is the password-cracking table. Passwords are definitely stronger when longer and more complex. Following NIST's guidance of

---

7   Strom, David. What Is Fido (Fast Identity Online)?: Definition from TechTarget. *Security*, TechTarget, 20 Mar. 2023, http://www.techtarget.com/searchsecurity/definition/FIDO-Fast-Identity-Online.

all characters, you would need to have a password of at least 16 characters since there is no complexity at all. This is a big caution. I can't recommend **not** using a complex password. A better solution is to use a sentence as a passphrase that is meaningful to you and make the first letter capital and last a special character such as a period, exclamation, or an asterisk. Once you think in terms of sentences you can see how a longer password is easier to create and remember. You should also add spaces or dashes between the words. An example of a strong password is I l0ve Country Music! You can check the strength of your password at `https://www.security.org/how-secure-is-my-password`. It's even better to have three or four unrelated words that mean something to you. The spaces are critical in adding more variation and strength to the password.

I totally disagree with the NIST guidance of including an eight-character password as acceptable. Now, with ChatGPT, your password needs to be much longer in length and complex. NIST got it right in recommending that two-factor authentication should be enabled and that passwords should never be reused. The new guidelines encourage using password storage tools such as password managers. The guidelines emphasize educating users about maintaining strong passwords and signaling them during account logins if their passwords do not meet the standard requirements.

NIST 800-63-3B does not want you to force a password change unless there is a known breach. If you force password changes frequently, research shows users will create a weak password.[8] I agree that fewer forced password changes are recommended, but I don't agree with no password change unless a breach happens. There could be a breach of the same password used on another site, but the user is unaware. I don't think you should force a password change every six weeks or quarterly. I do think a password change should be made at least annually in case of a breach, but the user is unaware. Now, depending on the governance that your organization must comply with, you must check with your compliance department. For example, PCI requires that passwords be changed every 90 days. If you aren't subject to PCI, then you probably could push out the forced change to 180 days or even once a year.

Application security

On the developer side, NIST 800-63-3B provides good recommendations as far as checking if a password has been compromised before allowing a user to use it and how to securely store the hash of the password. First of all, the guidelines do not want you to allow a user to store a password hint that could be accessible to an unauthenticated user. NIST also does not want you asking the user questions for authentication, such as, what is your first dog's name? Many applications and websites still use these types of personal questions for authentication. One of the problems with this is that if there is a breach where these answers have been stolen, then you will use the same one across different sites. Additionally, sometimes, people may put this information on their social media, such as what high school they attended. An attacker could use one of these compromised, reused answers to gain control of your account.

---

8   Cranor, Lorrie. Time to Rethink Mandatory Password Changes. *Federal Trade Commission*, 26 Mar. 2021, http://www.ftc.gov/policy/advocacy-research/tech-at-ftc/2016/03/time-rethink-mandatory-password-changes.

In addition, when a new password is entered by a user, the program should check it against dictionary words, weak passwords, and the *Have I Been Pwned* website before accepting the password. Ideally, you should rate the password so the user knows if it is strong or weak. You don't want to use repetitive letters or numbers for a password.

After a set number of incorrect logins, the application should lock the user out for a specified period of time. It is recommended to have at least a 15-minute lockout after five failed login attempts. NIST 800-63-3B allows for SMS to be used for out-of-band authentication, but beware, as I stated earlier, there are ways to compromise SMS.

When it comes to storing passwords, it's essential to keep them secure. One common way to do this is by hashing the password rather than storing it in plain text. This process involves converting the password into a cryptographic hash and then storing the hash instead of the actual password. When a user logs in, the password they enter is hashed again and compared with the stored hash. If they match, the user is allowed access.

NIST 800-63-3B has some guidance on how to securely store your password hashes. This way, hackers won't be able to break into your system easily. Additionally, it's imperative to ensure network devices and servers have strong passwords, and the password hash should be stored securely. Some of the secure password hashing algorithms are **Scrypt**, **Bcrypt**, **Argon2**, **PBKDF2**, and **Balloon**. Argon2 is memory hard and highly recommended. If your company has to meet FIPS 140, then use PBKDF2 with a minimum of 600,000 iterations.

These algorithms, such as **PBKDF2**, use a **password-based key derivation function** that uses a salted, iterative algorithm to derive a cryptographic key from a password. Argon2 is another password hashing algorithm designed to be resistant to attacks such as dictionary, brute-force, and precomputational attacks.

When implementing a key derivation function, it is important to use a one-way function that is approved and secure. The HMAC algorithm specified in FIPS 198-1 is recommended, as well as the **Secure Hash Algorithm 3 (SHA-3)**, which is outlined in FIPS 202.

NIST 800-63-3B also allows for several options, including **CMAC [SP800-38B]**, **Keccak Message Authentication Code (KMAC)**, **Customizable SHAKE (cSHAKE)**, and **ParallelHash [SP 800-185]**. To ensure maximum security, the output length of the key derivation function should be the same as the length of the one-way function output.

Additionally, a salt value of at least 32 bits in length must be used in conjunction with the key derivation function. The salt value should be selected randomly to reduce the likelihood of collisions among stored hashes. The salt value and the resulting hash must be stored securely for each subscriber using a secret authenticator.

The number of iterations used in the PBKDF2 function should be as large as performance allows, typically a minimum of 10,000 iterations per NIST 800-63B. With today's processors, the iterations should be a minimum of 600,000 iterations. It is also recommended that a second iteration of the key derivation function be performed that uses a secret salt value known only to the verifier. This salt value should be generated using an approved random bit generator and must provide at least 112 bits of security strength, as specified in SP 800-57 Part 1. The secret salt value should be stored separately from the hashed memorized secrets. Ideally, for high security, the secret salt value should be stored in a hardware security module. With this additional iteration, brute force attacks on the hashed memorized secrets are impractical as long as the secret salt value remains secret. The importance of high iterations is to make it so processor-intensive if a password database is stolen that the hackers cannot easily break the hashes to determine the passwords.

Your company should implement a security baseline that aligns with compliance requirements. We will cover security baselines in a later chapter. By doing so, you can ensure that your security policies are in line with regulatory requirements and best practices. Your entire company will have policies to follow to ensure consistency. In summary, by using secure password hashing algorithms and following NIST guidelines, you can keep your passwords secure and protect user data.

Password manager

I recommend using a password manager such as **Bitwarden**, **1Password**, or **LastPass**. By using one of these password storage applications, you can create individual strong and complex passwords for each application and website. You only have to remember the password manager's password. The password manager will also check the *Have I Been Pwned* (https://haveibeenpwned.com/) website to alert you if a password has been cracked and is posted on the dark web. You can check your email addresses and passwords on the site. A password manager is also a great way to securely store shared passwords. Ideally, you do not want to use shared passwords. There seem to always be some passwords that need to be shared within a team. These should be stored securely in a company-provided password manager and used sparingly. Ensure that these shared passwords are changed once a team member either moves to another department or leaves the company. This should be part of a formal process that your company follows to revoke access when an individual moves internally or leaves the company. If there is logic to your passwords, such as with I l0ve Country Music! and then I l0ve Rock and Roll!, then also change the logic when the team member leaves. Using individual accounts tied to a user identity is always the best course of action.

Quick reference

Ideally, your company's identification and authentication compliance should include the following:

- **Basic:**

  - Multi-factor authentication for every user

  - A 14+ character passphrase

  - Unique passwords

  - Password manager

- **Medium:**

  - Multi-factor authentication for every user

  - A 14+ character passphrase

  - Unique passwords

  - Passwordless

  - Context awareness

  - Password manager

- **Advanced:**

  - Multi-factor authentication for every user

  - A 14+ character passphrase

  - Unique passwords

  - Passwordless

  - Context awareness

  - Password manager

  - Device authentication

  - Hardware token

Summary

The NIST 800-63-3B guidelines have received a fair amount of criticism for contradicting the previous password guidelines imposed by NIST, such as password-expiration policies, using special characters, and complexity requirements. The guidelines have been criticized for allowing users to use passphrases as passwords without complexity, even though the strength of passwords based on characters only are technically weaker passwords. Even so, the guidelines do provide some good information. I recommend taking what is useful and marrying it with the latest information we have in order to secure your passwords.

In conclusion, using multi-factor authentication is imperative to prevent phishing and account attacks. The NIST 800-63-3B guidelines represent a move toward flexibility in password creation and emphasize education, but it is crucial to be cautious about where they may differ from previous password guidelines. The implementation of the guidelines should be a priority for technology companies and organizations to minimize the risk of data breaches through weak passwords, such as password123. However, it is crucial to weigh the risks associated with certain measures against the benefits they may provide. As such, it is important for businesses to revisit their password policies and ensure that they are in line with the latest guidelines and industry best practices.

In the next chapter, we will be covering security policies; when building a security program, security policies are one of the foundational building blocks. Where are the policies, and are they being used? If you don't have them, then creating a solid set of policies is essential.

3
Security Policies

This chapter is about security policies. I know it's not an exciting topic, but it is mandatory in building a solid information security program. We will be discussing how security policies meet the laws and regulations that are required by your industry. We'll cover the differences between policies, procedures, and guidelines. We'll discuss the fact that following your security policies shows due diligence. Finally, we'll discuss two major breaches and how policies played a role.

In this chapter, we're going to cover the following main topics:

- Where are your policies, and are they being used?
- Compliance begins with laws and regulations
- Importance of due diligence

Where are your policies, and are they being used?

One of your first tasks in building out an information security program is to review the company's information security policies. You need to ask the following questions:

- Where are the security policies?
- Are the policies being followed?
- When were they last updated and reviewed?
- Is there a documented sign-off for employees?

Your security policies set a baseline of security, including actions that the entire company must follow. They show due diligence and provide consistency across your organization. Policies are meant to be high-level so that they can be applied across departments and the entire organization. It's imperative the organization is aware of the policies and that they are followed. There needs to be an annual review of the key security policies that all employees sign off on after reviewing the policies. Alternatively, an "employee handbook" summarizing the policy can be written and signed off by all employees. The security policies aren't just a check mark; they provide consistency and an understanding of the processes and actions the entire company must take.

In the event of an audit or cybersecurity breach, the fact that there are policies and whether they are followed will be evaluated. If they are not being followed, then your organization will be cited in an audit. Even more important, in the event of a breach, it could be cited that the organization was not following its security policies, which means not showing due diligence. This can lead to higher fines and lawsuits.

A security policy provides the framework and basis of your company's security program. They are the guiding principles that your employees and company must follow to stay compliant and lower your company's risk. Before you start writing any policies, ensure there aren't any policies that already exist. Your company may already have a security policy. You should check with the **Chief Information Officer's (CIO's)** office to see if one already exists. If it does, then dust it off and make sure it is updated and current. You can even take it a step further and conduct an internal audit, ensuring employees and managers are aware of the policies and that their processes align with them. If your company doesn't have a security policy, then someone in your information security department should begin working on one. The good news is there are free templates available online to help get you started. Template.net has thousands of templates and a few generic security policy templates that can get you started. SANS also has some free information security policy templates[1] that are more specific, such as recommended password policies and recommended encryption policies. You can start with a general security policy template from template.net and then add more specific policy sections with the free SANS templates. Typically, you will want the following policies:

- Acceptable use policy
- Information security policy
- Backup policy
- Business continuity plan
- Disaster recovery plan
- Change management policy
- Data classification policy
- Encryption policy
- Logical access policy
- Data classification and labeling plan
- Risk management policy
- Security incident response policy and plan
- Software development lifecycle

---

1   https://www.sans.org/information-security-policy/

- Vendor due diligence policy
- Password policy

Some of these policies can be combined if it makes sense for your company. For example, the encryption and password policies could be sections in the information security policy. Auditors check for specific policies based on the standard or framework that your company adheres to. For example, an acceptable use policy is required for SOC2. I worked with one customer who had an in-depth code of conduct that was already part of their onboarding process. I updated a few items that differed from the acceptable use policy and added them to the code of conduct. I let the auditors know this was the case and that the code of conduct encompassed the acceptable use policy. If you don't have a separate policy that is required for compliance, then understand where that information is located and notify the auditors. Having said that, the acceptable use policy is a foundational policy that your auditors will ask for during an audit. Sometimes, it's easier for the auditor and you to have a separate policy for acceptable use. It's also important because it covers employee responsibilities, such as returning the computer hardware they were given when they were hired. Additionally, make your policies more general so that you can have overarching policies that govern the entire company. Your procedures can be more detailed and specific on how actions are carried out. Procedures aren't required for all compliance, such as SOC2, but are for other standards, such as NIST and ISO 9000. The only exception to this is when I prefer to include the cryptographic key sizes and algorithms that need to be used in either the information security policy or encryption policy.

The information security policy needs to be written in a manner that a non-technical employee can understand. Depending on the regulatory compliance your company needs to meet, the set of policies may slightly differ. The preceding list of policies are required for SOC2 Type 1 and Type 2. SOC2 is the mainstay compliance standard for commercial companies in the United States. NIST CSF is the standard framework that companies follow in the United States.

ISO27001 is the required compliance standard in Europe and internationally. ISO 27001 and SOC2 are 96% the same[2]. One major difference is that ISO27001 requires an internal audit. ISO27001 is prescriptive when SOC2 is customizable.

What do I mean by this? ISO27001 states that if your company is large, then often, the company will train individuals within the company to conduct an internal audit. When I worked at Cisco, they had a volunteer program to be part of the internal audit team to do internal ISO27001 audits. If your company must comply with ISO 27001, then you can use it as a guideline for your security policy. There is an excellent ISO 27001 working group that provides lots of great information and even a free toolkit. The site is titled ISO27k Information Security[3]. ISO 27001 and 27002 are the foundation of information security management systems. ISO 27002 is based on ISO 1779, which was based on the British Standard BS7799.

---

2   Irwin, Luke. *ISO 27001 VS SOC 2 Certification: What's the Difference? IT Governance Blog EU*, 23 Jan. 2023, http://www.itgovernance.eu/blog/en/iso-27001-vs-soc-2-certification-whats-the-difference.

3   https://www.iso27001security.com/index.html

Compliance begins with laws and regulations

No company says, "I love compliance because it makes my company more secure." Compliance is seen as a pain. Many people see it as something that slows your company down from what they need and want to be doing. As a CISO, compliance can be your ally. You can use it to bolster your security program. Maybe you want to segment your network to ensure it's not flat. In addition, you want to segment critical assets from the main network. Your company may not see segmentation as a priority. As the CISO, you can tie the risk of a flat network into your risk register. You can review the compliance standards for your company and use a standard or framework to give your idea more weight. As an example, if your company is using the **National Institute of Science and Technology (NIST) Cybersecurity Framework (CSF)** as their framework, then you could leverage control **PR.AC-5: Network integrity is protected**, which specifically calls out network segmentation. This control maps to many other standards and frameworks. NIST provides mappings to other control frameworks in The Cybersecurity Capability Maturity Model (C2M2) Tool[4]. The C2M2 Tool provides an easy way to do a self-assessment of your organization's IT network. The tool is in spreadsheet and html format. It maps back to the NIST CSF. NIST maps *PR.AC-5* to several other compliance frameworks:

- **CIS CSC**: 9, 14, 15, 18

- **COBIT 2019**: DSS01.05, DSS05.02

- **ISA 62443-2-1:2009**: 4.3.3.4

- **ISA 62443-3-3:2013**: SR 3.1, SR 3.8

- **ISO/IEC 27001:2013**: A.13.1.1, A.13.1.3, A.13.2.1, A.14.1.2, A.14.1.3

- **NIST SP 800-53 Rev. 4**: AC-4, AC-10, SC-7

- **NIST SP 800-53 Rev. 5**: AC-4, AC-10, SC-7

At this point, you may be thinking about all the other compliance regulations and frameworks not listed in the preceding list. All of the frameworks and standards map back to the controls in NIST 800-53B. I was making manual mappings for compliance when I worked at RedSeal. As people found out that I had mapped the product features to NIST 800-53B and PCI, suddenly, the requests kept coming in for other frameworks. Well, how do we map to SOC Type2, and what about HIPAA? NIST provides some cross-reference mappings but not to the extent of the hundreds of frameworks and standards that exist. I realized fairly quickly that all of the compliance frameworks and standards map back to the NIST 800-53B controls. I wrote a Python script along with another developer to make the process easier. There is also open source OSCAL that has carried out the same. There is also an amazing cross-reference mapping that the Secure Controls Framework has published that is free to use[5].

---

4   https://www.energy.gov/ceser/cybersecurity-capability-maturity-model-c2m2

5   https://securecontrolsframework.com/scf-download/

Compliance is required depending on the industry your company is in. Additionally, the compliance your company must meet may be determined by your customers and the compliance they must meet. Compliance at your company begins with the laws that it must comply with. The laws that apply to your company are based on the industry it resides in, the type of data, and the data's locality. Essentially, where is the sensitive data stored? Most importantly, where is your personally identifiable information (PII) or personal information (PI) data stored? Privacy professionals now call PI what cybersecurity professionals call PII. For example, if your company is located in the United States and is in the healthcare industry, then your company will be subject to the **Health Insurance Portability and Accountability Act (HIPAA)**. If your company stores data of Californians, then it is subject to the **California Consumer Privacy Act (CCPA)**. If your company stores information on European citizens, then it is subject to the General Data Protection Regulation (GDPR). It gets complicated in that it's not just what data you are storing but where they are stored. Depending on where your information on European Citizens is stored will also affect the strictness of the compliance. Essentially, where the data is stored affects the regulations on it. As an example, if your EU citizen data is stored in Germany, then the interpretation of GDPR is the most stringent. It all comes back to where the data is stored and what data you have. As you can see, it can get complicated fast. I heard from a privacy expert that many companies in the UK are storing their PI/PII data in Canada in order to avoid stringent interpretations of GDPR regulations. This is where a privacy expert comes into play. Essentially, where the data are stored affects the regulations.

The good news is that the privacy regulations have influenced the latest NIST 800-53b version 5, which has been expanded to include privacy controls. In even better news, all compliance, whether it be laws or frameworks, overlap and map back to NIST 800-53b. Yes, you heard me correctly; they all overlap. The efficient way to address these laws is to figure out the industry and location of the stored data, specifically any PII or sensitive data. When I say sensitive data, this can include health-related information. In addition, if your company is a software development company, then it would include source code, and those servers storing the source code would be considered critical assets. Whatever industry your company is in, its sensitive data can vary. Think of it as this: if the data are lost, could it bankrupt the company?

Nortel hack

The importance of understanding the sensitive data your company has and where they are stored is key. This goes back to Nortel, which was once a leading Technology Company. Nortel was a huge Northern telecom in Canada in the early 2000s. The **Canadian Security Intelligence Service (CSIS)**, which is similar to the United States **Central Intelligence Agency (CIA)**, noticed unusual network traffic coming from China. The agency saw very large downloads. They suspected that China was stealing Nortel's intellectual property, including sensitive documents, patents, and, essentially, the "keys to the kingdom" at Nortel. The CSIS set up a meeting with Nortel executives and warned that "*They're sucking your intellectual property out,*" but the Nortel Executives did nothing about it[6]. This is a warning to all companies: when you are alerted to a hack, whether by an internal team or government agency, you better take it seriously. Get your incident response team to do a thorough investigation. Nortel, once the largest telecom in Canada, went bankrupt because they did nothing. Soon after, hackers, directed by the Chinese government, had successfully brute force attacked the passwords of the executives up to and including Frank Dunn, the Chief Executive Officer (CEO). The CSIS discovered that "*someone using his login had relayed the PowerPoints and other sensitive files to an IP address registered to Shanghai Faxian Corp.*"

What were these hackers targeting? "*Nortel's prized optical unit, in which the company had invested billions of dollars[7].*" The hackers used a script called Il.browse to download massive amounts of Nortel's intellectual property, including "*Product Development, Research and Development, Design Documents & Minutes, and more. They were taking the whole contents of a folder—it was like a vacuum cleaner approach[8].*" What did Nortel do at this point? Unfortunately, not much; they did change the passwords that had been hacked but never did a root cause analysis on the hack and how they were breached in the first place. As a result, the hacks continued. It took a full 5 years for Nortel to go bankrupt, but it did nonetheless. What did the Chinese government do with all this newly found intellectual property? Well, they founded their own telecom company called Huawei.

Depending on the type of company you work for, the sensitive information could be different. PII data are the same, no matter what type of company you are at. The definition of PII may change based on the type of PII and where the data are stored. This also applies to data that are stored in the cloud. Your cloud service provider should be able to tell you where your data will be stored. To safeguard your data, ensure the data are encrypted at rest and that all remote sessions use TLSv1.2 or above. If your data are stored in the US and do not include EU Citizen data, then FIPS 800-60 is a good resource to follow. You also have to take into consideration the California Consumer Privacy Act (CCPA) if you store CA citizen data.

---

6   Obiko Pearson, Natalie. *Did a Chinese Hack Kill Canada's Greatest Tech Company?*

7   Obiko Pearson, Natalie. *Did a Chinese Hack Kill Canada's Greatest Tech Company?*

8   Obiko Pearson, Natalie. *Did a Chinese Hack Kill Canada's Greatest Tech Company?*

Importance of Due diligence

If you are a CISO, then you must ensure your company has a corporate security policy. Ideally, you should have a full set of security policies, as listed earlier in the chapter. If your company is hacked, whether you have a security policy or not, it can be used as evidence that your company has or has not done its due diligence to ensure the company's network is secure. After the notorious Equifax hack, in subsequent legal filings, Equifax was cited as having a poor security policy and not doing its due diligence in protecting its network. More specifically, the 2019 class action lawsuit states deficiencies such as using a username and password of "admin" on an externally facing portal that stored PII data. The lawsuit goes on to state Equifax was not using known good cybersecurity hygiene practices, such as multi-factor authentication, nor adequately monitoring its own networks[9]. It's bad enough getting hacked, but then to have to deal with a litany of fines and lawsuits that follow can not only harm a company's reputation but can take a toll on their financials, which, for Equifax, totaled up to an estimated USD 1.38 billion.

The Equifax breach was a complete breakdown of people, processes, and technology. The Apache struts vulnerability (CVE-2017-5638) was rated as a CVSS 10 and released to the public on March 7, 2017. An email about the CVE was sent to a high-level manager who was not responsible for patching. Notifications of vulnerabilities need to be sent to the patch management team in a timely manner. Critical CVEs such as this should be patched within 30 days. Ideally, you should be prioritizing your vulnerabilities so that critical devices and hosts, as well as internet-facing ones, are patched within 30 days. Moreover, factor in CISA's Known Exploitable Vulnerabilities (KEV). We'll talk more about this later in the book. Equifax had internet-facing servers that had this vulnerability, but since the server team responsible for patching these web servers was not notified, the servers remained unpatched into May. By mid-May, the hackers had leveraged the vulnerability to gain access to the Equifax network.

Since the Equifax network was not properly segmented, the hackers were able to break into the Equifax network from the unpatched web server. From there, they were able to find the usernames and passwords stored in plaintext. Moving laterally on the network, the attackers were able to find database servers and exfiltrated massive amounts of encrypted data. The IDS/IPS tool that Equifax was using had an expired certificate that hindered it from properly analyzing the data. As a result, the data exfiltration was missed by the tool. Massive amounts of PII data, including names, addresses, phone numbers, driver's licenses, and **social security numbers** (**SSNs**), were stolen. Security experts believe the attack was carried out by the Chinese for espionage purposes since the data were never ransomed or dumped onto the dark web.

Even more concerning is the CISO role, which is becoming the scapegoat when a large breach occurs. To be fair, the CISO role is responsible for the security and risk management of a company; however, it's on the executive management team to accept, mitigate, or transfer the risk. We'll get more into risk management later in the book. The Federal government is going after CISOs where there has been a big breach, and the CISO may be negligent. The latest example of this is the CISO of SolarWinds, which the **Security and Exchange Commission (SEC)** has brought charges against. The reason is that the "*SEC's complaint alleges that [Tim] Brown [the CISO of SolarWinds] was aware of SolarWinds' cybersecurity risks and vulnerabilities but failed to resolve the issues or, at times, sufficiently raise them further within the company*[10]." The complaint goes on to explain that Brown only raised generic risks in the SolarWinds risk report and didn't sufficiently document and explain the true risks within the company to the executive team and investors. The SEC is adamant in the complaint that strong cyber safeguards must be implemented in line with the company's risk posture.

Has your company decided on a standard framework for compliance? Depending on the industry, your company has to comply with specific laws and frameworks. If your company is in healthcare, then the **Health Insurance Portability and Accountability Act (HIPAA)** would apply. If your company processes credit cards, then the **Payment Card Industry (PCI)** will apply, specifically to the devices involved with processing payment card data. If your company has a software-as-a-service cloud offering, then SOC2 Type 2 is required. If your company is a startup planning to IPO, then you will have to go through a series of compliance steps, including SOC2 and SOX, two years before the IPO. For international companies, ISO 27001 is the main compliance. Moreover, companies in the US will use NIST CSF as a benchmark and will track their progress against it as they improve their information security program.

Depending on where your company is, as far as its compliance journey, the level of policies required may include the following:

- **Basic**: Startups

- **Medium**: Companies 3-5 years into their compliance journey

- **Advanced**: Companies who understand the importance of security and have aligned their risk management program with their business mission and objectives.

Ideally, your company's security policies should include the following:

- **Basic**:

  - Information security policy

  - Acceptable use policy

  - Backup policy

---

10   "Press Release." *SEC Emblem*, US Securities and Exchange Commission, 30 Oct. 2023, http://www.sec.gov/news/press-release/2023-227.

- Change management policy

- Password policy

- **Medium**:

  - Business continuity and disaster recovery plan

  - Reporting of risks and tracking up to senior management

  - Business continuity plan

  - Disaster recovery plan

  - Logical access policy

  - Risk management policy

  - Security incident response policy

  - Software development lifecycle policy

- **Advanced**

  - Business impact analysis

  - Data classification policy

  - Encryption policy

  - Vendor due diligence policy

A good place to get a good set of security policy templates is my website: `https://trustedciso.com/e-landing-page/ciso-guide-to-cyber-resilience/`.

Summary

In conclusion, having a solid set of security policies lays the groundwork for your security program. Your security policies should be reviewed annually and approved. A subset of your policies should be reviewed by all employees and signed off. This ensures that all employees are informed of what is expected of them and how the security practices of the company work.

In the next chapter, we will be covering security and risk management, which is the process of balancing cyber risks, the controls to thwart attacks, and a budget. As a CISO, it is a balancing act to decide on what to prioritize and what risks are acceptable.

4
Security and Risk Management

This chapter is about security and risk management. We will be discussing the importance of risk management and why you need it. Security and risk management is the process of balancing cyber risks, the controls to thwart attacks, and a budget. Business is about making money, and security and risk management is the process of choosing the controls that work for your company's budget. Your company can't be 100% secure, nor can there be 0% risk. Security is a balance of what is most important, what can wait, and what risks are acceptable to your business.

In this chapter, we're going to cover the following main topics:

- What is risk management?
- Identifying risks
- Monitoring your controls
- Key performance indicators (KPIs)

What is risk management?

Security and risk management is the process of balancing cyber risks and a budget. Business is about making money, and a business will always face constraints regarding its budget. Security is a balance of what is most important and what can wait (at least for now). When selecting the controls that work for your company, there may be areas where your company is subpar or where the budget requires a delay in implementation, as well as an exception to your security policies. These exceptions can be added to the **risk register**.

Security and risk management is a comprehensive approach to identifying, assessing, and mitigating potential risks and threats to an organization's assets, including its people, information, and physical infrastructure. It involves the systematic application of policies, procedures, and controls to minimize vulnerabilities and protect against potential harm. In addition, aligning your program with your company's mission and goals is imperative to achieve alignment from the top down. The communication of risk to senior management is necessary for appropriate managerial support, resources, and budget allocation. According to FIPS PUB 200, risk management is the process of managing risks to operations, assets, or individuals, which includes the following:

- Conducting a risk assessment

- Implementing a risk mitigation strategy

- Implementing continuous monitoring of IT controls

Identifying risks

The process of security and risk management begins with the identification and assessment of risks. This is also considered to be a **Business Impact Assessment**. This involves conducting a thorough analysis of the organization's assets, identifying potential threats and vulnerabilities, and evaluating the likelihood and impact of those risks. Risks can come from various sources, such as cyberattacks, natural disasters, human error, or even internal misconduct. An excerpt of a risk register with example risks can be seen in *Table 4.1*:

ID	Risk	Impact	Likelihood	Score	Treatment/Remediation
1	Malware	Moderate	High	50	• Follow patch management plan (Basic) • EDR deployed on hosts, servers, and end-user laptops (Moderate
2	New information security or privacy obligations introduced by laws and regulations, etc.	Moderate	Moderate	25	• Stay on top of the latest privacy laws and regulations
3	Severe Weather	High	Low	10	• Business continuity plan • Disaster recovery plan
4	Employee clicks on phishing email	Moderate	High	50	• Ensure all employees go through security awareness training • Email security filter

ID	Risk	Impact	Likelihood	Score	Treatment/Remediation
5	Unpatched servers that can't be upgraded are compromised by an attacker	High	Low	10	• Segment network so that these servers are separate from the regular network • Budget for new servers
6	Crown Jewel Asset is compromised	Critical	Medium		

Table 4.1 – Example risks

Risk assessment

A risk assessment needs to be done at least annually and re-evaluated each year. When I was a CISO, we initially did the impact analysis and risk assessment, and then we would re-evaluate where we were at quarterly intervals and communicate this to the executive management team. I also created a roadmap of red-yellow-green items that needed to be completed to improve the risk posture of the company. Watch out for "watermelon" reporting, which is when only the good green items are reported to executive management, thus hiding the red, high-risk items. This is one of the reasons that the SEC went after the CISO of SolarWinds. As long as you, as the CISO, are properly documenting the risks and communicating them to the executive management team, you have a paper trail. It's then on the executive management team to decide what actions are taken and what risks are accepted. It's the CISO's job to educate the management team about the risks. It can be daunting with the politics at the executive management level; the shift of burden should and must be on the executive management team. It is their responsibility to fund the IT and security budgets to properly mitigate, accept, or transfer the risks that the company is facing, not the CISO. I want to see this shift in the industry. If an executive management team refuses to address the risks as per the industry standards, then the CISO must leave. It's a hard decision for any CISO, and finding a new position takes time, but this is the reality in the current climate of prosecuting the CISO.

Figure 1, which is taken from NIST IR 8286, gives an overview of the entire risk management process. You can see how it's an ongoing process that needs to be re-evaluated at least annually. The upper tier outlines a six-step sequential process, each step leading to the next through visual arrows. The lower tier provides insights into the outputs generated by each step. A key feature at the figure's base highlights the ongoing processes of communication and consultation integral to every phase:

- **Context identification**: This step involves understanding the operating environment of the organization and the risks it faces.

- **Risk identification**: This involves recognizing a full spectrum of potential risks, both positive and negative, that could either support or hinder the achievement of objectives. This includes considering the risks associated with missed opportunities.

- **Risk analysis**: This step entails estimating the likelihood and potential impact of identified risks, aiming to understand the scale of their consequences.

- **Risk prioritization**: Here, risks are assessed based on their likelihood and potential impact to determine their overall exposure. Risks are then ranked according to their level of exposure.

- **Risk response planning and execution**: In this phase, suitable responses are formulated for each identified risk, guided by leadership's risk strategy.

- **Monitoring, evaluation, and adjustment**: This ongoing process ensures that the organization's risk profile remains within acceptable parameters as cybersecurity threats evolve, with adjustments made as necessary.

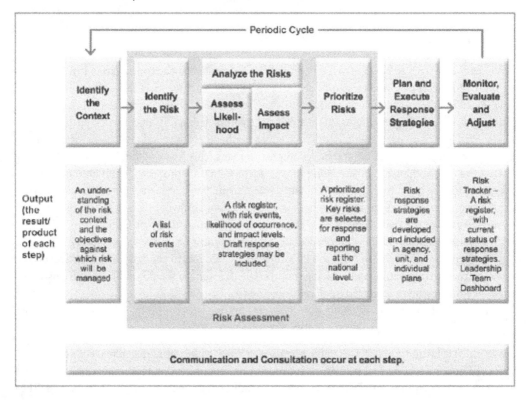

Figure 4.1 – NIST IR 8286 risk management cycle[1]

---

1   https://doi.org/10.6028/NIST.IR.8286

Impact and likelihood

Impact and likelihood should be assessed as part of the risk register. The impact and likelihood of each threat can be qualitative (high, moderate, or low) or quantitative (a numeric score). Risk can be quantitively defined by the following formula:

Risk = Impact * Likelihood

You need to select an Impact and Likelihood rating scale. NIST actually has a simplified scale in that both impact and Likelihood are based on low, moderate, high, and critical. You may see the scoring and impact levels with more levels and different scoring, which is fine as long as your organization's impact level and likelihood numeric scale (used in the risk register) are the same as those described in the risk management policy. The scoring example shown in *Table 4.2* is based on NIST scoring.

When filling out your risk register, you can use NIST FIPS PUB 199 definitions of low, moderate, and high. FIPS PUB 199 defines the Impact levels as low, moderate, and high, as described below.

Impact level evaluation

Low impact

A low-impact risk results in a limited adverse effect on an organization, such as the following:

- The organization will still be operating, but operations will be slowed
- Assets may receive minor damage
- There may be minor financial losses
- Minor harm to employees

Moderate impact

A moderate-impact risk results in a serious adverse effect on an organization, such as the following:

- Significant degradation of or reduction in mission and operations
- Assets may receive significant damage
- There may be significant financial losses
- Significant harm to employees

High impact

A high-impact risk will have a severe or catastrophic effect on an organization, such as the following:

- Severe degradation or loss of mission and operations
- Assets may receive major damage

- There may be major financial losses
- Severe or catastrophic harm to employees

Critical impact

A critical-impact risk will have a severe or catastrophic effect on an organization, such as the following:

- Severe degradation or loss of mission and operations
- Assets may receive major damage

Likelihood evaluation

The following list represents the criteria for likelihood evaluation:

- **Low likelihood**: Score a risk as low if there are more than two conditions that have occurred
- **Moderate likelihood**: Score a risk as moderate if two or more conditions have occurred
- **High likelihood**: Score a risk as high if one condition has occurred
- **Critical likelihood**: Score a risk as critical if the issue is already happening or there are zero conditions for it to occur

NIST scoring

For scoring your risks, you can quantitatively score the risks and likelihood in the risk register. In this case, we are using the NIST 800-30 method. In the following, you can see how to quantitatively score impact and likelihood: Low = 10, Moderate = 50, High = 100, and Critical = 150. For Likelihood, the scale is as follows: Low = 0.1, Moderate = 0.5, High = 1, and Critical = 1.5.

	Impact			
Likelihood	Low (10)	Moderate (50)	High (100)	Critical (150)
Low (0.1)	10*0.1 =1	50*0.1=5	100*0.1=10	150*0.1=10
Moderate (0.5)	10*0.5=5	50*0.5=25	100*0.5=50	150*0.5=50
High (1)	10*1=10	50*1=50	100*1=100	150*1=100
Critical (1.5)	10*1.5=15	50*1.5=75	100*1.5=150	150*1.5=225

Table 4.2 – Impact and likelihood quantitative scale[2]

If you are a small-sized firm, the qualitative scoring is adequate. As your company grows and the security program moves along with it, then quantitative scoring is recommended. I typically use both the qualitative and quantitative in the risk register. There is also a formal risk management and scoring

2   https://stateofsecurity.com/formula-for-calculating-cyber-risk/

system called the FAIR Materiality Assessment Model by the FAIR Institute. I won't be going into detail about FAIR in this book, but I want you to be aware that it exists and that larger organizations use it.

When you perform your risk analysis, you'll want to interview people from different areas of the company to understand their processes. If you don't have a tool or program to aid in performing the assessment, then you can use the NIST Cybersecurity Maturity Tool that allows you to assess your organization's network against the NIST Cybersecurity Framework. You can access the tool from here: `https://www.nist.gov/cyberframework`.

Once you complete the assessment, you'll have a better understanding of the deficiencies in your organization's information technology (IT) processes and technology. This is actually good because now, when you create your risk register, you can add risks related to the deficiencies. For example, in your assessment, you may have found out that a particular division has old servers that can no longer be upgraded. You can add it to the risk register, bringing visibility to the problem. The risk register needs to be presented to senior management in order to get support from the top down. In order to get the necessary budget and resources, upper management needs to be aware of the risk register and deficiencies and, ideally, create a plan of action and milestone (POA&M) system for each deficiency. Essentially, in the POA&M, you will track the deficiencies and the plans for when they will be fixed. For example, there may not be a budget to upgrade the servers until the following year or later. These details can be captured in the POAM.

Once risks are identified and assessed, organizations need to make decisions on how to manage them effectively. This involves selecting and implementing appropriate controls and measures to mitigate the identified risks. Controls can include technological safeguards, such as firewalls and encryption, as well as operational measures such as security policies, training programs, and access controls. The goal is to reduce the probability and impact of potential risks to an acceptable level.

However, it is important to note that achieving absolute security is not feasible or practical. Organizations must strike a balance between security measures, budget constraints, and operational requirements. There may be areas where a company's security measures are not optimal or where budget limitations require prioritization and the phased implementation of controls. In such cases, organizations can document these exceptions in a risk register, which serves as a centralized repository for tracking and managing identified risks and their associated mitigation plans.

A good representation of all your risks is a risk matrix:

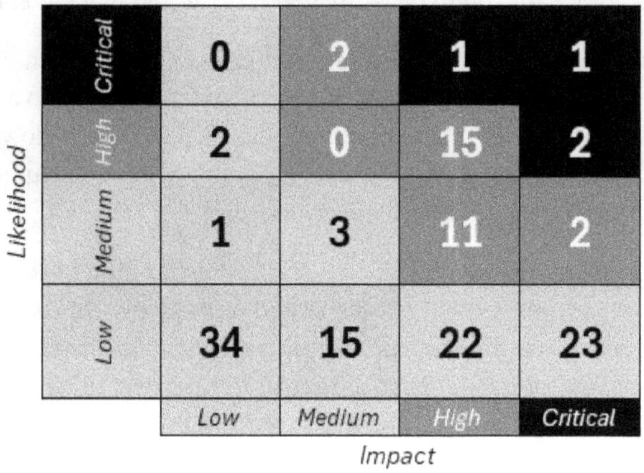

Figure 4.2 – Risk Matrix

Risk treatment

I've been talking about mitigations where you would, for example, patch an unpatched server. Risk treatment includes four separate actions:

- **Remediation**

  - To fix the deficiency

- **Mitigation**

  - To come up with another solution that may not fix the issue but will lessen the impact and likelihood of the risk

- **Acceptance**

  - Senior management decides to accept the risk

  - No remediation or mitigation is taken

- **Transfer**

  - Transfer the risk to some other entity

  - Transfer the risk to an insurance company, i.e., Cybersecurity Insurance

  - Risk avoidance:

    - This involves changing plans or approaches to completely avoid the risk. Typically, this involves changing the technology

- Risk sharing:

  - The risks are shared across several parties

The remediation of risks essentially means that you come up with a solution to fix the deficiency. Mitigation means you take action to lessen the effect of a risk. One form of mitigation could be updating a policy to change a process; it doesn't mean you have to purchase a product. For example, with unpatched servers that can't be patched due to old hardware, mitigation would be to segment these servers off of the regular network so that they aren't easily accessible. You definitely don't want them to have interfaces on the internet or in the DMZ. Ideally, segmenting these servers off of the regular network would be a good mitigation step until the hardware can be upgraded. Maybe the hardware can't be upgraded. Maybe the particular device only runs an old, outdated operating system, and there is no way to upgrade it. Again, segmentation is key for these devices. Let's say there is a risk that is so large that mitigating or remediating the risk would be cost-prohibitive. You have to remember that you are working for a business, which means they have a budget and must meet payroll. They may have to show a profit for shareholders. As a CISO, you have to think more like a business manager than a cybersecurity expert. There may be deficiencies that you know of and a product that would fix the issue, but upper management has deemed it is too expensive; so, in this case, management decides to accept the risk. Lastly, senior management can transfer the risk. Your organization can transfer the risk by purchasing insurance. Since the risk register is primarily about IT-related risks, it is important for your organization to have cyber insurance in order to properly transfer these risks to an insurance company.

Monitoring your controls

Security and risk management also involves the ongoing monitoring and review of implemented controls to ensure their effectiveness and to identify emerging risks. This includes regular security assessments, audits, and incident response planning to detect and respond to security incidents in a timely manner.

How you monitor your controls will follow the budget and priorities of your organization. You can manually do internal self-assessments at least annually. Ideally, at least annually, a third-party penetration test should be carried out on your network. At a more advanced level, you should bring in an outside third party to conduct an assessment of your network. If your organization has decided to comply with SOC2, then you would do at least one annual self-assessment, and an outside auditor would come in annually to do an audit.

At a more advanced level, you can carry out automated continuous monitoring of your organization's controls. The cloud makes this easier than ever. There are multiple compliance products on the market, such as **Drata**, **Secureframe**, and **Vanta**. These products will automatically monitor your cloud environment controls and map them to a specific framework or standard, such as SOC2 or NIST CSF. At least every 24 hours, the product will do a pull on your environment controls and will report whether you are in compliance or out of compliance. This is really great because you know if there was a change or if someone left the company and their access is still active. These continuous compliance real-time tools are great for ensuring not only that you are compliant with a specific framework or standard but also that you stay compliant on a day-to-day basis. "Continuous" compliance doesn't mean real-time compliance. It could be a weekly pull of your controls and a report or a daily one that is emailed to key stakeholders. Of course, this could go either way, where you get hourly pulls and checks or monthly regarding compliance. I would say that, at a minimum, you should be doing at least weekly pulls, and daily would be even better. Hourly would be great if you have a team that can act on these alerts. If your team is so small that you don't have time to address the hourly alerts, then daily is probably a better option. Of course, if you are a small- or medium-sized business, you may not even have a tool to monitor your controls. Most cloud services come with applications that can be used to monitor the cloud environment. If you can't afford a product to monitor your cloud controls, then I recommend using the cloud-provided tools. For example, for **AWS**, there is **Cloud Watch**, **Cloud Trail**, and **Guard Duty**. Each and every cloud service has tools you can use to monitor and report on the controls and determine if they are out of compliance.

Key performance indicators (KPIs)

A **key performance indicator** (**KPI**) is a measurable value that helps businesses or organizations evaluate their success in achieving specific objectives or goals. KPIs are quantifiable metrics that provide insight into various aspects of performance, allowing organizations to track progress, identify areas for improvement, and make data-driven decisions.

KPIs are typically established based on the strategic goals and objectives of a business or specific areas of focus within an organization. They can vary widely depending on the industry, department, or function being measured. For example, sales teams may track KPIs such as revenue growth, customer acquisition rates, or conversion rates, while customer service departments may focus on KPIs such as customer satisfaction scores or average response times. For the information security program, at a minimum, you need to select some good KPIs to report to senior management to show the progress of building out the information security program. Some good KPIs for tracking your security program are as follows:

- **Number of unresolved high/critical vulnerabilities**: Keeps track of vulnerabilities that pose a significant risk and remain unaddressed.

- **Phishing test click rate**: Percentage of employees who click on a simulated phishing email, providing insight into security awareness.

- **Monitor external risk posture**: Use an external risk-monitoring company, such as Security ScoreCard (free option), BitSight, or Censys.io.

- **Compliance timelines**: Progress toward meeting a framework or standard, such as NIST CSF, SOC2, or ISO27001.

- **Incident response time**: You could either provide the average time or you could have a service-level agreement (SLA) defining what is the expected, with a maximum response to an incident, and then report all incidents that are handled outside the SLA.

- **Number of security incidents**: Percentage of true positive security incidents.

- **Patch level**: Define your SLA for patching. Ideally, 100% of firewalls, routers, and servers should be patched within 30 days. A total of 90% of workstations should be patched within 30 days. More realistically, critical vulnerabilities should be patched in 30 days, high vulnerabilities in 60 days, and medium and low vulnerabilities as needed. We'll talk more about vulnerability prioritization later, in *Chapter 8, Vulnerability Management*. Having said that, if your company must meet StateRAMP, then all vulnerabilities have to be patched. Again, we'll talk about compliance and vulnerability management in more detail later in the book.

NIST offers a free NIST CSF Maturity tool that you can use to perform an assessment and track your progress. I recommend including these metrics in a quarterly presentation deck that will be communicated to senior leadership.

Providing a good risk management indicator to higher levels of management gives a holistic view of your information security program. Is it getting more or less secure? Many different products offer a risk index indicator. The important part is tracking it on regular basis, whether that's weekly, bi-weekly, or monthly, and understanding what makes it go up and down. For example, if your company just did a bunch of network device changes, then the score may go down, but you have a story to tell.

The continuous monitoring of your controls is paramount to ensure you stay in compliance. There are many products (especially for the cloud) that will do this, whether it's Drata, Secureframe, Vanta, Cypago or TrustCloud. There are other tools, such as CloudWize.io and Wiz, that provide full visibility into your cloud security risk posture.

Quick reference

Ideally, your company's risk management program should include the following:

Depending on where your company is in terms of building out its risk management program, the processes, planning, and remediation are as follows:

- **Basic**: Start-ups

- **Medium**: Companies 3–5 years into their compliance journey

- **Advanced**: Companies who understand the importance of security and have aligned their risk management program with their business mission and objectives

Ideally, your company's risk management should include the following:

- **Basic:**

  - Alignment with your company's budget

  - Asset inventory

  - Identifying risks and tracking them in a risk register

- **Medium:**

  - Co-ordination with senior-level management

  - Reporting of risks and tracking this up to senior management

  - Define your most critical assets

- **Advanced:**

  - Alignment with your company's mission and objectives

  - Key performance indicators (KPIs)

  - Monitoring of controls "continual compliance"

Summary

In conclusion, using risk management is imperative to creating a holistic information security program. You can't be 100% secure or have 0% risk. Balancing your controls with your organization's budget is required. It's very important to keep senior-level management updated on your security program. If your security and risk management program does not have the support of senior-level management, then it won't get the budget or resources necessary to be successful. Getting buy-in from top-level management is critical in getting funding and support for your initiatives. One of the best ways to get this support is to align your security program with your organization's mission and goals. Top companies such as Salesforce and Apple have done this successfully.

In summary, security and risk management is a continuous process that involves identifying, assessing, and mitigating potential risks to an organization's assets. It requires making informed decisions about which controls to implement and considering factors such as the organization's priorities, available resources, and risk tolerance. By taking a proactive approach to security and risk management, organizations can better protect their assets and minimize the potential impact of security incidents.

In the next chapter, we will be covering endpoint security. When building a security program, ensuring your endpoints are secure is a foundational building block. Are you managing your endpoints? Do they have anti-virus and endpoint detection and response (EDR)? What about mobile device management?

5

Securing Your Endpoints

This chapter is about **endpoint detection and response** (**EDR**). Here, we will be discussing the importance of securing your endpoints. Securing your endpoints is critical; this includes laptops and servers. With the move to remote work, people working out of their homes, and mobile working, it means endpoints are more at risk. Do your employees have a home firewall? When I worked at Cisco, they sent us configured firewalls with steps to complete the setup. Most companies can't afford to send out firewalls to everyone. There are solutions where you can test your home firewall setup to make sure it is configured properly.

In this chapter, we're going to cover the following main topics:

- Antivirus/anti-malware
- **Virtual private network** (**VPN**)
- Moving to remote work
- Testing your home firewall
- **Network access control** (**NAC**) and Zero Trust
- Application firewall
- Securing your browser
- Turning on your application firewall
- Okta hack

Antivirus/anti-malware

I'm sure you are familiar with antivirus and anti-malware. Every laptop, computer, and server should have a good antivirus installed, including every Apple MacBook. An antivirus is essentially a program that is installed on your laptop or server and scans your computer periodically for any virus or malicious software. Today, there is a new name for the latest antivirus and anti-malware software. It is called EDR or **endpoint protection platform** (**EPP**) software. Essentially, EDR software provides antivirus, anti-malware, and response capabilities. Let me explain; the best EDRs have levels of service that you can purchase along with the software. If you purchase the full capabilities with 24/7 customer support, then you will have access to an **incident response (IR)** help desk that will respond in case of an infection or attack. For example, with CrowdStrike, SentinelOne, Microsoft Defender for Endpoint, Bitdefender, Carbon Black, and Malwarebytes, if you purchase the full package including "R" response, then the IR support comes with antivirus and anti-malware. On the surface, it sounds great. If you are a small or medium-sized company and you don't have an **IR team (IRT)**, then your EDR can provide you with this support. Now, I have to caution you that CrowdStrike is considered the industry leader according to Gartner's *EPP Magic Quadrant*[1], but it is the most expensive. CrowdStrike comes with a 24/7 IR help desk. I only recommend CrowdStrike for large organizations, not small or medium-sized. You may be saying, "But wait! I want my customer to have the best one." I had a dear friend, Tony Pierce, who is the North American field CTO at Splunk, tell me, "Don't recommend CrowdStrike for a start-up; you'll get fired." Tony recommends SentinelOne for small and medium-sized businesses. Since I found out about Bitdefender, I recommend it for start-ups. A few weeks later, I attended the *RSA SANS CISO* boot camp. The first SANS speaker starts out talking about how he just got done talking with a start-up that fired their CISO because he recommended CrowdStrike! The SANS speaker said, "Your company may not need an expensive EDR." It was more confirmation of what Tony had cautioned me about already. This is why networking and knowing other people in the cybersecurity community is so important to bounce ideas off of them and find out what they are doing.

The good news is that Microsoft Defender for Endpoint comes free on Windows machines. Defender for Endpoint is rated very high on Gartner's EPP Magic Quadrant, almost the same as CrowdStrike. You do have to do research on the level of protection provided with the free version of Defender for Endpoint. For example, to have email phishing protection, you have to also purchase the Windows Defender for Office 365 Plan 1 add-on or purchase one of the premium **Microsoft 365 (M365)** packages. The base Microsoft Defender package doesn't include it. I know this because one client had gotten rid of Mimecast since they had M365 and they thought it provided email phishing protection, but the spam and phishing emails were exponentially increasing. When I researched the Windows M365 licensing, I realized that Microsoft Defender for M365 needed to be purchased separately. It's way more cost-effective to purchase the Microsoft Defender add-on rather than purchase the premium M365 license.

When you are looking at new products, ideally look at three. You can create a spreadsheet and explain the features, ratings, and cost. This way, you are showing due diligence by doing a product comparison of at least three products. In your EDR product comparison for the SMB space, you could compare MS Defender for Endpoint, Bitdefender, SentinelOne, and Malwarebytes. Even though MS Defender for Endpoint is free, there is a cost associated with the extra features. As discussed earlier, the most cost-effective way to get an email scanner is to purchase the MS Defender add-on package. If you have Macs, although MS Defender provides a Mac version, I have heard it is difficult to get it working. For businesses with Macs and Windows, I recommend using Bitdefender, SentinelOne, or Malwarebytes ThreatDown.

---

1   Gartner, December 2023

Virtual private network (VPN)

When securing your endpoints, a VPN is necessary when you are away from the office or traveling, unless your company has a **software-defined perimeter** (**SDP**). I cover SDPs and Zero Trust in *Chapter 11*. Your company may have a VPN set up if they have an on-premise data center. Typically, you will connect to the company VPN in order to get access to the on-premise servers and applications. As more and more companies move to cloud-first postures, your company may not have one set up. If your company is cloud-first, then every service it uses is a SaaS. Your employees log in to M365 or Google Workspace, for example. The remote session is already being encrypted with TLS 1.2 or above. As more companies move to this posture, they may not have a VPN that you connect to. A VPN is not obsolete. When you are out and about away from your home Wi-Fi or company network, connecting to guest Wi-Fi, then you need to use a VPN. Be suspicious of any free VPN except for Proton VPN. There are free VPNs that track and sell your data, but not Proton VPN. Ideally, your company would purchase a VPN and provide it to your employees unless using SDP or Zero Trust. If you are at a start-up or budget-conscious company, then I recommend using F-Secure VPN or Proton VPN when you are out and about connecting to public Wi-Fi networks. There are other good VPNs on the market; just do your due diligence and research.

What is phishing?

Email phishing is one of the top ways that hackers compromise people's computers. The hackers craft an email that looks legitimate, but it has a malicious attachment. Another tactic is to have an email that contains a link to a malicious website. If the unsuspecting person clicks on the link, then the user ends up on a malicious website not realizing malware has been automatically downloaded to their computer. The malicious software may be used to spy on you or, even worse, capture every keystroke on your computer.

Phishing has advanced, giving rise to multiple variations employing the following methods:

- **Vishing scams**: These occur via phone calls, voicemails, or **Voice over Internet Protocol** (**VoIP**) communications

- **Smishing scams**: These are executed through SMS (text) messaging

- **Pharming scams**: This variant involves the installation of malicious code on your computer, which redirects you to counterfeit websites

Email security scanners

Email security scanners will analyze your email before it hits the email servers and filter out infected emails by putting them in quarantine, preventing phishing and spam emails from being delivered to your employee mailboxes. Quarantine is a safe place to store emails without them executing malicious software. Your company can then turn them in to the FTC (`https://reportfraud.ftc.gov/#/`) or delete the phishing emails.

Microsoft **Exchange Online Protection** (**EOP**) or Defender for Office 365 Plan 1 can be used for email scanning. The base free version of Defender doesn't include an email scanner. This is important if you are also using M365, email phishing protection is not included in the base **Office 365** (**O365**). If you are using M365 for email, then you should upgrade to include the Defender for Office 365 Plan 1 package. It's cheaper to get the base M365 version and add the Defender package than to purchase the M365 E5 version.

Now, if your company is using Google Workspace for their email, then Google provides a high level of email phishing scanning, so the base Defender EDR would be fine. If your company is medium or large, then definitely look into a good email phishing filter product such as Abnormal Security, Proofpoint, Mimecast, Cisco **Email Security Appliance** (**ESA**), or Microsoft EOP. Definitely select at least three vendors to compare, and do your due diligence. You can find a software evaluation template at `https://TrustedCISO.com`. An example table is provided next:

Features	Mimecast	Microsoft Defender	Proofpoint
Windows client	Yes	Yes for Windows	Yes
Mac client	Yes	M365 for Mac*	Yes
SaaS	Yes	Yes	Yes
Email spoofing	Yes	TBD	Yes
URL protection	Yes	TBD	Yes
URL analysis	Yes	TBD	Yes
Ransomware email protection	Yes	TBD	Yes
Cost	$ TBD	$ TBD	$ TBD

Note: There is a Defender for Mac, but I heard it is difficult to get working.

Table 5.1 – Software evaluation email scanner

Similar to recommending EDRs based on your company size, it's the same for email security scanners. Based on price, Proofpoint is the highest rated and most expensive. I only recommend it for large organizations. Mimecast has a better price and makes more sense for small and medium-sized organizations. Microsoft's email scanner also makes sense for small and medium-sized organizations. Abnormal Security relies on **artificial intelligence** (**AI**) plugged into M365. It detects malicious emails that other email security solutions do not detect.

When securing your endpoints, typically **mobile device management** (**MDM**) comes up. I will be covering protecting your MDM later, in *Chapter 9, Asset Inventory*.

Moving to remote work

When COVID hit, there was a massive move from workers being in the office to working from home. Suddenly, your home network security became a higher priority. Now, we are in more of a hybrid work situation, but many companies are allowing their employees to continue to work from home. I think this is great. I have been working from home since 2001. I found it to be the best option for me. Prior to COVID, there was a move in tech to work in the office. I was super disappointed when I interviewed with IBM, which was one of the pioneers in working from home in the 90s and had completely abolished the ability to work from home. One bright spot of COVID is that it forced people to work from home, and companies saw it works. Everyone is different, so for some, being in an office works better for them. I think it should be a personal choice. Of course, for new college graduates, I think working from the office is paramount if able for the first 2 years. At the same time, with Zoom and all the great collaboration tools available, I don't see a difference between working in the office and at home. I work with teams from all over, which makes remote work the best option.

LastPass hack

The LastPass hack is a good reminder to make sure your company's end-user machines are secure. First, let's discuss how the breach occurred, and then we can talk about how it could have been prevented. The LastPass hack ended up being because a lead AWS administrator's home computer was breached because of an unpatched Plex server that had a remote code executable vulnerability. Essentially, if the LastPass employee had ensured auto updates were enabled on his home computer, then there would not have been a huge LastPass breach.

Let's get into the details of the hack. One of the most obvious issues is: Why would hacking his home computer cause a breach at his company? Well, once the hackers were able to compromise his home computer, they installed a key logger. At that point, the hackers were able to log every single keystroke on his home computer. You may still be asking yourself: How would that affect his company, LastPass? Well, some reports said he was also using his home computer to VPN into work. If this is accurate, then the employee had LastPass installed on his home computer and would type in his LastPass password to access his passwords for work. Now, the attackers had his LastPass password and had access to his LastPass password manager. If he'd had **two-factor authentication** (**2FA**) set up for LastPass, there would have been a chance that they couldn't get access to LastPass. Even with the unpatched Plex server, why was the attacker able to gain access to his computer in the first place? If the LastPass employee's home firewall had been properly configured, then the attacker would not have been able to gain access to his home network. Because this employee was a key AWS engineer supporting the LastPass cloud infrastructure, he had access to high-value administrator passwords and keys that allowed the hackers to gain access to the backups of customer LastPass vaults.

Key takeaways from the LastPass hack:

- Turn on auto-updates for patching
- Use 2fa
- Ensure the home firewall is properly configured

Testing your home firewall

You are probably thinking, is my home firewall properly configured? Cisco sent preconfigured firewalls to each employee. Most companies can't afford to send every employee a firewall. One way to ensure your employee's home networks are secure is to have them do a test on it. Steve Gibson's *ShieldsUP* web page provides a home firewall test that can be run: `https://www.grc.com/x/ne.dll?bh0bkyd2`. You could send this out to your employees to test their home firewalls. *HackerTarget* offers a way to test your external firewall also: `https://hackertarget.com/firewall-test/`. In addition, you can update your information security policy or **acceptable use policy** (**AUP**) stating that an employee can only connect to the company network with their company-assigned computer. Only phones or home computers can be used for checking email.

Network access control (NAC) and Zero Trust

Another option is to scan all devices that attempt to connect to your work network. Typically, this is part of Zero Trust offerings, but it's actually NAC that has been around since the late 2000s. NAC provides scanning, ensuring that the **operating system** (**OS**) is patched. In addition, NAC will ensure that your antivirus and anti-malware are up to date on all devices prior to being allowed to access your network. If your machine is company-issued, but the OS isn't patched or the antivirus needs to be updated, then NAC would place you on a separate network to upgrade the software. This was set up at Cisco years before the Zero Trust became a big topic. NAC is considered a building block of Zero Trust. At Cisco, if I brought in my personal laptop, it would not automatically connect to the Cisco internal Wi-Fi network. There was a website you would go to to register your device. NAC would scan your device to ensure the OS and antivirus were up to date. Even if the software on the device was patched and updated, the device would only be allowed to connect to the guest Wi-Fi. You can either attempt to set up NAC on your firewall for your network or purchase a Zero Trust solution. I always like to recommend Cloudflare's Zero Trust solution. The first 50 seats are free, so it is ideal for small organizations. Instead of using a traditional VPN to connect to your internal network, use Cloudflare One. Cloudflare originally developed it during COVID when everyone was working from home. Now, they offer it as a service. There are other Zero Trust offerings such as Cato, and Zscaler is a leader in the space.

Application firewall

To secure your endpoint, ensure the application firewall is turned on. The application firewall protects your computer from being attacked by another device on the same network. Whether you are running Microsoft Windows or macOS, the application firewall needs to be enabled. By default, Windows has the application firewall turned on; leave it that way. On macOS, the application firewall is off by default. You should ensure your baseline configuration for Macs is to enable the application firewall. Go to **Settings** | **Network** | **Firewall** to enable it. Some may say, "Well, I mainly connect to my work network, so it is secure." This is not always the case. Zero Trust means anyone could be an attacker. The reason is that a user's machine could have been hacked, and the user unknowingly is part of a botnet. What is a botnet? Essentially, hackers take over **Internet of Things** (**IoT**) devices such as cameras and lights that are directly connected to the internet. Likewise, hackers can compromise computers. Once the hacker has control of the device or computer, they can install malware that brings those devices and computers into a botnet. The botnet is a hacker-controlled assimilation of devices that the hacker will use to attack and break into other networks. For example, the hacker could have these devices and computers attack a specific server by overwhelming it with pings or attempted connections. This would be a **distributed denial-of-service** (**DDOS**) attack. IoT devices are particularly susceptible since many have default passwords that cannot be changed. They also have such small processors and storage space that providing encryption such as TLS 1.2 or above is not possible. The **National Institute of Standards and Technology** (**NIST**) is working on a lightweight cryptography standard that can be run on IoT devices to help solve this problem.

Mirai botnet

There were unintended consequences of the 2016 Summer Olympics that were held in Rio de Janeiro. Brazil wanted to provide a safe and smart city initiative for the Olympics. The unintended consequences were that all of these cameras and sensors installed throughout the city had default admin credentials that couldn't be changed. Hackers were able to install malware that made them part of the Mirai botnet. Mirai is a type of malware designed to compromise IoT devices running on ARC processors. Once infected, these devices are transformed into a remotely managed botnet, commonly used for executing DDoS attacks.

The IoT devices became a powerful hacker tool to execute DDoS attacks. You may think: Why not change the default password? Well, there is no option to change the password on these devices. They are so small, with little storage and processing power, that the only solution is to replace the sensors with ones that can change the password. IoT devices also can't encrypt remote sessions using TLS, SSH, or IPsec. As a result, the only solution is to replace the devices with new ones. When you are purchasing IoT devices, check and see what security features they have. At a minimum, you can change the administrator password. Another solution is to put all of your IoT devices on a separate subnet off of the internet. You need to do a discovery of all of your IoT devices in order to get them off of your internal network. They need to be segmented into their own network. There are tools such as Armis, Axonius, and Forescout that you can use to do the discovery to inventory all of the IoT devices. There are tools you can use to segment these IoT devices into their own networks, such as Illumio, Airgap, and Cylera.

Key takeaways to secure your IoT devices:

- Change default password
- Discovery
- Segmentation

Securing your browser

Everyone has a favorite browser, but I currently prefer Firefox. Brave is also a good browser that is based on Chrome; it has a lot of security functionality built in. Brave has built-in privacy. Brave provides safe browsing and search with a VPN (for an added fee). My only complaint is that it's so safe, sometimes even after whitelisting a site, it may not work properly. Firefox also has some good blockers built in to protect you. You can also add Ghostery to your browser to add further blocking protections. Essentially, when you go to a website, you may have to allow an action on the site. This will prevent your computer from being harmed by a malicious website. Also, make sure you configure auto-update so that your browser stays updated on software patches and upgrades. Based on Chromium, Enterprise Browser is a web browser designed specifically for enterprise use. It features core security controls embedded within the browser itself, such as anti-phishing, a malware scanner, and web filtering.

Turning on your application firewall

Traditional firewalls are devices, but there are also software firewalls. A firewall is typically a device that sits between your internal network and external network (internet). The network firewall filters the network traffic. Software firewalls are applications you install such as in the cloud, in VLANs, or residing on your OS that filter traffic going into and out of the device that could be virtual. By default, you want to deny/deny traffic versus allow/allow.

Ensure the application firewall on your OS is enabled. macOS does not enable the application firewall by default. Go into your Mac's **System Settings | Network | Firewall** and enable the firewall. By default, on Windows OS, the firewall is enabled. Open the Control Panel, then select **Windows Security | Firewall and Network Protection | Firewall on**.

Okta hack

The Okta hack was one of the biggest hacks of 2022. A tweet was sent on Twitter where the LAPSUS$ hacker group was bragging that they had hacked Okta. The tweets included screenshots of a customer support engineer's computer:

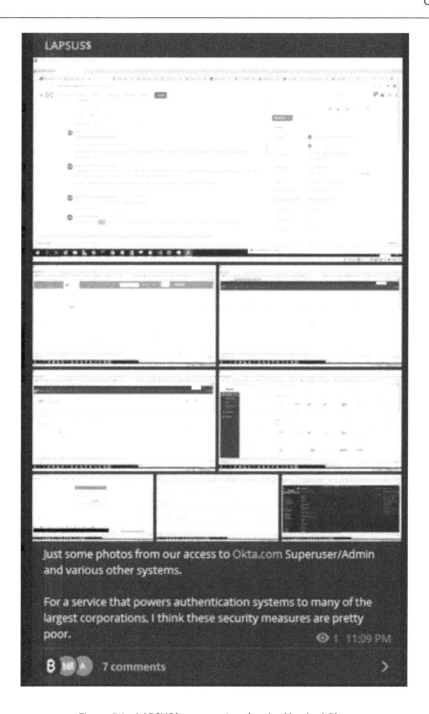

Figure 5.1 – LAPSUS$ announcing they had hacked Okta

Within the screenshots was a picture of the hacker logged in as a Cloudflare employee.

I was a CISO at this point, and someone at my company forwarded the tweets to me. Twitter (or X, as it is now called) is a good place to stay up on all of the latest hacks since hackers will brag on X. Also, there is a great number of cybersecurity researchers who post information on the site. If your company has an incident, then you need to do a write-up of the incident, detailing how you found out about it and the steps you took to address it. When there is an active incident at your company, you need to create a Tiger team or IR interim working group to focus on the Okta hack and how it may affect your company. You need to document a detailed timeline of when you found out about the hack or potential hack and the steps taken to address and remediate the issue. One of the first things we did was change our administrator passwords to be safe. Someone else suggested we force a password reset on all user accounts. The Tiger team decided to wait to force a password reset until we received more information about the hack. One of the problems is that it took Okta several days to respond publicly, which left Okta users wondering how to protect themselves and how bad the hack was. The hackers were making it out to be way worse than it actually was. The whole time, I documented what was happening and any steps taken.

The Tiger team checked for any signs of compromise to the company's systems and found nothing. The Tiger team literally started doing Google searches to get more information on the hack, and I found the best actionable information posted by Cloudflare. The Cloudflare blog explained that Cloudflare uses Okta internally for their employee **single sign-on** (**SSO**). Since a Cloudflare employee's account was in a tweet showing the hacker was using it, Cloudflare temporarily suspended the user's account. Cloudflare's IRT did a thorough investigation by pulling a list of all employees who requested a password or **multi-factor authentication** (**MFA**) reset from December 1, 2021, through March 22, 2022. Cloudflare forced a password reset for these employees in case a hacker had requested a password or MFA reset. Okta notified Cloudflare that morning that there was no evidence of compromise for Cloudflare's Okta instances.

Cloudflare went on to explain that there is a setting within Okta that allows Okta Customer Support to have escalated privileges and recommended disabling this access. In the final blog that Cloudflare posted about the Okta hack, they removed the information about Customer Support access. Cloudflare also explained it reviewed its Okta logs and stores the Okta logs on-premise so that they have access to them past 90 days, which is what the Okta dashboard provides. Okta explained they searched for the following in the Okta logs:

```
user.account.reset_password, user.mfa.factor.update, system.mfa.factor.
deactivate, user.mfa.attempt_bypass, and user.session.impersonation.
initiate
```

In addition to searching their Okta accounts for password resets, they also reviewed their Google Workspace accounts for resets during the December through March timeframe and forced password resets on those accounts.[2] As a CISO, I was so grateful for Cloudflare to have posted such detailed and helpful information publicly to help other Okta customers. It took Okta several days to respond to even acknowledge the hack, let alone provide guidance to its customers.

Quick reference for endpoint security

Based on company size, your company's endpoint security strategy may consist of the following:

- **Basic:**

  - Antivirus

    - Windows Defender (Windows devices)

    - Bitdefender (Mac devices)

    - Malwarebytes ThreatDown Core (Mac devices)

    - SentinelOne Core (Mac devices)

  - VPN

    - Proton VPN (free) when on guest Wi-Fi

    - F5 SecureFreedom

    - ExpressVPN

    - Surfshark

  - Security and awareness training and phishing campaigns (*Chapter 7*)

    - Curricula

- **Medium:**

  - Antivirus

    - Windows Defender (Windows devices)

    - Bitdefender (All devices)

2   Graham-Cumming, John, et al. "Cloudflare's Investigation of the January 2022 Okta Compromise." The Cloudflare Blog, Cloudflare, 14 June 2022, blog.cloudflare.com/cloudflare-investigation-of-the-january-2022-okta-compromise/.

- Malwarebytes ThreatDown Advanced or Elite (All devices)
- SentinelOne Control or Complete (All devices)
  - VPN
    - F5 SecureFreedom
    - ExpressVPN
    - Surfshark
    - Cisco
    - Palo Alto
    - Check Point
  - Email scanner
    - Defender EOP
    - Mimecast
  - Security and awareness training and phishing campaigns (*Chapter 7*)
    - KnowBe4
    - Curricula
    - NINJIO
- **Advanced:**
  - EDR
    - Windows Defender (Windows devices)
    - Bitdefender (All devices)
    - Malwarebytes ThreatDown Elite or Ultimate (All devices)
    - SentinelOne Commercial or Enterprise (Mac devices)
  - VPN
    - Cisco
    - Palo Alto
    - Check Point

- Email scanner

  - Defender EOP

  - Proofpoint

  - Cisco ESA

- Security and awareness training and phishing campaigns (*Chapter 7*)

  - KnowBe4

  - Curricula

  - Ninjio

Summary

In summary, securing your endpoints is imperative to lower your company's risk. Whether an employee takes their work laptop and connects it to a public Wi-Fi or clicks on a suspicious email, there are risks with your endpoints. Ideally, you want an advanced antivirus and anti-malware solution such as an EDR. Having a good EDR will both secure the endpoint and will alert you and your security team if an event occurs.

In the next chapter, we will be covering backups. When building a security program, ensuring you have good offline backups is critical. Whether an employee makes a mistake or your company gets attacked by ransomware, you need good offline backups and a **business continuity plan** (**BCP**).

6

Data Safeguarding

This chapter is about backups. I know it sounds so boring. A chapter about backups, really? Yes, because good *offline* backups are paramount to securing your company's data, ensuring your company's data and computers are available, and keeping your company running. We will be discussing the importance of backups, testing your backups, and business continuity.

In this chapter, we're going to cover the following main topics:

- Offline backups
- Testing your backups
- Availability in the cloud
- Business continuity
- Disaster recovery

Offline backups

I was at a security conference, and I heard a talk by Sean McCloskey, the Chief of Cybersecurity for the **Cybersecurity and Infrastructure Security Agency** (**CISA**) Region 4. Sean spoke about the importance of good offline backups. He said that every single company that has suffered a ransomware attack where he was part of the incident response did not have good offline backups. Whenever I talk about backups, I always stress that they must be offline. You're probably asking, What's the deal with offline backups? Well, with ransomware, it will encrypt all connected online drives. If you are using iCloud or SharePoint as an online backup drive, it will also be encrypted if ransomware is run on your computer. Likewise, any online USB-connected drives will be encrypted.

It's paramount that you have good offline backups. The way to do this is to configure incremental backups and disconnect access to the drive in between. Windows has a built-in incremental backup that can be configured. There are also backup-as-a-service offerings that will provide incremental backups. Remember, if you have a Mac computer, time machine provides this also. For a company, you will want to use managed Apple IDs so that the company can manage the corporate-owned Macbook computers. Apple provides free small business services in the United States, so that is something to consider. Even if your current backup was online and connected when ransomware is run on your computer, you can then go back to the last incremental backup and restore your data. The incremental backup can be set up and sent to an alternate server, cloud service, or a local storage device.

If you use a local backup drive, then only connect it periodically. I will say that some people advise keeping it connected all the time but periodically saving a backup to an offline drive. There are applications that can disconnect the drive when not backing up the computer. For compliance purposes, it is not recommended to allow for backups to local portable storage. **NIST 800-53B control MP-7: Media Use** restricts the use of portable storage for no identifiable owner. Essentially, unless your organization assigns a USB device to you, you should not use it. The reason is two-fold: you don't want an unauthorized USB drive that could potentially have malware on it plugged into your computer. On the other hand, by allowing your employees to back up their computers to a local portable storage device, there is the potential that sensitive documentation might go with them once they leave the company.

When I was at Cisco, they would purchase a backup drive for each of the team members who worked from home. Once Cisco was trying to get FedRAMP certification, everything changed. They moved to a SaaS-based backup solution. I highly recommend the various SaaS backup services such as **CrashPlan**, **Veeam**, or **Rubrik**. **CrashPlan** is a no-frills backup solution that is cost-efficient at a low price and works well for backups with unlimited storage. It is a good solution for small- and medium-sized companies. There are large Fortune 500 companies using CrashPlan, so I don't want you to think it is not a solution for large enterprises. They were the first to offer a SaaS backup solution. Veeam and Rubrik offer additional backup features that are more at the **Advanced** Enterprise level. *Table 6.1* provides a comparison of three backup-as-a-service solutions. Another option I wanted to mention is **Backblaze**. It started out as a cloud-based backup solution for Silicon Valley customers but is now also a competitor of AWS, offering S3 bucket-type services at a much lower price:

Features	CrashPlan	Veeam	Rubrik
Windows client	Yes	Yes	Yes
Mac client	Yes	Yes	Yes
SaaS	Yes	Yes	Yes
Encrypted at rest	Yes	Yes	Yes
Incremental backups	Yes	Yes	Yes
Backup and recovery	No	Yes	Yes
Disaster recovery	Yes	Yes	Yes
Alerts and notifications	No	Yes	Yes
Cost	USD TBD	USD TBD	USD TBD

Table 6.1 – Software evaluation backup-as-a-service

How does your company fulfill this as a startup or small company without the budget for a SaaS backup service? First of all, encourage all of your employees to save all of their company documents on the platform you use for document sharing. For example, if you are an M365 shop using SharePoint and Teams, then encourage your employees to work off of the server. There are options to open documents and spreadsheets that reside on the server on your desktop application, such as Word or Excel. The document is then stored and updated on the server.

Depending on the size and maturity of your security program, you can handle restricting local storage. First, for startups and small companies, you can address this in your security policy or backup policy. In the information security policy, you can state that local backups to a portable device are not allowed. This is a simple way to address the threat of data loss prevention by use of local storage devices. Definitely caution your employees not to trust USB drives or charging cables received in an unknown manner, such as found on the ground. This should be part of your security awareness training. We'll cover this in more detail in *Chapter 7*.

Ideally, you will want to use a backup-as-a-service whether you are at the **basic**, **medium**, or **advanced** level. Remember, companies are in business to make money. Especially for small- and medium-sized businesses, you can forgo the backup-as-a-service if you are a cloud-first company. The cloud and SaaS have built-in availability, snapshots, and backups that can be relied upon. Based on your company's budget, risk management, and cloud usage, you may be able to forego the backup-as-a-service.

Based on company size, your company's backup solution may include the following:

- **Basic**:
  - Use company-managed Windows Backup and iCloud for endpoints
  - Inform employees to work off of the server or upload work.
    - SharePoint
    - Teams
    - Git
  - Inform employees not to use unidentified USB sticks or local backups
  - Rely on SaaS and cloud-based availability and backups
  - Ensure backups of data center servers and device configurations
- **Medium**:
  - Ensure compliance mandates for your industry are met
  - Offsite storage of backups can be stored in the cloud

- **Advanced:**

  - Ensure offsite backup-as-a-service for endpoints and servers

  - Provide company-purchased USB drives to employees

  - Use software or implement Windows GPO to disallow USE use and local storage devices

  - Use **data loss prevention (DLP)** software

Testing your backups

When I was a CISO at RedSeal, the **Chief Executive Officer (CEO)** came back from a training session with a Venture Capital firm. It was a security and leadership conference for all of the CEOs in the Venture Capital Company's ecosystem. The CEO immediately reached out to me with the top actions that our company needed to take in order to be protected against ransomware. I had already done a lot of research on ransomware for a presentation that I did at the **Healthcare Information and Management Systems Society (HIMSS)** Conference, which is one of the largest IT Health conferences in the world.

Having good offline backups, as well as testing your backups, was a must. Many times, when it comes to being time to recover from a backup, the company realizes too late that they either don't have good offline backups or their backups are corrupted in some way. Possibly, the data they thought were being backed up weren't.

The best way to prepare for having to recover from your backups is to test them regularly. You can do this daily, weekly, monthly, or quarterly, depending on your company's time and resource availability. I recommend testing the backups at least quarterly, along with the account reviews that have to be done for compliance. The account reviews ensure that the accounts of employees who have left the company have been disabled. There should be a regular process for this, but it is good to do a quarterly review of accounts to ensure one wasn't missed. The account reviews can also be automated.

High-value data that would have a severe effect on the company if lost should be tested at least monthly. You should rotate the backups that are tested. If a subset of backups has been tested, ensure you rotate them. You don't want the engineer always testing the same backups each time. Set a recurring task to ensure these are done based on the company's agreed-upon timelines. Ensure your policies are properly updated to reflect the review and testing times. When your company is audited, the auditors will read your policies and request evidence that it was done. The evidence can be on a wiki or notion page with dates and the person doing the review.

Critical infrastructure servers, such as **domain controllers**, should be system-backed up and tested. In the case of ransomware, the domain controllers will most likely be compromised. Having a backup of domain controllers for a s system prior to the attack can drastically reduce the recovery time. Restoring a Windows domain from bare metal should be part of the backup tests.

Testing and validating your backups can be automated. By automating the testing and validation of your backups, you can easily move the timelines up for your most critical data to twice a day. Even by automating the testing, you should schedule a manual review of the backups at least quarterly or even monthly. This review can be done along with your account reviews. It is good for the administrator to take a look at the backups. It's possible the testing passed, but there could be formatting or other changes to files or data. As part of your automation, if you compare the hashes of files, you should be fine. A cryptographic hash is similar to a digital fingerprint of the file or data.

When looking at best practices, such as meeting SOC 2 Type 2, you will test the failover and availability of your cloud or backups. You need to review the stored data. Take a look at the backup; do you see the correct logs and document information? Consider this:

- Are they readable?

- Do the dates look accurate for the backup day?

Ensure your company has either a backup policy or this information is included within the information security policy. Additionally, have the engineer performing the backup testing write a procedure so that if they leave the company, a written procedure will be in place for how the backups will be tested each quarter.

Cryptographic hashing

While we are talking about hashing, I wanted to explain what it is and why you want to use it. Ensure your company is using **SHA-256** or above. SHA-1 has been deprecated due to a SHA-1 collision. A SHA-1 collision occurs when two distinct pieces of data hash to the same message digest. If an attacker can craft a collision, they can use it to create two different files that share the same SHA-1 hash value[1].

Although SHA-1 has been deprecated, hmac-sha-1 is still okay to use since it is a secret keyed hash value. What a hashing algorithm provides is integrity. It doesn't actually encrypt the data, so you can't read them. Hashing runs a mathematical function on the document that essentially fingerprints it. If anything in the document changes, then the hash value will also change, alerting you to the change. The reason this is important is that you know that the data or email has not changed while in transit.

If you have two documents with the same information in them and you run the SHA-256 hash on them, the hash value, which is 256 bits, will be the exact same. If anything changes in the document, even a space being added, then the hash value will change. This provides integrity. In *Figure 6.1*, you can see that two documents with the same information will result in the same 256-bit hash value:

---

1   Stevens , Marc, and Elie Bursztein. Announcing the First Sha1 Collision. *Google Online Security Blog*, Google, 23 Feb. 2017, security.googleblog.com/2017/02/announcing-first-sha1-collision.html.

What is SHA-256?

SHA-256 (Secure Hash Algorithm 256) is a <u>cryptographic hash function</u>

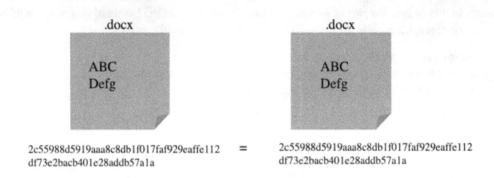

Figure 6.1 – SHA 256 hashing example for matching

In *Figure 6.2*, you see where one document had "De" deleted and the hash value changes. Now, when the hashing validation is done and the two values are compared, the change causes the values to no longer be equal. The application will cause an error saying the hash value is invalid. This alerts the user that something has changed in the document, image, or application:

What is SHA-256?

SHA-256 (Secure Hash Algorithm 256) is a <u>cryptographic hash function</u>

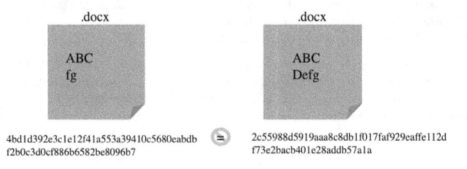

Figure 6.2 – SHA 256 hashing example for different

In a real-world example, the sender runs the SHA-256 hashing algorithm, and then, when the receiver opens the email, the same hashing algorithm is used to run the email. The original hashing value is encrypted with the sender's private key. The recipient is able to decrypt the value with the sender's public key. Next, the recipient will run the same hashing algorithm on the email. If they are not equal, then an error is received. When the hash value is encrypted, it's called a digital signature. This also provides non-repudiation so that the person who "signs" it or encrypts the hash value can't say that they didn't send the email. This is why digital signatures that use secure hashing algorithms tied to the user can be upheld in court as an actual signature. This is how Docusign-signed documents work.

Availability in the cloud

One of the great things about the cloud is that availability is built in. All of the cloud services provide this. Amazon's **relational database service** (**RDS**) automatically backs up your database instance to Amazon S3 for the duration that you specify. Additionally, you have the option to manually create snapshots, which are retained until you choose to remove them. The snapshots are the same as full backups. In addition, in AWS, they have regions, and within each region, there are availability zones. There is built-in availability with automatic failover within the regions. This is a great cost savings for cloud-first startups. They can use these built-in availability cloud features and not have to purchase an additional backup-as-a-service.

The other thing to think about is that each SaaS service that you use provides automatic backups of the data within their service. For example, SalesForce provides at least 30 days of backups. For small- and medium-sized companies, you can rely on that. For a more robust backup solution, you can do your own backups of the data for forensics purposes. Large companies will have additional backups. You also have to remember to align your backup policy with any compliance that you have to meet. The SEC requires that event and incident logs be retained for up to 5 years. Not all logs need to be retained, but ones specific to an incident must be retained.

Business continuity

Business continuity is keeping your business running in the event of an incident. We've all heard of the nightmare ransomware attacks where companies have to literally stop work until they are able to stop and recover from the attack. Your business continuity plan covers the roles and responsibilities of the individuals involved as well as a line of succession or who will be contacted and in what order. The business continuity plan is typically more general in that you don't list people's names but their job titles. For example, under the line of succession section of the plan, it can be said that the CEO is responsible for the safety and security of the employees and will ensure the business continuity plan is followed during a disruption. Next, there might be a description of the Head of Engineering being responsible for recovering the IT infrastructure in the event of disruption. Additionally, explain what happens if the CEO is unavailable; who can fill in for them? An example would be a sentence about the Chief Operating Officer filling in for the CEO.

Recovery time objective (RTO)

The **recovery time objective** (**RTO**) is the maximum acceptable length of time that a system can be down after a failure or disruption. It defines how quickly you need to restore a system to maintain business operations. For a small company or startup with one SaaS, a single RTO for your company can be set; for example, an RTO of 8 hours. This means in the event of a major disruption, at most, the company can only be down for 8 hours. Your company has to plan and prepare for availability measures that will ensure you can recover your systems and get operational within 8 hours.

For larger companies that have multiple products, the RTO can be broken out so that higher-impact systems have a shorter RTO than lower-impact systems. This can also be derived from the **business impact analysis** (**BIA**) and the categorization of assets. For example, a critical system such as the customer-facing SaaS may have a 3-hour RTO. The server where your source code is stored may be able to be down for 4 hours. Your HR systems may be able to be down for 6 hours. Remember, if you are using Github SaaS, then you can review the availability that the SaaS service provides.

Recovery point objective (RPO)

The **recovery point objective** (**RPO**) is the maximum age of files that an organization must recover from backup storage for normal operations to resume after a disaster. It defines how much data loss is acceptable. You can think of this as an incremental backup that you can recover. For example, if you do incremental backups every hour, then you can recover back to the last hour. If your incremental backups are every 6 hours, then you can recover back to 6 hours. An RPO of 6 hours means that your company accepts that you can lose 6 hours and that it is acceptable to recover from that point in time. I recommend 3 hours.

The RPO quantifies the acceptable age of data that must be recovered in the event of a system failure. When defined in a time-based metric, an RPO of 4 hours implies that the data restored should be no older than four hours. This metric is calibrated considering the data's importance, the time needed for restoration, and the potential business impact of data loss.

The RPO plays a crucial role in shaping an organization's disaster recovery plan. Setting the RPO too high could leave the organization vulnerable to unacceptable levels of risk.

Maximum tolerable downtime (MTD)

The **maximum tolerable downtime** (**MTD**) is the longest period of time that a system or business process can be unavailable without causing irreversible harm to the organization. It's a metric used in business continuity planning to assess the impact of downtime and guide recovery strategies. MTD encompasses both RTO and RPO, providing a comprehensive view of tolerance for operational disruptions. MTD includes the time when you discovered there was an incident and have begun to assemble the incident response team. The MTD includes this time, so if your RTO is 8 hours, then the MTD has to be at least 10 hours, but it could be longer, such as 48 hours.

Succession planning

Succession planning in cybersecurity refers to the strategic process of identifying and developing new leaders who can replace old leaders when they leave, retire, or are unable to fulfill their duties due to unforeseen events. This is an essential component of business continuity planning, as it ensures that there is no loss of knowledge or leadership in the event that a key employee is no longer available.

This planning involves understanding the critical roles within the organization and ensuring that there are trained and capable employees ready to step into these roles at a moment's notice. Succession planning ensures operational resilience and mitigates the risks associated with the loss of experienced leaders who hold critical cybersecurity knowledge and capabilities. It also includes cross-training employees, creating detailed job descriptions with the critical functions documented, and ensuring knowledge is shared and not siloed.

In the context of cybersecurity, succession planning is crucial because it prepares the organization for a smooth transition of responsibilities that includes maintaining the integrity and security of IT systems and sensitive data. This helps to preserve the organization's defensive capabilities against cyber threats, even during periods of transition.

AWS DDOS attack

Even AWS, which provides 99.999% availability, has incurred major DDOS attacks in the past that slowed response times for various regions. In December of 2021, AWS-East1 suffered a major DDOS attack that affected multiple customers who run their companies in AWS-East-1. It was reported that Netflix, iRobot, Ring, and Disney were affected because their foundational services, such as internal DNS, monitoring, and authorization, are provided to AWS-EAST-1. When the DDOS occurred, affecting a large number of AWS clients, auto-scaling was triggered at an alarming rate, which overwhelmed this internal network, causing communication delays[2].

AWS engineers realized the congestion and one of the first things they did was move the DNS to another subnet, allowing customer traffic to connect to the DNS. This allowed them to review logs and figure out the root cause of the disruption. The engineers also disabled the auto-scaling while troubleshooting until they could properly remediate the issue. AWS has since made changes to its architecture in order to ensure an outage like this does not occur. The point is that even if a service or SaaS that your company relies on has given you 99.999% availability, it can still have delays. When you are deciding on your RTO, you should take this into account. This particular disruption affected AWS customer support from 7:33 PM to 2:25 PM PDT, which is 7 hours. AWS-East-1 wasn't completely down, but customer communications were delayed and slowed. This is why you want to give yourself some time for the RTO. I recommend 8 hours. Most customers want to see that you have a business continuity plan with RTO, MTD, and RPO. If a potential customer doesn't sign because you have an 8-hour RTO, then you can revisit and decide if you want to lower the number.

---

2   Applegate, Katherine. Summary of the AWS Service Event in the Northern Virginia (US-EAST-1) Region. *Amazon*, Amazon, 2020, aws.amazon.com/message/12721/.

> **Important note**
>
> DNS is a foundational service used in networking. It translates domain and host names to IP addresses. When you go to `https://www.google.com`, this URL has to be translated to an IP address in order for you to communicate with Google. If the DNS goes down, then you won't be able to communicate on the web. I was a DNS administrator at IBM in my early career. Most people don't understand what an important role it plays in being able to connect over the internet. An easy way to check if your DNS is working properly is to open a command prompt (or terminal on Mac) and type `www.google.com` in lookup to see if you are reaching your DNS. You can easily build in availability with your DNS by adding two to your configuration. On a Mac, you go to **Settings | Network | Wi-Fi | Details | DNS** to verify you have two DNS servers configured. Typically, these will be given to you when you connect to your Wi-Fi. On Windows, you can right-click on the Windows button | **Settings | Network & Internet | Wi-Fi | Hardware Properties | Edit**.

Disaster recovery

Disaster recovery is extremely important to keep your company running in case of a disaster. It can be a natural disaster such as a flood, earthquake, or hurricane. It could also be man-made, such as a ransomware attack, that brings your company to a halt. Before the cloud, you had to have a secondary data center from your primary one that had a hot, warm, or cold setup. The secondary site would be in another region. For example, if your primary site was on the East Coast, then your secondary backup site would be in the Central time zone. Ideally, a disaster recovery site is located in a geographically separate region, far enough from the original site to not be affected by the same disaster (such as a flood or earthquake) but close enough to be reached in a timely manner if physical access is needed. The choice between a hot, warm, or cold site is a balance between cost, speed of recovery, and the importance of the systems that are being protected.

Hot site: A hot site is a replica of the original site of the organization, with full computer systems and near-complete backups of user data. Hot sites are fully functional data centers that companies can move to with little or no downtime in the event of a disaster. These are the most expensive to operate.

Warm site: A warm site has the necessary hardware and connectivity but does not have live data. Companies may have backups on hand at the warm site, and the recovery time is slower than with a hot site but faster than with a cold site. Warm sites are a cost-effective solution that provides a compromise between hot and cold sites.

Cold site: A cold site is the most basic type of recovery site for an organization. It does not have the hardware and software systems pre-installed. Instead, a cold site is simply a space where the infrastructure (e.g., space, power, and networking) is available. Companies using cold sites typically have a longer recovery time, as they need to set up systems or transport them from the affected site.

With the advent of the cloud, disaster recovery has gotten much easier because the cloud includes built-in availability and failover. The one detail to consider is that the built-in availability and failover are within the same region, only a few miles apart. If there was a flood in that region or another major event, your failover servers may be affected. Many companies just rely on the built-in failover and redundancy in the cloud. For best practices, I recommend configuring an automated backup to another region. All cloud services have this option for a fee. You can also backup to cold cloud storage, which is an inexpensive option offered by AWS. I've even heard that if your primary cloud is AWS, then some companies use AWS for their backup storage and vice versa. Apparently, at one point, two Azure regions went down at the same time.

Redundancy in architecture

When doing your disaster recovery planning, you have to think about redundancy in the architecture of your data center, and infrastructure refers to the incorporation of additional or duplicate systems, components, or functionalities within an IT infrastructure to ensure continuous operations in the event of a failure or disaster. The objective is to create a fail-safe environment where the system can rely on backup components without experiencing a significant interruption in service.

In practical terms, this can include multiple power sources, redundant data storage solutions (such as RAID arrays), clustered servers, or duplicated network paths and components. Redundancy can be applied at various layers of an organization's architecture, including data, hardware, and connectivity.

The key aspect of redundancy is that it's proactive; instead of reacting to a failure, systems are designed to automatically switch to standby systems that take over the load with minimal to no downtime. This approach is crucial for mission-critical applications where even a short period of unavailability can have significant adverse effects on the business.

Disaster recovery roles and responsibilities

In the case of a disaster, all staff, including contractors, are to assist in the recovery of IT systems to re-establish standard operations. Responsibilities are assigned as follows:

- **Executive Team**

  - Declare the company as being in a state of disaster

  - Evaluate information to determine the maximum tolerable downtime

  - Authorize contracts essential for resuming operations

- **IT Team**

  - Re-establish network services either at a secondary location or in the primary office location

  - Determine which servers or services are not functioning and re-establish functionality

- Order the equipment necessary to re-establish services
- Install and implement any tools, hardware, software, and systems
- **Operations Team**
- Directing employees to their respective work locations
- Restoring and ensuring the functionality of telephone and internet services
- Managing the conference call system and scheduling as required
- Provisioning essential supplies for disaster response
- Providing ample computer and laptop resources for the resumption of work

Testing disaster recovery

Testing your disaster recovery is made up of forcing a failover to ensure the availability of critical parts of your network. It can include testing your generators if you manage your own data center. We only had to test the generators when I worked at IBM, and we operated our own data centers. With the advent of the cloud, most companies simply test the failover of their critical assets in the cloud.

Tabletops are used to test your disaster recovery and incident response plans. A table top exercise is essentially a discussion-based simulation of a disaster. Key team members will discuss their roles during an emergency and walk through a specific disaster scenario to assess the plan's effectiveness.

Summary

In summary, good backups, availability, business continuity, and disaster recovery are imperative to ensure that your company can maintain operations in the event of a disaster. Whether a natural disaster, terrorist attack, or man-made disaster occurs, your company will be prepared with thoroughly tested business continuity and disaster recovery plans.

In the next chapter, we will be covering security awareness training. When building a security program, ensuring you build a culture of security awareness is important. You can have excellent security safeguards, but one click on the wrong link or having a hacker trying to tailgate could open your company to attack.

7
Security Awareness Culture

This chapter is about developing a security awareness culture. No matter what tools and security controls you have deployed, you still need security awareness training for everyone in your company. You'll want to make it fun. It's great to come up with a slogan. I took the *MIT Sloan Executive Education Cybersecurity for Managers: A Playbook* class, and one of the big points was to come up with a slogan for your company. You can make it fun or in a way that fits well with your company's culture. Gamifying your security awareness is another way to make it more interesting for your employees.

In this chapter, we're going to cover the following main topics:

- Security awareness training is foundational
- Cybersecurity awareness training products
- Security is everyone's responsibility
- Security awareness is mandatory and tracked

Security awareness training is foundational

Security awareness training is mandatory for all companies under any compliance framework. It doesn't matter what standard or framework your company adheres to; security awareness training is required. You can see this in *Table 7.1* which maps security standards and frameworks to the sections that cover security awareness training:

Standard/Framework	Section
NIST CSF	PR.AT-1
NIST 800-53	AT-2, PM-13
CIS	14
PCI	12.6
HIPAA	164.308(a)(5)(i)

Standard/Framework	Section
CMMC	AT.L2-3.2.3
	AT.L2-3.2.1
ISO 27001	A.7.2.2, A.12.2.1
GDPR	Data Protection Officer Responsibilities
	Art 39
SOC 2 Type 1 and 2	CC5.3
	CC1.4
CCPA	No specific details on awareness training
NERC-CIP	CIP-003-6 R1
	CIP-004-6 R1
FedRAMP (Low, Moderate, High)	AT-1
	AT-2
	AT-2(2)
NIST 800-171	3.2.1
	3.2.2
	3.2.3

Table 7.1 – Security awareness training and compliance

One security awareness training program can cover all of these standards. If your company wants to obtain SOC 2 Type 2, then creating a security awareness program will cover this, as well as other compliance standards and laws such as HIPAA, ISO 27001, and GDPR.

Depending on the size of your company, you can vary your approach as to how you create your cybersecurity awareness training program. For example, if your company is a start-up, you can take a more simplistic approach of instituting annual cybersecurity awareness training for all of your employees. Larger companies may want to come up with a slogan and have a more cohesive culture shift around security; for example, *Every October is Cybersecurity Awareness Month in the United States*. Putting flyers around the office in common areas and displaying cardboard cut-outs near elevators can raise awareness. Whether your company is small or large, simply having mandatory cybersecurity awareness training for all of your employees will suffice.

When I worked at Cisco, they put out these security monster cutouts and had slogans for each, such as *Don't get hooked by phishers*. You can also use well-known slogans such as *Stop. Think. Connect.* This is a global campaign to protect children from online dangers. There is also *Stop-Think-Click*, which is an organization that provides information about cybersecurity training. Other government agencies are also using the slogan. You can Google cybersecurity awareness slogans also to get more ideas.

Cybersecurity awareness training products

There are a number of excellent cybersecurity awareness training products on the market. I've used several different ones. I like KnowBe4, but also NINJIO is really good and fun. KnowBe4 is the industry leader at the moment. With every publicly traded company having to meet compliance requirements, there are a lot of cybersecurity awareness training companies that jumped into the market.

If your company decides to use a compliance product such as Drata, then it has security awareness training bundled into the product. In that case, you wouldn't have to purchase a separate product. Drata provides continuous compliance for your cloud environment. If your company is primarily on-premise, then a product such as Drata would not be useful to you.

Of the security awareness training I have used, I really like KnowBe4. With Kevin Mitnick having sold the company and now having passed away, I'm not sure what the future of KnowBe4 is. I'm sure KnowBe4 will keep the videos updated, just without Kevin in them. However, basic security awareness isn't going to change much. Ninjio was referred to me by another **virtual CISO (vCISO)**. I've seen a demo of the videos. Ninjio hires Hollywood actors to do the voices in the training videos. They also send out monthly short awareness training so that it is continuous throughout the year. Curricula is perfect for companies that have a tight budget or are smaller, such as a start-up. *Table 7.2* provides a comparison of features of Curricula, KnowBe4, and Ninjio:

Features	Curricula	KnowBe4	Ninjio
Awareness training	Yes	Yes	Yes
Email phishing	Yes	Yes	Yes
Monthly ongoing training	Yes	Yes	Yes
Quarterly ongoing training	Yes	Yes	Yes
Physical training	Yes	Yes	Yes
Ransomware prevention	No	Yes	Yes
Email phishing campaigns included	Yes	Yes	Yes
Gamification	Yes	No	Yes
Cost	$ Free 1st 1,000 users	$ TBD	$ TBD

Table 7.2 – Software evaluation cybersecurity awareness training

> **Note**
>
> A vCISO oversees and manages the security functions of an organization. A vCISO may also be called a fractional CISO. Companies not ready to hire a full-time CISO but that need advisory services to lower their company's cyber risk, as well as meet compliance such as SOC 2, ISO 27001, HIPAA, CMMC, or FedRAMP, will need to hire a vCISO to advise their company. A vCISO can be hired for a number of hours per week, such as 10 or 20 hours per week or even per month. Also, if your CISO has been promoted from within, it's good to hire an outside CISO to get another perspective. I provide these services as part of TrustedCISO.

How does your company fulfill the security awareness training as a start-up or small company without the budget for a security awareness training program? I was pleased to learn about Curricula since it is free for the first 1,000 users and provides automated phishing campaigns. This is perfect for start-ups and smaller companies on a tight budget. They offer two videos for security awareness training that will meet your needs for security awareness training and also provide SOC 2 training. Curricula also includes a phishing simulator at the free tier. A phishing simulator allows you to set up phishing campaigns. Phishing is when an attacker sends an email that is bogus or malicious in nature. Typically, there will be a sense of urgency for you to do something fast. It also will most likely include a link to a malicious website where malware will automatically be downloaded to your computer or an attachment that contains malicious macros or malware. The phishing simulator will allow you to automatically send out fake phishing emails to your employees on a regular basis, such as quarterly. It will track who clicks on the link or opens an attachment. If the employee fails the phishing simulator, then they are required to retake the phishing training video. This gets employees used to being cautious and analyzing emails on a regular basis.

In *Figure 7.1*, you will see an attempted phishing attempt from someone masquerading as Microsoft. When analyzing an email, you want to review the entire email message beginning with the subject and sent email address:

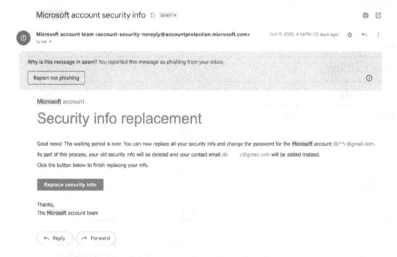

Figure 7.1 – Microsoft account phishing email

Beginning at the top of the email, review the subject, "*Microsoft account security info*," which by itself should make you take notice. The title should definitely give you pause in that it is from Microsoft and has *security* in it. Next, look at who sent it. It says *The Microsoft account team*. Anyone can create their own email name to display, so the actual email address is most important: *account-security-noreply@accountprotection.microsoft.com. The Microsoft.com domain is a legitimate domain, but they have added a subdomain "accountprotection" subdomain to it.*

Note

Domain Name Servers (DNS) are used to make IP addresses into human words. This is how you can open a browser and type in `google.com` and not the IP address of the Google server. For example, if you open a Terminal window on a Mac or a cmd window on a Windows machine and type `>nslookup google.com`, you will first see the DNS server that is doing the translation between IP addresses and hostnames. Next, the IP addresses of the Google.com servers are listed:

```
db@MacBook-Pro-8 ~ % nslookup google.com
Server:         192.168.220.7
Address:        192.168.220.7#53

Non-authoritative answer:
Name:    google.com
Address: 209.85.201.102
Name:    google.com
Address: 209.85.201.138
Name:    google.com
Address: 209.85.201.100
Name:    google.com
Address: 209.85.201.139
Name:    google.com
Address: 209.85.201.101
Name:    google.com
Address: 209.85.201.113
```

Figure 7.2 – DNS query – nslookup

A DNS domain typically has two components: the domain name and the top-level domain (TLD), separated by a dot (.). For example, in "*google.com*," "*google*" is the domain name, and "*.com*" is the TLD. "*Accountprotection*" is considered to be a subdomain. Subdomains can be hacked if a server has a vulnerability or is misconfigured. A subdomain takeover is a security flaw that arises when a subdomain points to an inactive or improperly configured service such as a Content Delivery Network (CDN) or cloud host. This vulnerability allows attackers to seize the subdomain and exploit it for malicious activities, such as phishing or malware distribution.[1]

---

1   Sah, Rocky. "*Subdomain Hacking: Understanding the Threat, Methodology, and Prevention Strategies.*" Codelivly, 1 Sept. 2023, http://www.codelivly.com/subdomain-hacking-understanding-the-threat-methodology-and-prevention-strategies.

The body of the Microsoft email says, "*You can now replace all of your security info and change the password for the Microsoft account*". Why would I want to change all of my security info? I have it there for a reason and definitely do not want to change it along with my password. Secondly, it is referring to a Google email and not a Microsoft email. This is a red flag. Next, it says, "*your old security info will be deleted*". Why would I want to do that? This would allow a takeover of my entire account. In the same sentence, it says that it will add the same non-Microsoft email to my Microsoft account. This makes no sense. I reported this email as phishing. I could have hovered over the **Replace security info** button to inspect the link, but the whole email had so many red flags it seemed unnecessary. I reported it as spam and a phishing attempt. It's important to flag it not only to make it so that the button is not clickable but to alert Google to review and report on it. Google will alert Microsoft, and the bogus subdomain can be shut down.

Lately, Microsoft has suffered some data breaches. In Microsoft's most recent SOC 2 Type 2 report, they had several exceptions. This won't stop people from using Microsoft's products. When you are that large, you are kind of too big to fail. Companies aren't going to stop using Microsoft because they have multiple exceptions in their SOC 2 report or suffered a data breach. You need to use multiple products and different vendors to provide a layered defense. This is called **defense in depth** (**DiD**). If you have M365 even with the email phishing protection at E5, ideally you should have a separate product such as Proofpoint to scan your emails. Smaller start-ups can't afford all these products, so they will ensure they have the M365 E5 subscription with the Windows Defender email phishing scanning included. Many start-ups use Google Workspace because of the cost savings and built-in phishing features.

Based on company size, your company's security awareness solution may include the following:

- **Basic:**

  - Use *Curricula.org*

    - Free for up to 1,000 users

    - Provide security awareness training

    - Provide email phishing training

    - Provide SOC 2 training

  - Ensure training is delivered when an employee is hired

  - Ensure annually all employees complete the security awareness training

  - Track the training and ensure all employees have completed it

- **Medium:**

  - Use KnowBe4 or Ninjio or check out G2 for other options

    - Provide security awareness training

- Provide email phishing training

- Ensure training is delivered when an employee is hired

- Ensure annually all employees complete the security awareness training

- Ensure all employees review and sign pertinent policies; for example:

  - Information security policy

  - Code of conduct

  - **Acceptable use policy (AUP)**

- Track the training and ensure all employees have completed it

- Provide ongoing quarterly training via email covering various topics such as the following*:

  - Email phishing

  - The latest well-known breach and how it relates to your company

  - Password tips

  - Ransomware awareness

- *Ninjio automatically sends out monthly security updates

- You can also set up an automated email or Slack channel that lists the latest breaches and cybersecurity news or Cybersecurity and Infrastructure Security Agency (CISA) alerts

- Run phishing campaigns at least quarterly

- **Advanced:**

  - Use KnowBe4, Ninjio, or another product

    - Provide security awareness training

    - Provide email phishing training

  - Ensure training is delivered when an employee is hired

  - Ensure annually all employees complete the security awareness training

  - Ensure all employees review and sign pertinent policies; for example:

    - Information security policy

    - Code of conduct

    - AUP

- Track the training and ensure all employees have completed it
- Provide ongoing quarterly training via email covering various topics such as the following*:
  - Email phishing
  - The latest well-known breach and how it relates to your company
  - Password tips
  - Ransomware awareness
- *Ninjio automatically sends out monthly security updates
- You can also set up an automated email that lists the latest breaches and cybersecurity news and send those out periodically; that is, monthly
- Run phishing campaigns at least quarterly
- Provide application security training for developers on OWASP top 10 annually

Security is everyone's responsibility

When I was a CISO at RedSeal, the company had already built a culture of security that was great to build upon. Every employee was referred to as a cyber warrior. This made it easy for me to build upon this security-minded culture. One thing that everyone needs to know is that security is not simply the information security team's responsibility. Security is everyone's responsibility, from the CEO down to every employee. As more and more regulations are enacted, security being everyone's responsibility is becoming more laser-focused and required.

The Security Exchange Commission (SEC) issued a final rule on July 26, 2023, which requires disclosures on "cybersecurity risk management, strategy, governance, and incidents."

The SEC ruling mandates that material cyber incidents be reported on Form 8-k item 1.05. In addition, the board and executive management need to be fully aware of the actual risks your company faces. In the SolarWinds SEC case against the CISO, Timothy G. Brown, it specifically explains that the CISO was not reporting the actual risks the company faced up to executive management. The SEC filing states that *"SolarWinds allegedly misled investors by disclosing only generic and hypothetical risks at a time when the company and Brown knew of specific deficiencies in SolarWinds cybersecurity practices."*[2] For every CISO to be compliant with the SEC, it needs to be fully transparent in their risk register and reporting the risks up to executive management and the board.

---

2   https://www.sec.gov/news/press-release/2023-227

Materiality assessment

Registrants must use judgment to determine the materiality of cybersecurity incidents. The concept of "materiality" in the context of the new SEC Form 8-K, Item 1.05, does not adhere to a strict percentage of revenue or any other quantitative benchmark. Instead, materiality is determined based on whether the information about a cybersecurity incident would be considered important by a reasonable investor when making an investment decision. This assessment involves a qualitative judgment that can vary depending on the specific circumstances of the incident and its potential impact on the company's financial condition, operations, or reputation. In determining what cyber incidents to report, the CFO, CISO, and executive management should discuss and consider what incidents would be considered material to investors.

Materiality is based on various factors, such as the following:

- Violations of a company's security policies or procedures could lead to legal liability. *Note*: This is due diligence, as discussed in *Chapter 3*.

- Events that negatively impact a company's reputation, products, or services, including production delays or decreases.

- Incidents that financially affect a company, either directly or indirectly, through costs such as ransom payments, remediation fees, lost revenue, or damage to competitiveness.

- Issues that disrupt a company's relationships with customers or suppliers, such as accidental or intentional data exposure or compromise.

- Events that impair a company's operations, including unauthorized access to or loss of control over business information or systems.

- A series of smaller incidents that, when considered collectively, become material and thus warrant disclosure.[3]

Disclosure requirements

Under the updated regulations, entities must report any cybersecurity incidents deemed material by disclosing them on Form 8-K's new Item 1.05. This disclosure involves detailing the incident's characteristics, including its nature, extent, and timing, alongside the actual or potentially significant impact on the entity. Typically, the submission of an Item 1.05 Form 8-K is required within four business days following the entity's recognition of the incident's materiality.

---

3   Johnston, Jeff, et al. *"What Makes a Cybersecurity Risk or Incident Material? A Look at the SEC's Proposed Rules on Cybersecurity: Insights: Vinson & Elkins LLP."* Vinson & Elkins, 7 Nov. 2023, http://www.velaw.com/insights/what-makes-a-cybersecurity-risk-or-incident-material-a-look-at-the-secs-proposed-rules-on-cybersecurity/

Governance and management

In addition, the new SEC Form 8-K, Item 1.05, mandates detailed reporting on cybersecurity and risk management. This requirement emphasizes the necessity for the board to be fully aware of cybersecurity threats and for management to have effective processes in place for assessing and mitigating these risks.

Detailed disclosures about the board's and management's roles in cybersecurity risk oversight are required

The board must be informed of the actual cybersecurity risks, and management must have processes for assessing and responding to these risks. Typically, the CISO should report up to executive management on a quarterly basis. The CISO should be tracking the risks and risk treatment over time showing the red risks turning green as mitigations and controls are applied. Your company may have exceptions where old equipment cant be patched, then mitigations such as segmentation should be used to lower the risk. These exceptions should be tracked and signed off by executive management.

Third-party involvement

When a cybersecurity breach occurs in the systems of a third-party service provider that your company relies upon for its operations, you must evaluate the materiality of the incident in the same manner as it would for an incident within its own systems. If the incident is determined to be material, the company must disclose it under Item 1.05 of Form 8-K. This disclosure includes providing details about the nature, scope, and timing of the incident, as well as its material impact or the reasonably likely material impact on the company. Keep in mind for third-party disclosure, the following:

- Registrants are not exempt from disclosing incidents on third-party systems
- They may need to design disclosure controls related to communication with third-party **service providers (SPs)**[4]

Security awareness training is mandatory and tracked

Once your company begins on its compliance journey, whether it is SOC 2 Type 2 or ISO *27001*, you will need records showing that every employee has taken annual security awareness training. Don't worry if you haven't been doing this in the years prior to getting SOC 2 Type 2 or ISO *27001*. When you are ready to go for compliance, the security awareness training is mandatory once you are in your audit window. It is good to start doing security awareness training as soon as possible, and using one of these great platforms such as Curricula, KnowBe4, or Ninjio will make the process super easy. One thing to be aware of is that once you are in an audit period (for example, with SOC 2 Type 1), it

---

4   *"SEC Issues New Requirements for Cybersecurity Disclosures (July 30, 2023)."* DART, Deloitte, dart. deloitte.com/USDART/home/publications/deloitte/heads-up/2023/sec-rule-cyber-disclosures. Accessed 30 Oct. 2023.

is a **point-in-time** (**PIT**) audit. The auditors come in and check the controls for a particular day and conduct the audit. For SOC 2 Type 2, you will decide on an audit reporting period from 3 months to 1 year. During that audit reporting period, you need to demonstrate meeting the requirements and controls. Most requirements have to be met during that period, such as the **disaster recovery** (**DR**) and **incident response** (**IR**) tabletop. Your annual pen test doesn't have to be within the audit period, but it is ideal if it can be. Once you obtain SOC 2, then the reporting period will start for the following year, and it's easier to ensure all requirements are met within the reporting period. As for the security awareness training, as long as it is done within the year of the audit, it will meet SOC 2. Every employee must take the training, and you must track it.

Summary

In summary, security is everyone's responsibility, from the CEO down to the lowest-ranking employee. In order for everyone in the organization to understand, be trained, and be prepared to defend the organization, they need security awareness training. Clicking on one bogus link could potentially launch ransomware and cause a major disruption for your company. Even seasoned information security professionals need refreshers on what to look out for when it comes to phishing emails. Everyone can get in a hurry and click on that link that they shouldn't have.

In the next chapter, we will be covering vulnerability management. Did you know that the most critical Common Vulnerability Scoring System (CVSS)-scored vulnerabilities may not be the first ones you need to patch? Well, it depends on several factors, such as asset location, asset rating, and whether it has been exploited in the wild.

8

Vulnerability Management

This chapter is about vulnerability management. In order to build a strong security program and lower your company's risk, you must patch security vulnerabilities. If you stay up with the latest threats, you will understand that it's not easy to keep up with patching all those thousands of vulnerabilities. We'll be discussing practical strategies to prioritize vulnerability patching.

In this chapter, we're going to cover the following main topics:

- What are software vulnerabilities?
- Prioritizing your remediations
- Securing your code

What are software vulnerabilities?

A software vulnerability is a flaw or weakness in a software program that can be exploited by hackers to compromise the system's security. Software vulnerabilities can be introduced in several ways, such as the following:

- A developer not trained on the **Open Worldwide Application Security Project (OWASP)** Top 10
- An old vulnerability that has been patched is mistakenly reintroduced in the code
- Sometimes, hackers discover how to exploit the code after it has been published

When I was at RedSeal, I voluntarily created a Threat Response team. What we did was review the latest vulnerabilities, decide on the most severe, and write up a blog post about how our customers could use RedSeal to quickly discover, act, and patch the vulnerability. One thing you will realize once you begin taking notice of the latest vulnerabilities over a period of time is the same vulnerabilities come up again and again. Even though it seems like thousands of new vulnerabilities, there is actually a reoccurrence of the same vulnerabilities again and again.

Common Vulnerabilities and Exposures

MITRE is a nonprofit organization that operates research and development centers, providing cybersecurity expertise and solutions to the US government. MITRE originally began tracking public software vulnerabilities in 1999 as a community effort. `https://cve.mitre.org` is the legacy website. It is being transitioned to `https://cve.org`. With the support of the U.S. Department of Homeland Security and the **Cybersecurity and Infrastructure Security Agency** (**CISA**), as well as other industry companies and leaders, MITRE continues to play a vital role in the identification and classification of public vulnerabilities.

In a nutshell, the following applies to **Common Vulnerabilities and Exposures** (**CVEs**):

- A list of information security vulnerabilities and exposures specific to a product

- Assigned a unique identifier, CVE ID

- Scored using the **Common Vulnerability Scoring System** (**CVSS**)

- Used to share data across separate tools, databases, and services within the cybersecurity community

What is the NIST definition of software vulnerabilities?

The **National Institute of Standards and Technology** (**NIST**), an agency within the U.S. Department of Commerce, provides measurement standards, including cybersecurity frameworks. In 2005, NIST started the **National Vulnerability Database** (**NVD**), found at `https://nvd.nist.gov`. NIST began tracking CVEs, scoring them using the CVSS, and linking to company websites that provide details on how to patch and/or mitigate the vulnerability.

NIST defines a vulnerability as *"a weakness in the computational logic (e.g., code) found in software and hardware components that, when exploited, results in a negative impact to confidentiality, integrity, or availability. Mitigation of the vulnerabilities in this context typically involves coding changes, but could also include specification changes or even specification deprecations (e.g., removal of affected protocols or functionality in their entirety)."*[1]

---

1   "Vulnerabilities." National Vulnerability Website, NIST, 3 Aug. 2023, nvd.nist.gov/vuln.

CVSS

CVSS is an open industry standard for assessing the severity of computer system security vulnerabilities. CVSS provides an objective measure to help in the prioritization of response efforts. Each vulnerability is scored from 0 to 10 under the CVSS scoring system. CVSS v2.0 is the first version of scoring that has since been updated and is now CVSS v4.0. The big difference between the scoring systems is that CVSS 2.0 does not have a "*Critical*" designation. You can see the differences in *Table 8.1*:

CVSS v2.0		CVSS v3.0		CVSS 3.1		CVSS v4.0	
Severity	Base Score	Severity	Base Score	Severity	Base Score	Severity	Base Score
Low	0-3.9	Low	0.1-3.9	Low	0.1-3.9	Low	0.1-3.9
Medium	4-6.9	Medium	4-6.9	Medium	4-6.9	Medium	4-6.9
High	7-10	High	7-8.9	High	7-8.9	High	7-8.9
		Critical	9-10	Critical	9-10	Critical	9-10

Table 8.1 – CVSS scoring[2]

From CVSS v3.0 to 4.0, there are no changes in the base number scoring. There are a lot of different qualifications that go into the CVSS scoring. The CVSS scoring allows you to see what are the worst and, therefore, highest-rated vulnerabilities. This is one part of the vulnerability prioritization. You will logically want to patch the most critical vulnerabilities first, such as CVSS-rated 10. It's not that simple because where the asset is located relative to the internet, and asset criticality, also plays a factor. We will be discussing this in more detail later in the chapter.

One of the big changes between CVSS v3.1 and v4.0 is taking into account **threat intelligence** (**TI**) and environmental metrics for more accurate scoring. In addition, CVSS v4.0 has incorporated more metrics to better cover the **Internet of Things** (**IoT**) and **Operational Technology** (**OT**). Previously, the scoring was defined for Information Technology. IoT is the sensors and devices such as cameras, or even your refrigerator if it has Wi-Fi. OT is more about industrial systems and manufacturing such as **Supervisory Control and Data Acquisition** (**SCADA**). In CVSS v3.1, exploit maturity was in a separate *Temporal* group, but now is in its own *Threat Metric Group*. There is a new *Supplemental Metric Group* that has been added. To see all that goes into the CVSS scoring v4.0, see *Figure 8.1*:

---

2   "Vulnerability Metrics." National Vulnerability Database (NVD), NIST, nvd.nist.gov/vuln-metrics/cvss. Accessed 3 Nov. 2023.

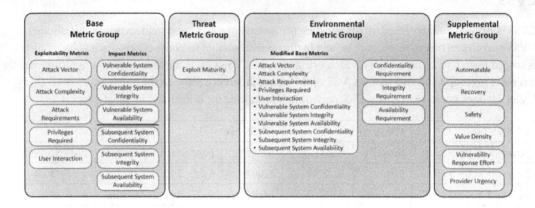

Figure 8.1 - CVSS metric groups[3]

Even though the CVSS base scoring as shown in *Table 8.1* hasn't changed much, the other metric groups as shown in *Figure 8.1* have changed. Since CVSS v4.0 was released on November 1, 2023, it will take a few months for products to integrate it into their scoring. I checked NVD in November 2023, and it is still using CVSS v3.1.

Common Weakness Enumeration

If we are talking about CVEs, then we need to discuss the **Common Weakness Enumeration** (**CWE**). These are weaknesses that can lead to vulnerabilities. CWE was developed by MITRE, working with the broader cybersecurity community, to provide a standardized list of software and hardware weakness types to facilitate effective discussion, description, and management of software weaknesses. One difference between CWEs and CVEs is that CWEs are not specific to a particular product like CVEs are.

In a nutshell, the following applies to CWE:

- A category system for software weaknesses that can lead to vulnerabilities that are introduced during code development

- A common language for describing software security weaknesses in architecture, design, or code

- Used to help in the development of tools and systems that can identify, mitigate, and prevent these weaknesses

---

3   "CVSS v4.0 Specification Document." First Improving Security Together, FIRST.org, 1 Nov. 2023, http://www.first.org/cvss/v4.0/specification-document.

Known Exploited Vulnerabilities

The **Known Exploited Vulnerabilities** (**KEV**) Catalog is maintained by CISA, part of the U.S. Department of Homeland Security. The KEV catalog was officially launched in November 2021 as part of **Binding Operational Directive** (**BOD**) *22-01*, aimed at driving urgent and prioritized remediation of vulnerabilities posing significant threats. KEVs are vulnerabilities in software and hardware that have been identified as being actively exploited by malicious actors. These vulnerabilities are typically cataloged and highlighted by cybersecurity organizations, including government agencies, to inform and prioritize patch management and security measures for organizations and individuals to protect against known threats.

CVE, CWE, and KEV

All those acronyms can be confusing. In summary, CWE provides a categorization of types of vulnerabilities, CVE provides specific instances of vulnerabilities, and KEV highlights which of the CVE-listed vulnerabilities are currently being exploited in the wild.

What we're up against

There are thousands upon thousands of public vulnerabilities published every year. As you see in *Figure 8.2*, vulnerabilities keep trending up year over year. SecurityScorecard's *CVE Details* site (`https://cvedetails.com/`) gives good information related to CVEs. Vulnerabilities for 2023 surpassed 25,000:

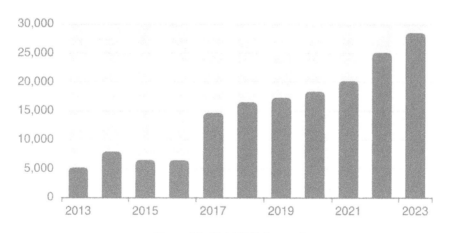

Figure 8.2 – Total CVEs by year[4]

---

4   https://cvedetails.com/

Prioritizing your remediations

Vulnerability prioritization is the only way to properly deal with the enormous number of vulnerabilities that are published on a daily basis. Just because a CVE is rated as a 10 doesn't necessarily mean that it is the highest priority to remediate at your company. I know this seems counter-intuitive, but there are several factors you need to take into account when prioritizing vulnerabilities:

- CISA's KEV Catalog
- CVSS metrics:
  - Attack Vector
  - Attack Complexity
  - Privileges Required
- CVE score

CISA's KEV Catalog

CISA created a known exploited vulnerability catalog that is invaluable when deciding which vulnerabilities to patch and by when. Essentially, when it's discovered that hackers are exploiting a specific vulnerability, CISA will add it to the catalog with a due date. As you can see in *Figure 8.3*, CISA has the CVE ID, vendor, description, action to take, and due date. The **due date** is critical and needs to be part of your vulnerability prioritization process. Once a vulnerability is known to be exploited, it means there most likely is a hacker script making the vulnerability easily exploitable. These exploit kits are offered for sale on the dark web:

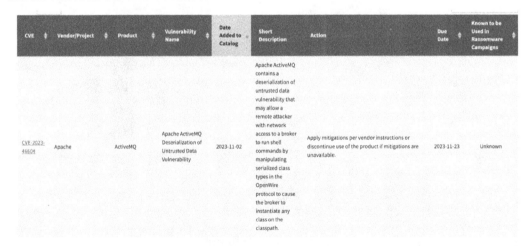

CVE	Vendor/Project	Product	Vulnerability Name	Date Added to Catalog	Short Description	Action	Due Date	Known to be Used in Ransomware Campaigns
CVE-2023-46604	Apache	ActiveMQ	Apache ActiveMQ Deserialization of Untrusted Data Vulnerability	2023-11-02	Apache ActiveMQ contains a deserialization of untrusted data vulnerability that may allow a remote attacker with network access to a broker to run shell commands by manipulating serialized class types in the OpenWire protocol to cause the broker to instantiate any class on the classpath.	Apply mitigations per vendor instructions or discontinue use of the product if mitigations are unavailable.	2023-11-23	Unknown

Figure 8.3 – CISA KEV Catalog

Understanding the assets your company owns, both software and hardware, is critical in prioritizing what to patch. We'll be covering asset management in *Chapter 9, Asset Inventory*. At a basic level, you need to at least keep an inventory, even if in a spreadsheet, so that you can search for these vulnerabilities and know what to patch. Of the thousands that get released, most won't apply to your environment. Being able to quickly review and know what does apply to your company is critical. We will be discussing the tools and products that can automate this process later in the chapter.

CVSS metric – Attack Vector

One of the most important metrics to review as part of the CVSS score is the Attack Vector, AV:N. The attack vector of the CVE with an "N" is the most attackable over the network, including the internet. This is also referred to as **remote code execution** (**RCE**). Attack vector refers to how to get *access* to the asset in order to exploit the vulnerability. For example, if your company has a web server that is externally facing the internet and it has a vulnerability that can be exploited via the network, then you need to patch the server *as soon as possible*. Your asset is a ticking time bomb of when hackers will discover that your asset that has the vulnerability is accessible via the internet.

For Attack Vector, there are three indicators that I always use to decide the prioritization of the CVE. We will be using the v3.1 CVSS metrics since the v4.0 is so new that NIST is not using it yet. The metric values for v3.1 and v4.0 are the same, so even under v4.0, these same metrics will apply:

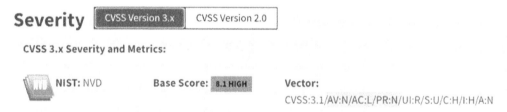

Figure 8.4 – CVSS Severity and Metrics v3.x – CVE-2020-0601[5]

In CVSS scoring, the attack vector is defined as follows:

- **Network (N)**: This category of vulnerability is exploitable over the network, up to and including the internet. This is deemed the riskiest of vulnerabilities and is referred to as RCE because the attack can be launched over a network.

- **Adjacent (A)**: This means the attack is limited to logical proximity. For example, the attack needs to be launched over Bluetooth, Wi-Fi subnet, or the same network subnet.

- **Local (L)**: For local, there is no way to exploit the vulnerability over the network. The exploit is able to read, write, and execute processes. This exploit can be carried out if a user has physical access to the vulnerable asset and can use the keyboard, console, or even compromised SSH keys or credentials.

---

5   (ISC)2 2022 Cybersecurity Workforce Study, (ISC)2 , Nov. 2022, https://www.isc2.org/research.

- **Physical (P)**: The only way to conduct a physical attack is to gain physical access to the asset. Once an attacker is able to physically gain access to the data center or to a laptop in a hotel room, they can then execute multiple attacks to gain access to a device's data. If someone has physical access to a device, it is 100% hackable. If a vulnerability can only be exploited with physical access, then it is considered a lower risk. This is why you have data centers with multiple physical defenses, such as locked doors, badge access, security cameras, and security guards.

Essentially, if the Attack Vector is *Network*, then you need to prioritize this vulnerability to be patched within 30 days unless CISA has a sooner due date, but we will look at a few more metrics before we make our final designation. We'll use this table to decide on the prioritization:

Metric	ID	Comment	Patch Timeline
KEV (Yes/No)	Y	If Yes, then it is known to be exploited in the wild, so patch within CISA's prescribed due date.	If Yes, follow CISA's guidelines. Patch by the assigned due date.
CVSS Metric: Attack Vector	AV:N	This means it is exploitable from the internet. This is the easiest attack method to exploit a vulnerability.	Within 30 days unless not exposed to the internet, then 60 days or if on KEV, follow CISA's due date.
CVSS Metric: Attack Complexity	AC:L	This means it is easily exploitable. The attacker does not have to be highly trained.	Within 30 days unless not exposed to the internet, then 60 days, or if on KEV, follow CISA's due date.
CVSS Metric: Privileges Required	PR:N	The attacker does not need to have access privileges to exploit the vulnerability.	Within 30 days unless not exposed to the internet, then 60 days, or if on KEV, follow CISA's due date.
Asset Location		On the internet	Within 30 days ,or if on KEV, follow CISA's due date.
Asset Criticality		Critical assets should be multiple hops into your network and ideally on a segmented network.	Within 60 days

Table 8.2 – Vulnerability Prioritization – CVE-2020-0601

CVSS metric – Attack Complexity

This metric pertains to the external conditions that must be met for an attacker to successfully exploit a vulnerability. Essentially, the attack complexity classifies whether the vulnerability can be exploited by a less trained hacker (AC:L) or by an expertly trained hacker (AC:H). The easier it is to exploit the vulnerability, the lower the skill of a hacker is needed to exploit it. These conditions, which are outside the attacker's direct influence, might involve gathering additional details about the target system or exploiting specific computational anomalies. It's crucial to note that this metric's evaluation does not consider any user interaction that might be necessary to execute the exploit. Attack Complexity metrics are as follows:

- **Low (L)**: There are no unique or mitigating conditions required for an exploit. An attacker can reliably expect to succeed every time they target the vulnerable component.

- **High (H)**: An attacker's success is contingent upon factors they cannot directly control, meaning that an attack is not guaranteed to work on demand. Instead, the attacker must expend a certain amount of effort in either preparation or execution to exploit the vulnerability effectively. For instance, a successful attack might require the attacker to do the following:

  - Acquire specific knowledge about the target's environment, such as configuration settings, sequence numbers, or cryptographic secrets

  - Manipulate the target environment to increase the chances of a successful exploit, which could involve bypassing sophisticated mitigation techniques

  - Position themselves within the communication path between the target and a requested resource to intercept and potentially alter the data being transmitted, as seen in **man-in-the-middle (MitM)** attacks

CVSS metric – Privileges Required

This metric is based on the privileges required to carry out an attack and leverage the vulnerability. For example, if the attacker needs to be signed in as an administrator (PR:H), then it is a harder attack to carry out than if the attacker does not need to be signed in at all (PR:N). In the first case, an example would be if the attacker has to have the login credentials of an administrator on the asset. The Privileges Required CVSS metric is defined as follows:

- **None (N)**: The attacker does not possess any prior authorization and does not need access to the system's settings or files to initiate the attack.

- **Low (L)**: The attacker must have privileges that grant basic user rights, which are typically limited to altering user-owned settings and files. Alternatively, an attacker with low-level privileges may only be able to interact with non-sensitive resources.

- **High (H)**: The attacker needs to have high-level privileges, such as administrative rights, which allow comprehensive access.

CVE priority

CVE scoring is a great indicator to consider when deciding on how to prioritize your vulnerabilities. As described earlier in the chapter, the CVE score is from 0 to 10. 10 is the worst, called *Critical* for v3.x. Of course, a CVE with a score of 10 needs to be patched within 30 days, unless the CISA KEV has a sooner date or the asset is located in a location that does not have access to the internet or next hop.

Starting with vulnerability scans

Your company needs to be running vulnerability scans on a regular basis. It can be daily, weekly, or monthly. I highly recommend running the scans at least monthly and ideally weekly. The three big vulnerability scanners are Qualys, Rapid7, and Tenable. Ask your team if they have a preference. When I was managing security at a company, I checked with my team, and they had specific experience with different scanners. Two of the people really liked Rapid7, so we went with that. All of them do a good job. I did hear that Tenable has a lot of false positives from someone who had previously worked at a large government agency. Of course, I filled out a software evaluation form for the three vulnerability scanner products doing my due diligence. Remember to do your due diligence and to fill out a software evaluation form for three products. All three of these products will identify the vulnerabilities in your software and will be prioritized by CVSS. In a later chapter, we'll get into more detail about tying your vulnerability data into another tool that will give you more visibility into vulnerability prioritization.

Making it fun

If you are beginning your vulnerability scanning journey, then you will have thousands of vulnerabilities to patch. Make it fun. You can offer a bonus to a team or a person who patches the most vulnerabilities. Of course, you need to get your manager involved so that funds can be available to pay the bonus.

In the cloud

If your company has a cloud network, did you know that by using AWS Lambda, all of the operating system and below vulnerabilities will be automatically patched by AWS? Depending on the cloud your company uses, there is a similar offering. Yes – it's more expensive, but instead of having a security team patching these vulnerabilities for you, you are having the cloud provider do the patching. All you have to worry about is patching the applications that you run in Lambda. If your company is developing a product, then you will need to do code scanning for vulnerabilities. We'll talk more about that in the next section.

Securing your code

If your company develops code, then you need to scan the code for vulnerabilities and test the code prior to release. With **continuous integration**, **delivery**, and **deployment**, also known as **CI/CD**, you must automate the code. First, **Infrastructure as Code (IaC)** must be used to provide consistency. In addition, scanning and testing your code as part of your secure development life cycle is mandatory. There are several tools that you will want to use as part of this testing: **static application security testing (SAST)**, **dynamic application security testing (DAST)**, **interactive application security testing (IAST)**, and vulnerability scanning of your code. You will need to do this to ensure your code doesn't have vulnerabilities in it.

IaC

IaC leverages DevOps methodologies and version control, employing a descriptive model to manage and provision infrastructure components such as networks, **virtual machines (VMs)**, load balancers, and connection topologies. This approach ensures consistent environment deployment, akin to how identical source code consistently produces the same binary.[6]

SAST

At a minimum, you need to do SAST scanning of your source code while it's in development. A SAST tool will scan your code for vulnerabilities. *Static* means that it scans the code while it is not in use. The best way to use SAST is to configure it to scan the code every time a pull is done. This way, a developer isn't introducing a new vulnerability with a new code update. A free SAST tool is GitHub's code scanning tool. Using SAST for code scanning offers both advantages and disadvantages, such as the following:

- **False positives and negatives**: SAST tools analyze source code based on predefined assumptions, which can lead to incorrect identifications, false positives, or erroneous alerts.

- **Lack of contextual understanding**: SAST tools may not fully grasp the context of the code, especially when it comes to unsanitized user input. While such input is a significant security concern, the fix might occur in a different part of the application, such as the backend, even if the issue appears in the frontend. Since frontend and backend code might not be located in the same repository, SAST tools could flag this as an issue erroneously, prompting developers to address a problem that has already been mitigated elsewhere.

- **Dependence on the programming language**: The effectiveness of SAST is closely tied to the programming language in use. While there is an abundance of SAST tools for widely used languages such as Java and C, options are limited for less common languages such as ReScript.[7]

---

6   Jacobs , Mike, et al. *"What Is Infrastructure as Code (IAC)? - Azure DevOps."* Azure DevOps | Microsoft Learn, 28 Nov. 2022, learn.microsoft.com/en-us/devops/deliver/what-is-infrastructure-as-code.

7   "SAST Testing: How It Works and Why Do You Need It?" Snyk, 20 Apr. 2021, snyk.io/learn/ application-security/static-application-security-testing/#vs.

DAST

DAST tests the code while it is running. You can think of it similar to a pen test when it's done manually, or as a vulnerability scan when it is set up to run automatically. OWASP Zap is a free DAST tool that you can use to scan your code. Snyk is highly recommended and provides both SAST and DAST functionality.

Advantages of DAST include the following:

- **Runtime detection**: DAST identifies security flaws such as exploitable vulnerabilities, misconfigurations, and improper security headers that manifest during the application's runtime

- **Framework and language independence**: It is compatible with applications and APIs irrespective of the frameworks or programming languages used

- **No source code needed**: DAST can evaluate all operational components, including dynamic dependencies, without requiring access to the source code

Limitations of DAST include the following:

- **Running application required**: It necessitates an operational version of the application for testing, even if it's just a basic prototype

- **Scope of testing**: The testing is confined to the parts of the code that are active during the assessment period

- **Issue location**: The pinpointing of issues may not be as accurate as with other testing methodologies

IAST

IAST combines the strengths of SAST and DAST. Before you think that it can replace SAST, it still has its limitations. One of them is that it scans the program while running, similar to DAST. When a developer is making updates to code, it won't scan the code, the same as SAST when doing a code pull. An advantage it has over DAST is that it can map the vulnerability back to the source code, similar to SAST.

IAST provides the following advantages:

- **Real-world scanning**: IAST's primary strength lies in its ability to scan code in its live, production state. Unlike SAST, which can overwhelm developers with false positives, IAST hones in on genuine issues, bypassing those that have been resolved elsewhere in the code base.

- **Development phase scanning**: Beyond production, IAST proves invaluable during development. Certain IAST tools integrate with your **integrated development environment(s) (IDE(s)**, providing developers with immediate feedback on the security of new features. This "shift-left" approach makes fixing issues more cost-effective.

- **Efficient issue resolution**: IAST excels in pinpointing exact code locations linked to issues, a clear edge over DAST. It guides developers through the application to troubleshoot problems and suggests swift fixes. However, untested code segments can still harbor vulnerabilities, so developers must still use SAST.

Yet, IAST is not without limitations:

- **Language limitations**: IAST's dependency on programming languages is a significant limitation. Although some tools don't necessitate specific code, they remain tied to certain technologies that may not align with less common languages.

- **Time commitment**: IAST requires building and running the application, unlike SAST, demanding a substantial time investment. Quick feedback during development mitigates this, but extensive testing for production releases can be time-consuming.

- **Incomplete code coverage**: By focusing only on the code that executes, IAST may miss vulnerabilities in untested code segments. This approach reduces false positives but risks overlooking areas not covered by **quality assurance** (**QA**) tests, which could be critical in a production environment.

Software composition analysis

Software composition analysis (**SCA**) provides scanning of open source that resides in your code and ensures it is up to date and patched. Renovate is a Snyk tool that will automatically scan all of the **open source software** (**OSS**) used in your code and will update it accordingly. This is critical to keep your code up to date and secure.

OWASP

I would be remiss if I didn't touch on OWASP, which is the de facto standard when it comes to application security. OWASP is community-driven and provides various top 10 vulnerability lists that cover the following types of applications:

- Web
- API
- Mobile

There are lots of resources on the OWASP website. I recommend to all my clients to use OWASP ZAP, which is a free DAST tool that you can use to scan your web applications. It scans your code for the OWASP top 10 vulnerabilities and weaknesses.

Based on company size, your company's vulnerability prioritization and management program may consist of the following:

Basic:

- Vulnerability scan both on-premise and cloud environments with the following tools:

  - Nessus
  - Nuclei

- For patching, do the following:

  - Follow CISA KEV due dates
  - Review CVSS metrics:

    - Attack Vector
    - Attack Complexity
    - Privileges Required

  - Keep in mind the following:

    - Asset location
    - Proximity to internet
    - Next hop
    - Criticality of server

- For code scanning, use the following:

  - SAST – GitHub's code scanning tool
  - DAST – OWASP ZAP
  - SCA – Snyk Renovate

- Test external internet -acing servers using Qualys or Nessus free scan unless you must meet compliance (for example, SOC 2, ISO *27001*), then you would need a third-party pen tester. *Note*: Ideally a third-party pen tester should be used, but a pen testing tool or assessment may be conducted. For example, CloudWize provides a pen testing feature and reporting for cloud environments that is sufficient for SOC 2.

Medium:

- For vulnerability scans on both on-premise and cloud environments, use the following:

  - Nessus
  - Nuclei

- Qualys
- Rapid7

- For patching, do the following:

  - Follow CISA KEV due dates
  - Review CVSS metrics:

    - Attack Vector
    - Attack Complexity
    - Privileges Required

  - Keep in mind the following:

    - Asset location
    - Proximity to internet
    - Next hop
    - Criticality of server

- For code scanning, you can use the following:

  - SAST – GitHub's code scanning tool
  - DAST – OWASP ZAP

    - IAST
    - SCA – Snyk Renovate

- Annual pen test

  - For compliance, this should be done by a third party

Advanced:

- For vulnerability scans on both on-premise and cloud environments, use the following:

  - Nessus
  - Nuclei
  - Qualys
  - Rapid7

- For patching, do the following:

  - Follow CISA KEV due dates

  - Review CVSS metrics:

    - Attack Vector

    - Attack Complexity

    - Privileges Required

  - Keep in mind the following:

    - Asset location

    - Proximity to internet

    - Next hop

    - Criticality of server

- For code scanning, use the following:

  - SAST – GitHub's code-scanning tool or other product

  - DAST – OWASP ZAP

  - IAST

  - Fuzzing

  - SCA – Snyk Renovate

- Annual pen test

  - For compliance, this should be done by a third party

Summary

In summary, unpatched vulnerabilities can lead to multi-million dollar losses. Of course, having that one vulnerability on an external web server that lets the hacker in is a major concern. Also, consider the cost of a vulnerability that is not immediately found prior to the release of the code is going to cost your company a lot more in having to deal with fixing it after the fact, and it will also cause friction for your customers.

In the next chapter, we will be covering asset inventory. You have to know what assets you have in order to protect them.

9
Asset Inventory

This chapter is about asset inventory. In order to know what to protect, you have to understand what assets you have whether they are software, hardware, or ephemeral. Asset inventory is foundational in a cyber-resilient organization. The reality is an asset inventory tends to be an afterthought. You need a good asset inventory so that you know what is on your network, whether on-premise or in the cloud.

In this chapter, we're going to cover the following main topics:

- Asset inventory
- Change management
- **Mobile device management** (**MDM**)
- Knowing your network

Asset inventory

An asset inventory is a listing of software and hardware assets at your company. It can be as simple as a spreadsheet with the software versions, hardware with serial numbers, and an asset owner. Who wants to have to manually keep up with this information? You will definitely want to use a product to help with keeping an accurate list of your company's assets. Having a good asset inventory will enable you to do the following:

- Quickly search the assets you own and figure out if a CVE applies to your company
- Have asset owners assigned for each hardware asset
- Understand if an unauthorized asset is on your network

An asset inventory is mandatory for all compliance. Many times, companies don't get serious about their asset inventory until it is time for the company to be compliant, whether it's SOC 2, ISO *27001*, or HIPAA. See *Table 9.1* to see a mapping of asset inventory to various compliance standards and frameworks:

Standard/Framework	Section
NIST CSF	PR.DS-3
NIST 800-53B	CM-8
CIS	1
PCI	2.4, 9.5, 9.6, 9.7, 9.8, 9.9
HIPAA	164.310 164.310(a) 164.310(a)(1) 164.310(a)(2)(ii) 164.310(d)(2)(iii) 164.310(d)(1) 164.310(d)(2)
CMMC	AM.4.226 PE.2.135
ISO 27001	A.8.2.3, A.8.3.1, A.8.3.2, A.8.3.3, A.11.2.7
GDPR	Not specifically, but you do need to understand which assets store personally identifiable information (PII). Art 32.1, Art 32.2
SOC2	CC6.1, A1.2

Table 9.1 – Mapping of frameworks to asset inventory

Identifying your assets

In building an information security program, you would normally start with asset management, which is essentially an inventory of all of your assets. It sounds easy enough to identify your assets, but it's a massive task that is ongoing. With every upgrade, new purchase, and deprecation, your asset inventory changes.

What is the NIST definition of asset inventory?

In NIST *800-53B* and NIST SP *800-128*, asset inventory falls under System Component Inventory *CM-8*. Essentially, NIST requires that all assets including software and hardware are inventoried. Each asset must have an owner. Typically, each hardware asset is assigned an owner. The granularity of the inventory is up to the organization. For hardware, you will have the serial and model numbers. Some organizations may want to track all parts of an asset.

To make asset inventory useful, it must be maintained. As changes are made, such as software patching, as well as new hardware being deployed, these must all be updated in the asset inventory. This also includes the deprecation of software and hardware. Is it properly disposed of and updated in the asset inventory? You can quickly see how the inventory can become a major task to keep up.

Automating your asset inventory

There are several products that will automate your asset inventory. ServiceNow is the dominant player for large enterprises in the **Information Technology Service Management (ITSM)** space. ManageEngine ServiceDesk Plus and Atlassian Jira are alternatives in the space. Jira is popular since DevOps uses it for Agile development. I've heard good things from another vCISO about ManageEngine in general, and ServiceNow is the industry leader used by most large organizations. Here's a table comparing all their features:

Features	Jira	ManageEngine	ServiceNow
IT support enablement	Yes	Yes	Yes
Asset management	Yes	Yes	Yes
IT knowledge management	Yes	Yes	Yes
Service reporting and resource management	Yes	Yes	Yes
Service configuration management	Yes	Yes	Yes
Workflow automation and integration	Yes	Yes	Yes
Cost	$ TBD	$ TBD	$ TBD

Table 9.2 – Asset inventory and change management software

Change management

Change management is ensuring all changes to your IT environment are managed, approved, and documented throughout the entire process. This ensures orderly software and hardware changes are made in your environment. When I worked at IBM in the 1990s, I was part of the Network Team supporting the IBM Southeast Geoplex. I really learned about the change management process while at IBM. I was mentored by two different people on changes who each had their own way of performing changes. The first person who trained me on doing changes would put in a ticket, get approval, and then we would show up during the change window and figure out and make the change. You don't want to do this. The second person I worked with had a very different and much better approach. Of course, we would enter a ticket into the ITSM system. We would get approval to do the change during off hours. We would send out an email notification related to the change to potentially affected users. We would test the change a few days prior in the lab environment to make sure the change would be successful. We would have everything prepared prior to the change window. If it was an upgrade, we would have it on the domain nameserver ready to be installed and would only have to reboot the server. We would have already tested the new code in the lab and would only need to reboot the IBM AIX server. For **Domain Name Servers (DNS)**, everyone should have two, primary and secondary DNS servers configured in their network configuration. Making a change on one DNS server should not cause an outage. There would invariably be that one person working late, and they wouldn't have two DNS servers configured, causing an outage for the user while the DNS server rebooted. The second change management process is so much better because you aren't scrambling to get whatever is needed ahead of time. Everything is ready to go for the change, making it a seamless and more likely successful change.

Your company needs a change management process. It could be as simple as you create a ticket, and another person reviews and approves the change. If it is a more involved architectural change, then you need to have a discussion with several people, possibly in more than one department, to discuss the new architecture and approve it. Large companies will have change management boards. The important thing is that there are other people reviewing the change and approving it.

NIST security-focused change management

NIST covers the following four phases as part of security-focused configuration management in NIST *800-128*. First is planning, then implementing secure configuration baselines. I will be covering this in a later chapter. Next is change management, and finally monitoring. We'll review each phase:

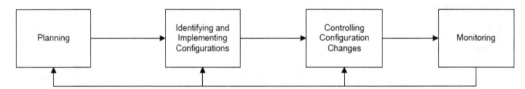

Figure 9.1 – Security-focused change management

Phase 1 – Planning

Planning is incorporating the phases into your company's policies and procedures. If your company doesn't have a change management policy, you can create one. The change management policy should cover at a high level your company's change management process, such as the following:

- Scheduled and unscheduled changes
- A ticket must be opened
- Architectural changes must be approved by a manager

- Exceptions to unscheduled emergency changes being approved after the change is implemented

- Rating scale for the impact of changes based on the number of users it can affect if it goes wrong

Phase 2 – Identifying and implementing configurations

Baseline configurations and secure configurations of all of your assets are paramount in building a cyber-resilient company. Having secure baseline configurations is low cost and will build security from the ground up. You are probably thinking, Why am I just hearing about this now? Well, it's not easy to build a secure baseline and ensure all of your devices are configured accordingly and keep them aligned to your stated configuration. Once you decide on a baseline to follow, then you can make baseline images for each type of asset. For example, for Windows laptops, you will have a baseline image with specific authorized software and secure configuration. Once you have that baseline image, you can ghost it. I'm sure the programs used today are different, but essentially, that same image will be used again and again for any Windows laptops issued by your company. An example of a baseline configuration for a Windows host using **Center for Internet Security (CIS) Implementation Group (IG)** 1 includes the following:

- A specific version of Windows with necessary patches

- Windows M365

- Anti-virus or EDR; for example, Windows Defender

- Password manager; for example, Bitwarden, 1Password, or LastPass

- Have automatic patching configured

- Enable Windows BitLocker

- VPN; for example, Proton VPN or one configured for your VPN

In the commercial space, CIS is the default for secure configuration. CIS makes it easy to select a configuration baseline. They have the controls referred to as cybersecurity safeguards categorized according to three levels and grouped as follows:

1. **CIS IG1**:

   - Designed for small and medium-sized businesses with limited resources and cybersecurity expertise.

   - Focuses on a basic set of security controls that can significantly reduce risk and are manageable for smaller teams.

   - Includes foundational controls that are essential for every organization, regardless of size, to protect against common threats.

2. **CIS IG2:**

   - Aimed at medium-sized organizations with more resources such as IT and Security teams with greater cybersecurity expertise than those in IG1.

   - Builds upon the safeguards in IG1 with additional controls to enhance security.

   - Suitable for organizations that have the capacity to implement a more comprehensive security program.

3. **CIS IG3:**

   - Targeted at large, resource-rich organizations with advanced cybersecurity needs.

   - Encompasses all the controls from IG1 and IG2, plus additional advanced controls.

   - Designed for organizations that are likely targets of sophisticated cyberattacks and have the resources to implement complex and comprehensive cybersecurity measures.

In the federal government, the required secure configurations for all devices, hosts, and cloud assets are called **Security Technical Implementation Guides** (**STIGs**). These configurations are the baseline configuration for all assets used in the federal government whether on-premise or in the cloud. In the commercial space, very few companies use STIGs. When I do come across a company that has made STIGs a baseline configuration for their assets, I am super impressed. Essentially, for any operating system, computer, device, or host, there is a defined secure configuration that is followed. One of the features of RedSeal is that it automatically audits all of your assets against STIGs and reports whether you are in compliance or not. Don't select STIGs if you are in the commercial space unless there is a requirement such as you are providing services to the Federal Government.

Phase 3 – Controlling configuration changes

You will also want to decide on what tools will be used to track changes for IT assets. You need to plan, track, approve, and manage each IT change. For small and medium-sized companies, you need to ensure changes are approved by a second individual and not the same person. For larger changes that would have a high impact if they fail or architectural changes, then you should assemble a group of cross-functional stakeholders such as two to three from different areas (IT, Security, Architecture) to review the change and approve it. For smaller organizations, you don't need a formal **Configuration Control Board** (**CCB**) but should pull a few members from different areas (IT, Security, Architecture) in order to review and approve any high-risk or large-impact architectural changes and network changes.

For very large companies, you will want a more formal CCB known as a change management board that will meet on a regular basis to discuss larger changes, architectural reviews, and do post-mortems when large or high-impact changes fail.

> **Note**
>
> Even if your company has a CCB, not all changes have to be reviewed by the CCB. For example, "pre-approved" changes such as applying security patches provided by the vendor, updating anti-virus signatures, and the replacement of defective peripherals or internal hardware components are categorized as pre-approved changes. These changes are recognized as routine maintenance activities essential for maintaining operational integrity and security and, therefore, do not require prior approval for each instance. Add a section to your change management policy describing these pre-approved changes.

The CCB should be composed of three or more key stakeholders to ensure a comprehensive perspective while maintaining efficiency in decision-making. It is recommended for members to come from cross-functional groups within your organization; they typically include the following:

- **Software engineering representative**: Provides insights on software development, integration, and maintenance

- **IT representative**: Provides insights into the potential impact and understanding of the change

- **IT security representative**: Provides insights into the potential security impact of the change

- **CCB chair**: An individual designated to lead the CCB, ensuring efficient proceedings and decision-making

This composition balances the need for cross-functional perspectives with the necessity of a streamlined group for prompt and effective decision-making.

Phase 4 – Monitoring

The monitoring strategy is for after your configuration management program is up and operational, ensuring the organization is following your change management policy and processes. You can track changes and the number that fail and are successful. You should be able to run reports using your tracking tool such as Jira or ServiceNow. In addition, track the secure baselines and how you are keeping them compliant. There are tools that will report on whether your assets are in compliance with CIS and STIGS. Once you have CIS IG1 implemented, you can start moving toward implementing CIS IG2. You can also track compliance with the CIS level, such as the percentage of assets in and out of compliance.

Mobile device management (MDM)

As part of your asset management strategy, you need to consider managing mobile devices. If you are a small company, a cost-effective way to do this is to use Apple's Business Essentials for small businesses if your organization uses Apple products.

Microsoft's Intune is great for asset management and mobile device management and also will manage Apple and Android devices.

A more traditional means of managing mobile devices is to use **network access control** (**NAC**). When I worked at Cisco, they used NAC for MDM. If you tried to connect to the Cisco internal network with your own device, it would automatically be put on the guest network. As for **Internet of Things** (**IoT**) devices, these should be on separate network segments since they are easily hackable and not internet-facing.

Knowing your network

It's important to have visibility into your network. Understanding where devices sit, whether on the internet, several hops into your network, or even in a lab, is important. Understanding your network and where assets reside is important, especially to your vulnerability prioritization plan. Many companies have network diagrams, but having a tool that will give you an actual view of your network is super valuable, whether it is on-premise, hybrid, or in the cloud. There are visibility tools such as Datadog, Dynatrace, and New Relic that will map your network automatically. For the cloud, each service offers its own tools for asset discovery and inventory, including visualization of your assets. There are separate tools that will provide visibility into multi-cloud environments that combine multiple features into one product. CloudWize, Wiz, and RedSeal provide multi-cloud visibility with vulnerability and attack vectors. Wiz is the dominant leader in the space for large enterprises. CloudWize is a start-up that offers a myriad of cloud visibility, vulnerability management, and compliance. RedSeal Stratus offers a free version to see visibility and attack vectors in multi-cloud. We'll talk about these more in a later chapter.

Quick reference for asset management

Based on company size, your company's asset management program may consist of the following:

- **Basic:**
  - Spreadsheet with assets listed
    - Hostname
    - Hardware serial number
    - Software installed
  - Cloud inventory
    - AWS Systems Manager Inventory
    - Azure Resource Manager
    - GCP Cloud Asset Inventory

- Cloud visualization

  - Amazon Neptune and AWS Config

  - Azure Resource Graph

- Change management program

  - Process of reviewing and approving changes

  - Keeping asset inventory updated

- Configuration baseline

  - CIS IG1

- **Medium:**

  - Asset inventory tool

    - Microsoft Intune

    - Hardware serial number

    - Software installed with versions

  - Cloud inventory

    - AWS Systems Manager Inventory

    - Azure Resource Manager

    - GCP Cloud Asset Inventory

  - Cloud visualization

    - Amazon Neptune and AWS Config

    - Azure Resource Graph

  - Change management program

    - Process of reviewing and approving changes

    - Keeping asset inventory updated

    - Using Tool

  - Configuration baseline

    - IG2

- **Advanced:**

  - Asset inventory tool

    - ServiceNow

    - Hardware serial number

    - Software installed with versions

  - Cloud inventory

    - AWS Systems Manager Inventory

    - Azure Resource Manager

    - GCP Cloud Asset Inventory

  - Cloud visualization

    - Amazon Neptune and AWS Config

    - Azure Resource Graph

  - Change management program

    - Process of reviewing and approving changes

    - Keeping asset inventory updated

    - Using Tool

  - Configuration baseline

    - CIS IG3

Summary

In summary, having a good asset inventory is critical in building your security program. It is usually step 1 in frameworks, but in reality, it becomes an afterthought. Whether you use a tool such as Jira, ManageEngine, ServiceNow, or even a simple spreadsheet, you need to maintain an asset inventory. As part of establishing an asset inventory, a change management plan and processes should be used, as well as developing a configuration baseline.

In the next chapter, we will be covering data protection. The most important action every CISO must take is to encrypt your company's data, whether in transit or at rest.

10
Data Protection

This chapter is about data protection. Did you know if an attacker is able to break into your company's network and steal critical data and the data stolen is encrypted, then it is not a breach? Yes – that is correct even under GDPR; if the data is encrypted, then it's not considered a breach. Of course, if an attacker hacked their way into your network, they now have knowledge of it and will come back to try to find more data to steal. This is why you want layers of security built into your security program, known as **defense in depth (DiD)**. Encrypting data alone is not enough, but it is an important step.

Understanding where your critical data is located and encrypting data at rest and in transit is critical to protect your organization.

In this chapter, we're going to cover the following main topics:

- Encrypt your data!
- What is PII? It depends…
- Third-party risk management

Encrypt your data!

I was first trained in cryptography in the United States Air Force where I held a Top- Secret Clearance. My career continued in the cryptography space when I joined Entrust Technologies, which is now Entrust Datacard. Entrust is a **public key infrastructure (PKI)** development company. I was trained in PKI and encryption. With all of the advances in cryptography, we're still using algorithms that were developed 30 years ago. Granted, the key sizes are larger, and NIST has begun a quantum-resistant algorithm search. We'll talk more about quantum computing and encryption later in the chapter.

Introduction to encryption

Even in the cybersecurity space, encryption knowledge is limited. Throughout my career, I've been the person on the team that has been the go-to person when it comes to encryption algorithms that should be used. I've also realized that the cybersecurity community in general lacks the knowledge and know-how of encryption. I'm going to start with an encryption introduction.

History of encryption

At its most basic form, encryption ensures that you can't read information in plain text. This is why encryption provides confidentiality. Encryption has been around for thousands of years. One of the earliest forms of encryption was when Julius Caesar used a substitution cipher to send secret messages to his generals. It substituted each letter of the alphabet with the letter three positions over in the alphabet. For example, "A" becomes "D" and wraps around the alphabet so that "X" becomes "A."

Encryption basics

The two main types of encryption in use today are symmetric and asymmetric encryption. Symmetric encryption uses a symmetric algorithm such as the **Advanced Encryption Standard (AES)** with key sizes such as 128 or 256. AES-256 is preferred to be used, but AES-128 is still safe to use in case the speed and processing that must be done requires AES-128. It is considered symmetric because the same key is used to both encrypt and decrypt the data.

Typically, symmetric and asymmetric encryption are used in tandem. A symmetric key is used to encrypt and decrypt the data. An asymmetric key is used to encrypt the symmetric key to securely share it with the individual who is intended to read the encrypted data. The person receiving the encrypted data has a private key stored locally that is used to decrypt the symmetric key, thus allowing them to decrypt the data. Typical asymmetric algorithms are as follows: RSA 2048 or above; ECC using P-256, P-384, or P-521. See *Table 10.1* for a detailed listing of algorithms and key sizes recommended. You can also see recommended algorithms and key sizes on the *Crypto Done Right!* website standards table (`https://cryptodoneright.org`):

System/Type of Data	Tools and Protocols	Encryption Algorithm
PKI for authentication	OpenSSL, OpenSSH, TLS, SSH, IPsec	RSA 2048 ECC P-256, P-384, P-521
Data encryption keys	OpenSSL, OpenSSH, TLS, SSH, IPsec	AES-128 or above
Virtual private network (VPN) keys	OpenSSL, OpenVPN, IPsec	AES-128 or above
Website SSL certificate	OpenSSL, X.509 Certificate, TLS	AES-128 or above

Table 10.1 - Recommended cryptographic algorithms and key sizes

Figure 10.1 shows how, using asymmetric encryption, Alice can encrypt an email for Bob:

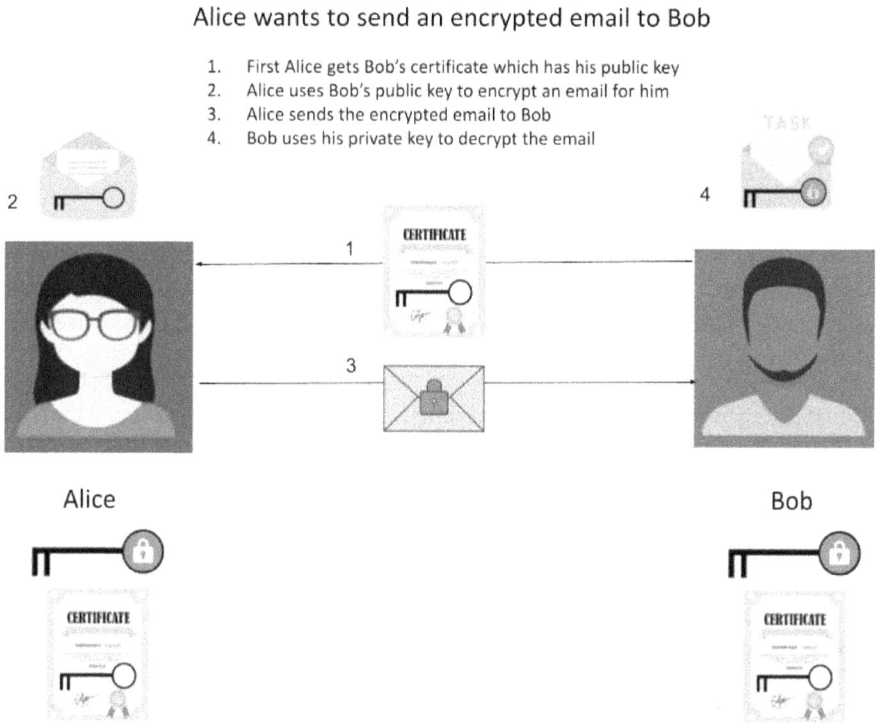
Alice wants to send an encrypted email to Bob
1. First Alice gets Bob's certificate which has his public key
2. Alice uses Bob's public key to encrypt an email for him
3. Alice sends the encrypted email to Bob
4. Bob uses his private key to decrypt the email
2
4
1
CERTIFICATE
3
Alice
Bob
CERTIFICATE
CERTIFICATE

Figure 10.1 - Asymmetric encryption

Encrypted data means there is no breach!

Encrypting your data, especially critical **personally identifiable information** (**PII**) data both in transit and stored, can save your company potentially millions in fines. Under GDPR, fines can go up to €20 million or up to 4% of the annual worldwide revenue of the preceding financial year, whichever is greater. If there is a data breach, but the data is encrypted and unreadable, then notification of the breach under GDPR is not required. *Article 34* of GDPR states the following:

"The communication to the data subject referred to in paragraph 1 shall not be required if any of the following conditions are met:

...the controller has implemented appropriate technical and organisational protection measures, and those measures were applied to the personal data affected by the personal data breach, in particular those that render the personal data unintelligible to any person who is not authorised to access it, such as encryption..."[1]

Encrypting your company's data both at rest and in transit is paramount in building a resilient cybersecurity program. Here are some things to bear in mind.

Be cautious with data encryption. Although almost all standards require data encryption at rest, many do not specify exactly where the encryption should occur. For instance, consider a database containing data you wish to protect through encryption. You have several levels at which encryption can be implemented:

- You could place your database on a self-encrypting hard drive that encrypts data at the hardware level. This method only protects against hardware theft.

- You could use an encrypted filesystem, such as Microsoft BitLocker, which safeguards against hardware theft and some very specific types of attacks.

- You can encrypt the database file itself. Microsoft's **Transparent Data Encryption** (**TDE**) does precisely this, offering protection against hardware theft and unauthorized database access from another system.

- Ideally, and most securely, you would implement encryption at the field level within the database. This means encrypting individual fields within tables, which in turn are within the database. This approach ensures that even if someone gains online access to your database, they would not be able to read the contents of the fields simply by executing an SQL query.

While all these encryption methods can make you compliant with most security standards, only field-level encryption effectively protects against threat actors.

What is PII? It depends...

PII is personally identifiable information. In a nutshell, it is information that identifies a person. This can be information alone that maps back to you, such as your **Social Security Number** (**SSN**). This is called direct PII because only one person can have a specific SSN. To make it more confusing, the privacy community now refers to this data as **personal information** (**PI**). NIST and the cybersecurity community still use PII to refer to personal information. You need to work very closely with the Legal and Compliance departments. They should be the ones formally defining PII. Before we go on, I need to add a legal disclaimer that when classifying your data, a consultation with a privacy professional is recommended. Depending on the type of data, the location of a company's headquarters, and where

---

1   *"Art. 34 GDPR – Communication of a Personal Data Breach to the Data Subject."* General Data Protection Regulation (GDPR), EU, 30 Aug. 2016, gdpr-info.eu/art-34-gdpr/.

the data is stored (that is, in which country), the definition of PII may change. For example, if the data is stored in Germany, then the definition of PII is the most stringent of all interpretations! A privacy professional told me that IP addresses alone are considered PII in Germany. If you are on a tight budget, I recommend you follow the instructions in this chapter, inventory your PII data, and classify the impact of it. Once you have done this and mapped the data flows, hire a privacy expert to review what you have done to ensure your plan and security safeguards are sufficient.

NIST's definition of PII

NIST and the cybersecurity community still use PII to define personal information. If you are developing policies and a security program for the US Federal Government or companies that process PII for the Federal Government, then follow NIST *800-122*, *Guide to Protecting the Confidentiality of Personally Identifiable Information (PII)*, which defines and describes how to classify PII. In a nutshell, PII is data that can identify an individual. There is PII data that can directly identify an individual, such as their full name or SSN, but there is also indirect or linked PII, such as birth dates. Since so many people can share the same birth date, it is not considered PII by itself. But if this date is linked in a database to the person's name, then it is considered to be PII. The date is considered to be linked even if it is stored in a different database or the same host. Under GDPR, a birth date is considered to be PII. We'll discuss this more in the next section. As part of doing analysis on your sensitive data and classifying it as PII, you need to map how PII data flows in your network so that you can see where the information traverses and is stored in order to protect it.

Linked versus linkable data

Linked data is data that may not be directly traceable to an individual but can be linked or associated with them. This other linkable data then becomes PII. This can be, for example, a person's date of birth. Many people have the same birth date, but when linked to a person's full name, it becomes PII. There is also linkable data, where information about a person such as their full name can be linked to other data, such as medical records or financial information.

Impact level

Under NIST *800-122*, the impact level of the loss of **confidentiality, integrity, or availability (CIA)** of PII determines how you protect PII data. You may think all PII data should be protected at the highest level, but not necessarily. Impact level is what is the impact of the loss of CIA if the PII data is stolen. The risks stemming from the compromise of PII are significant and varied. For individuals, this includes the risk of blackmail, identity theft, potential physical harm, discrimination, and emotional distress. On the organizational front, a breach of PII confidentiality can lead to considerable challenges. These encompass a wide range of issues, not limited to the administrative complexities of managing the breach, substantial financial losses, erosion of public trust and reputation, as well as legal liabilities.

The following low, moderate, and high impact levels are defined in FIPS *199* and pertain to any attack, disruption, or breach whether the data is PII or not. Even though these aren't specific to PII, they still are similar. A **low-impact** scenario typically leads to limited adverse effects on a federal agency. In such instances, the agency's operations are likely to continue, albeit with some degree of slowdown. The agency's assets might sustain minor damage. Financially, the agency could face minor losses. Additionally, there's a possibility of minor harm to employees.

A **moderate-impact** scenario is likely to lead to serious adverse effects on an agency. This could include significant degradation or a notable reduction in mission-critical operations and activities. In such situations, the agency's assets are at risk of incurring considerable damage. Financial repercussions are also likely, with the potential for significant monetary losses. Moreover, this level of impact may result in substantial harm to the agency's employees.

A **high-impact** scenario can lead to severe or even catastrophic consequences for a federal agency. This level of impact could result in significant degradation or complete loss of mission-critical operations. The agency's assets might face major damage, and there could be substantial financial losses. Furthermore, such a scenario poses a serious threat of severe or catastrophic harm to employees such as law enforcement.

In NIST *800-122*, the definitions of low, moderate, and high impact regarding PII and the loss of CIA are as follows:

- A **low-impact** breach concerning the confidentiality of PII typically results in issues no more severe than minor inconveniences, such as the need to change a telephone number.

- However, at the **moderate-impact** level, the consequences of a PII breach become more substantial. They could encompass financial losses due to identity theft, denial of benefits, public humiliation, discrimination, and even the risk of blackmail.

- In cases of a **high-impact** PII breach, the ramifications escalate significantly, potentially leading to serious physical, social, or financial harm. This could include dire outcomes such as loss of life, substantial loss of livelihood, or even wrongful physical detention. This typically has to do with law enforcement PII.

Once you have determined the impact level of the potential loss of the PII data, you can select the level of NIST controls to properly protect the data. There are privacy impact analysis templates that you can use to analyze and classify the data you have, as well as the risk of the loss of PII data. The characteristics to consider when classifying the data are as follows:

- **Identifiability**: This is how easily the data can identify an individual. For example, *direct* data such as full name, SSN, and fingerprints can uniquely identify someone. *Linked* data is indirect in that you need other data to make it PII. Examples, of indirect data are zip codes and birth dates. Even if two databases reside on the same host, one with full names and the other with indirect data, then the indirect data should be considered PII.

- **Quantity of PII**: The amount of PII that is at risk of being exposed also affects the impact level. If you have 25 full names and SSNs stored, then it would have a lower impact rating than 25 million names and SSNs.

- **Data field sensitivity**: Each data field should be analyzed for impact, and all of the data fields together. If the person's full name with their email address or phone number is stored, it may have a lower rating than if the full name and SSN are stored.

- **Context of use**: This context refers to the specific purposes for which PII is collected, stored, processed, or shared, such as for statistical analysis, determining eligibility for benefits, benefits administration, research, tax administration, or law enforcement activities. The context can lead to varying confidentiality impact levels for the same types of PII. Consider an organization that maintains three lists, each containing identical PII data fields such as names, addresses, and phone numbers. The first list is for subscribers to a general-interest newsletter, the second for individuals who have filed for retirement benefits, and the third for undercover law enforcement officers. The potential risks to individuals and the organization differ markedly across these lists. Based solely on the context of use, these lists would likely warrant low, moderate, and high impact levels, respectively.

- **Obligations to protect confidentiality**: Depending on your company's industry, location, and where the data is stored, it is subject to various regulations. For example, if you are a healthcare company, then you are subject to HIPAA. If you are doing business in the EU and storing information on European citizens, then your company is subject to GDPR. In addition, your company's own privacy policies need to be followed. When determining the impact levels, these regulations and policies must be considered.

- **Access to and location of PII**: Organizations should factor in the nature of authorized access to PII when assessing its confidentiality impact level. The frequency and breadth of access to PII – by numerous individuals, systems, or both – inherently increase the risk of confidentiality breaches. Additionally, the context in which PII is accessed plays a significant role. For instance, PII accessed or stored on teleworker devices, through external web applications, or off-site, such as on laptops or removable devices that are not under the direct control of the organization, presents a higher risk. Given these factors, it is prudent for organizations to assign a higher impact level to PII that is widely accessed, as a measure to counterbalance the elevated risk.

There are some good examples in NIST *800-122* of how to determine the impact level. We are going to go through one as an example. Remember – where PII is stored is critical. If it's stored in the EU, then you need an EU privacy expert to review your impact analysis. If PII is already available publicly, then you can set the impact level to be low. For example, the name and phone number of someone in a phone book would be considered public information. Law enforcement PII is typically marked as high impact. In general, PII is classified as moderate impact.

Example to determine impact level

An organization operates an intranet site for employee use and maintains a web-use audit log with the following data:

- User IP addresses

- Referring URLs (the URL of the last visited site before accessing the intranet)

- Dates and times of site access

- Records of accessed web pages or topics within the intranet (for example, organization security policy)

In determining the PII loss impact level, the following categories should be considered:

- **Identifiability analysis**: While the log itself doesn't contain directly identifiable information, there is an associated system log with domain login records, including user IDs and IP addresses. Administrators with access to both systems can potentially correlate data to identify individual users. This capability extends to most users accessing intranet resources.

- **Quantity of PII**: The log encompasses a substantial volume of records that link to PII.

- **Data field sensitivity**: The log details which internal web pages and topics are accessed. Some content, such as searches for substance abuse program information, could be sensitive. However, the risk of embarrassment or harm is limited due to the intranet's scope.

- **Context of use**: The log's creation aligns with the organization's **acceptable use policies** (**AUPs**), known to all staff. Disclosure of this information is unlikely to cause significant harm, with the exception of potential embarrassment for a few users.

- **Access and location of PII**: Access to the log is restricted to a limited number of system administrators for operational troubleshooting and **incident response** (**IR**) personnel for investigating incidents. Access to the data is restricted through the organization's internal systems using **role-based access control** (**RBAC**) and **identity and access management** (**IAM**).

Impact-level determination

Considering these factors, the organization assesses that a breach of the log's confidentiality would likely result in minimal harm. Consequently, it assigns a **low** PII confidentiality impact level to this data.

I created the following table to help demystify the classification of PII. I have to give the warning that once you classify the impact level of your PII data, especially if the data is stored in the EU and contains EU citizen PII or PI, please consult a privacy expert. Depending on where the data is stored in the EU, the interpretation of GDPR changes:

NIST direct PII	NIST linked/linkable data (info that is linked or linkable to direct PII)	GDPR personal information (personal information)*	Linkable data (info on its own is not personal data)
<ul><li>Full name</li><li>SSN</li><li>Birth date and place</li><li>Mother's maiden name</li><li>Biometric data</li><li>Home address</li></ul>	<ul><li>Medical</li><li>Education</li><li>Financial</li><li>Employment records</li><li>Date of birth</li><li>Place of birth</li><li>Race</li><li>Religion</li><li>Weight</li><li>Activities</li><li>Geographical indicators</li></ul>	<ul><li>Full name</li><li>Identification number</li><li>GPS coordinates</li><li>Online identifier</li><li>Physical</li><li>Physiological</li><li>Genetic</li><li>Mental</li><li>Commercial</li><li>Cultural</li><li>Social identity natural persons</li></ul>	<ul><li>Age</li><li>Height</li><li>Weight</li><li>Telephone number</li><li>Credit card</li><li>Personnel number</li><li>Account data</li><li>Number plate</li><li>Appearance</li><li>Customer number or address</li><li>Time a person starts and stops work</li><li>Work breaks</li><li>IP address</li></ul>

Table 10.2 - Types of PII and PI

*Under GDPR, along with personal information such as full or last name, the following is also considered to be personal information: time the user visits a website, phone number, what a person ate, what kind of clothes a person wears, and how many children they have.

Third-party risk management

Third-party risk management is critical. If a critical vendor you rely on is compromised, then the breach may also affect your company. We have talked in *Chapter 8* about using Snyk's `renovate` package to ensure your open source code is up to date and patched. Also, use GitHub's **static application security testing** (**SAST**) code scanning tool to ensure your code doesn't have vulnerabilities. What if the tool you use has been compromised? This is exactly what happened with the SolarWinds attack. This is why third-party risk management, also known as supply chain management, is so critical.

SolarWinds attack

SolarWinds has a network Monitoring product called Orion. It was used throughout the commercial and federal government. SolarWinds suffered a major cyber-attack in 2020. What makes the SolarWinds attack so devastating is that the attackers were able to gain access to their source code and introduce malware that would allow them to backdoor into SolarWinds at customer sites.

Since Orion is a network management platform, it has privileged access to network devices and logs. It was one of the industry leaders in its space, making it a prime target for hackers. This led to the largest supply chain hack on record. Hundreds of companies and government agencies were hacked as a result of the backdoor in the Orion code. This hack was a nation-state attack by a foreign country. This attack also highlights why you need to vet your third-party critical vendors such as vendors, contractors, partners, and sub-contractors.

Vendor management policy

To begin with, you need a vendor management policy. The policy will cover the overall vendor risk program your company has. You will have sections covering the following:

- Vendor inventory of third-party vendors

- Criteria for rating the vendors: high, moderate, or low

- Ensuring all critical vendors are properly vetted with either an audit report (that is, SOC 2, ISO *27001*) or a security questionnaire

- General contract-related information

Vendor management contract clauses

For contracts, you need to ensure that there are security-related descriptions that your vendor or contractor has to meet. For example, add a clause requiring that the vendor does background checks on its employees. Next are some common contract clauses that you can add. Don't use all of them for all vendors because this will leave you with very few vendors that you can use. For example, a small one-person company that isn't processing sensitive data shouldn't have to meet the same stringent requirements as a company processing sensitive data for your company. Some security and privacy-related contract clauses follow:

- **Right to Audit**: The Organization reserves the right to audit and test the Vendor's security controls periodically or upon significant changes to the relationship. This includes access to audit reports, security testing results, and relevant documentation to ensure ongoing compliance with agreed-upon security standards.

- **Notification of Security Breaches**: The Vendor is required to promptly notify the Organization of any security breaches, ideally within 72 hours of discovery. This notification must include details of the breach, affected data, and steps taken for mitigation, in compliance with applicable data breach notification laws.

- **Adherence to Security Practices**: The Vendor must adhere to the Organization's specified security practices. Any inability to adhere to these practices must be communicated immediately to the Organization, along with proposed measures to address any resultant security gaps or conflicts.

- **Response Time to Vulnerabilities**: The Vendor is obligated to promptly address known critical vulnerabilities that may impact the Organization's business, with responses and remediation efforts communicated and implemented in a timely manner, not exceeding 30 days from identification of the vulnerability.

- **Demonstration of Compliance**: The Vendor shall provide independent evidence of compliance with the contractual requirements, including but not limited to third-party audits, certifications, and compliance reports, as mutually agreed upon by the Vendor and the Organization.

- **Management of Supplier's Supply Chain Risks**: The Vendor is responsible for ensuring that its supply chain adheres to the same security standards and clauses applied to the Vendor, including conducting regular audits and requiring similar compliance evidence from its suppliers.

- **Communication of Changes**: The Vendor must inform the Organization of any changes in its operational environment that may impact the Organization's business. This includes changes in technology, business processes, or security practices, with a commitment to reassess and realign with the Organization's security requirements.

If the contractor is processing PII data, then you could add more stringent items such as all employees and subcontractors assigned to directly work with the data have background checks completed. The use and non-disclosure of confidential information must be agreed upon. Typically, this will also be in a separate non-disclosure document.

Critical vendors

When setting up your new vendor management program, you have to evaluate each of your vendors as high, medium, or low risk. At the very least, you have to decide on what vendors your company relies on that are considered to be critical. Now, when I first did this at RedSeal, I asked for a list of all vendors, and it was thousands. RedSeal is a medium-sized company. Larger companies would have so many more. You don't have to rate *EVERY* single vendor. This can be tricky, but there are some general rules. What you have to do is think about all the vendors that your IT, security, and development staff rely upon: the vendors that are critical to the service or product your company provides. For example, if your company has a SaaS product that runs in AWS, then every vendor that could potentially cause a disruption to the platform is critical. As an example, this would include AWS, Terraform, Jira, and GitHub. You need to think about any vendors that provide services or a platform; if it goes down, that would affect your SaaS product. Next, thinking about your on-premise assets and company as a whole, think of your critical vendors. For example, if you are a Google Workspace company or M365, either one would be a critical vendor. If your company uses a shared data center space, then the company providing the data center would be critical. If your company has outsourced its IT, then they would be considered critical. You can either create a spreadsheet or use a tool such as Drata, Vanta, Secureframe, or OneTrust. Table 10.3 below is an example of a Third-Party Risk Register. It can be a simple spreadsheet or table where you track the third party vendors that you rely upon as seen below:

Vendor Name	Type	Risk	Login Used
AWS	Cloud provider	High	SSO
Microsoft	Email and collaboration	High	SSO
Stripe		Low	Username/password

Table 10.3 - Vendor list

Train your staff

Train your staff who work with new vendors to ask them upfront if they have a third-party audit report such as SOC 2 Type 1 or 2 or ISO *27001*, and if not, send a security questionnaire to be filled out. If your company has a CRM, you can add a section that lists their compliance. When I was at RedSeal, we added some fields to Salesforce so that for each vendor, there were fields that said SOC 2, ISO *27001*, ISO *9000*, or compliance that could be selected with a date for checking. This way, you can run a report with the list of vendors to show the auditors and also keep track of when you vetted the vendor. You have to review your vendors' compliance annually.

Vendor risk rating

There are two platforms where you can search for your vendor and get a risk rating. These platforms are SecurityScorecard, which has a free option, and Bitsight. Both allow you to see your own company's risk profile and your third-party vendors. How it works is these companies do passive penetration tests on the external (internet-facing) assets and interfaces of these companies' networks and provide risk ratings. Many times, you will have customers ask you to respond if your risk rating on SecurityScorecard or Bitsight is below a specific threshold. When I was at RedSeal, we used the SecurityScorecard ratings of RedSeal to track and give metrics to the board.

Data loss protection

At the most basic level for **data loss protection** (DLP), you don't want to allow your employees to back up their laptops to an external backup drive. It may seem counterproductive with all of the remote work being done now, but you have to consider that your company data may be going along with that person when they leave your company. Protecting your company data may be as simple as adding this to your security policies and notifying your employees via email. This includes using unapproved or company-assigned USB sticks for storage. In addition, ensure your employees use company-owned and approved storage and not personal cloud storage such as iCloud. As your company grows, you can provide a **Backup-as-a-Service** (**BaaS**) such as Veeam. For advanced protection, you can use an EDR solution that restricts the use of USB portable storage. This prevents corporate data loss as well as protects from insider threats.

Insider threats – the hidden danger

While external cyber threats often steal the spotlight, insider threats lurk within organizations, posing a significant risk to cybersecurity and resilience. These threats can emanate from current or former employees, contractors, or business partners who have intimate knowledge of an organization's systems and operations. Insider threats may be intentional, such as disgruntled employees seeking to inflict harm or individuals with malicious intent. However, unintentional insider threats are equally prevalent, stemming from employees' inadvertent actions or negligence. Whether through negligence or malice, insider threats can lead to data breaches, **intellectual property** (**IP**) theft, or disruption of critical operations. In this book, we have discussed many strategies and best practices to detect, mitigate, and prevent insider threats, ensuring your organization's cyber resilience is fortified from both external and internal adversaries. From your security policies to enforcing RBAC, data encryption, and the **principle of least privilege** (**PoLP**), this book has shown you a multi-pronged approach to securing your data from both internal and external threats.

I wanted to give a personal example of an insider threat. I worked at IBM in the 90s as a DNS/IP management Team Lead. An IBM engineer got mad and attacked the research lab where he worked. He deleted all the data and work that resided in his research lab. Since I was a member of the IBM network team, we heard about the massive data recovery that had to be done. Something like this can happen to any company.

Quick reference for data protection

Based on company size, your company's third-party risk management program may consist of the following:

Basic:

- Encrypt data in transit and at rest
    - TLS v1.2 or above
    - AES 256
    - IPsec
- Third-party risk management
    - Vendor management policy

- High-level description of the program
- Inventory of vendors
- Common contract clauses

- Spreadsheet with vendors listed and risk rated

  - Name

  - Type

  - Risk

  - Login used

- External posture tool

  - Censys.io

  - SecurityScorecard

Medium:

- Encrypt data in transit and at rest

  - TLS v1.2 or above

  - AES 256

  - IPsec

- Data discovery

  - Where is PII located?

  - Map data flows of PII within the network/cloud

- Impact level of PII

  - Low

  - Moderate

  - High

- Third-party risk management

  - Vendor management policy

    - High-level description of program

- Inventory of vendors
- Common contract clauses
- Tools
  - Drata
  - OneTrust
  - Vanta
  - Secureframe
- External posture tool
  - SecurityScorecard
  - Bitsight

Advanced:

- Encrypt data in transit and at rest
  - TLS v1.2 or above
  - AES 256
  - IPsec
- Data discovery
  - Where is PII located?
  - Map data flows of PII within the network/cloud
- Impact level of PII
  - Low
  - Moderate
  - High
- Third-party risk management
  - Vendor management policy
    - High-level description of the program
    - Inventory of vendors
    - Common contract clauses

- Tools

  - Drata

  - OneTrust

  - Vanta

  - Secureframe

- External posture tool

  - SecurityScorecard

  - Bitsight

Summary

In summary, encrypting your data in transit and while stored is critical in building your security program. In order to ensure that data is encrypted, it should be part of your security baseline. For example, all laptops and servers should be configured to ensure the hard drives are encrypted. Also, disable protocols such as Telnet. Understanding where PII is stored and processed within your network is important to protecting it. Finally, vetting your critical third-party vendors is important to lowering your company's risk.

In the next chapter, we will be covering security resilience: taking your security program to the next level. We will discuss more advanced security measures that you can take to level up your security program.

Part 3:
Security Resilience:
Taking Your Security Program
to the Next Level

In this part, you will learn how the traditional antivirus system has been taken to the next level with **Endpoint Detection Response (EDR)**. We'll demystify **Extended Detection And Response (XDR)**, **Managed Detection And Response (MDR)**, and Zero Trust. Next, we'll discuss the importance of creating a security baseline. We'll also cover the importance of classifying your critical assets. In the last chapter, we cover artificial intelligence: the good, the bad, and the ugly. Finally, we'll cover Responsible AI, exploring both the European take and that from NIST, and what actions your company needs to take to be compliant.

This section contains the following chapters:

- *Chapter 11, Taking Your Endpoint Security to the Next Level*
- *Chapter 12, Secure Configuration Baseline*
- *Chapter 13, Classify Your Data and Assets*
- *Chapter 14, Cyber Resilience in the Age of Artificial Intelligence (AI)*

Taking Your Endpoint Security to the Next Level

This chapter is about taking your endpoint security to the next level. We've covered the basics in *Chapters 1–10*. You know you need an antivirus and VPN. In this chapter, we'll get into more advanced topics while demystifying EDR, MDR, and XDR. Next, we'll cover zero trust and how it's not all about buying a new product. Later in the chapter, we'll talk about some more advanced cloud tools.

In this chapter, we're going to cover the following main topics:

- Endpoint detection and response (EDR) – Focusing on the "R"

- Managed detection and response (MDR)

- Extended detection and response (XDR)

- Cloud security posture management (CSPM)/Cloud-native application protection program (CNAPP)

- Zero trust vs. software-defined perimeter

- DNS protection

Endpoint detection and response (EDR) – Focusing on the "R"

We already covered the latest advanced antivirus and anti-malware, which is called endpoint detection and response (EDR), in *Chapter 5*. It takes the traditional antivirus to the next level. Products such as CrowdStrike, SentinelOne, and MalwareBytes' ThreatDown will sell the products based on multiple levels. Each level offers more protection, with the "R" actually providing your company with a 24/7 help desk for your employees' endpoints. The help desk is there to provide you with help in the event of an endpoint-related incident and to get your endpoints back online. If an employee downloads malware or ransomware, then the help desk will help you recover the laptop and get back online. In some cases, the "R" acts as a remote **Security Operation Center** (**SOC**) for your company. Remember, when protecting your endpoints, this doesn't just include your employee laptops but servers and company-approved mobile devices.

As we discussed earlier, having a mobile device management (MDM) solution is important to isolate mobile devices that are not approved to connect to your network. Having a solution that can recognize these unauthorized devices and put them in a separate network segment, such as the guest network, is important. Since MDM solutions scan any device connecting to your network, even approved devices that are not patched or have malware will be quarantined and patched before being allowed on the corporate network.

We saw when we covered the LastPass breach how an employee used his personal computer to log in to work, and it led to a breach of the LastPass corporate network. The computer was not managed by the company. As a result, it was not maintained with the proper security safeguards. The employee had installed the company VPN on his personal computer. Since the employee also had an unpatched Plex server on his home network, the attacker was able to gain access to his home network and, ultimately, his personal computer. We don't know whether the Plex server was on this personal computer or another computer on his home network, but we do know the employee's personal computer did not have the proper safeguards installed. If there was an EDR solution installed on it, then it would have alerted when the hacker installed malware on his computer. Having a network access control solution or zero trust, which we will talk more about later, would have stopped this unapproved computer from accessing the LastPass network.

Managed detection and response (MDR)

MDR is essentially a virtual SOC. If your company doesn't have a SOC, or even if it does, having an MDR solution is useful. Now, you have a remote SOC that is monitors threats across the globe, as well as the EDR clients on your network. When an alert is sent, the remote SOC analyst reviews the alert and determines whether it is a false positive. Once it is determined that the threat is not a false positive, then the team will reach out to your company and either guide your own IT security team in how to address the issue or remediate the issue.

MDRs offer several advantages:

- They provide 24/7 coverage, which can be complex and costly to implement in-house
- They possess expertise that may not be available internally
- They must handle the high turnover rates of their cybersecurity analysts
- They can distribute the costs of expensive security tools across all their clients
- They can oversee your log retention needs
- They have access to global threat intelligence, which might be challenging to obtain locally
- They offer quick setup and the ability to scale up or down as needed

However, MDRs also have limitations:

- They may not understand your systems as intimately as you do, potentially leading to overlooked alerts or unnecessary escalations

Assessing the quality of an MDR service can be difficult. It's advisable to assign a dedicated individual to manage the MDR relationship. Ideally, this person should independently verify the MDR's findings, providing a dual-layered security approach. Unfortunately, satisfaction levels among CISOs with their MDR services tend to be low.

Extended detection and response (XDR)

XDR is a product, typically a SaaS, that takes all of your vulnerability and threat data plus alerts and analyzes this with **machine learning (ML)** and **artificial intelligence (AI)**. Most XDR services combine EDR as part of the service. Typically, the XDR will analyze the logs from EDR clients. The XDR will filter through the alerts, reducing false positives and allowing your SOC and security teams to focus on actual incidents. Typically, XDR is bundled as part of the response for the EDR.

SOAR

SOAR, which stands for security orchestration, automation, and response, is a cybersecurity solution that automates and streamlines security operations. It integrates various security tools and systems, typically the EDR/XDR, allowing for more efficient and effective incident response and threat management.

The core components of SOAR include orchestration, automation, and incident response. Orchestration connects different tools and systems to allow for seamless data sharing and process execution. Automation enables the execution of tasks without human intervention based on predefined playbooks and workflows. This not only accelerates incident response but also reduces the likelihood of human error. Incident response within SOAR involves managing and responding to security incidents with the help of automated workflows, ensuring that each incident is addressed promptly and effectively.

For organizations facing sophisticated and evolving cyber threats, SOAR offers a way to enhance their security operations with greater efficiency, speed, and intelligence. By automating routine tasks and orchestrating complex workflows, SOAR empowers security teams to stay ahead of threats and maintain a strong security posture. SOAR is the ultimate management of security alerts. It requires a lot of expertise and very deep knowledge of your system.

Cloud security posture management (CSPM)/Cloud-native application protection program (CNAPP)

CSPM and CNAPP tools are essentially the same. CSPM was the first name for these products, and then CNAPP became the way to describe the same tools. CSPM provides compliance with secure configurations such as the **Center for Internet Security (CIS)** or **Security Technical Implementation Guide (STIGS)**. Some also provide compliance with regulatory frameworks and standards such as NIST, PCI, and ISO. Depending on the product, review the specific features it provides. Other features include exposure and vulnerability management. CNAPP takes all of the CSPM features and adds to them, such as **infrastructure-as-code (IaC)** scanning. Again, with all of the hype, I think CNAPP was a way to differentiate from all the other cloud security tools. You should do a product evaluation with at least three products, comparing the features and cost. I have included a product evaluation template at `https://trustedciso.com/e-landing-page/ciso-guide-to-cyber-resilience/`.

I'm sure vendors will complain when I say CSPM and CNAPP are essentially the same because the vendors who claim they are a CNAPP were trying to differentiate themselves from the CSPM vendors. The new buzzword is CNAPP.

What is CSPM/CNAPP?

CSPM/CNAPP tools are amazing. What they do is hook into your cloud and provide mapping, visibility, compliance, threat analysis, and the automated configuration of your cloud. What makes CNAPP so great is it can quickly scan and analyze multi-clouds and alert you to the following:

- Asset inventory changes
- Misconfigurations
- Threats
- Unintended exposure to the internet
- Real-time threats
- Identity and access control changes
- Compliance

Purchasing a separate product, such as Wiz.io or Cloudwize.io, makes it easy to quickly see and remediate misconfigurations and threats. Wiz.io is the leader in this space. CloudWize.io is a smaller startup. There are native tools within each of the cloud platforms that can also be used to get similar results. With a separate CSPM and or CNAPP tool, you have the ease of one dashboard providing a cohesive view of your security posture in your multi-cloud environment. Remember that each tool used within AWS, Azure, or GCP has an associated cost. When you are deciding whether you want to use a separate product, such as Wiz.io or CloudWize.io, take into consideration the ease of one dashboard vs. the cost of each cloud tool. For example, in AWS, you need AWS Security Hub, AWS Inspector, AWS Access Analyzer, AWS GuardDuty, and AWS CodeWhisperer to get all the same features as Wiz.io or CloudWize.io. In *Table 11.1*, I have compiled a list of tools for each cloud service provider that will give you CSPM and CNAPP features.

Item	Tool
Risk assessment	AWS Security Hub
	Azure Microsoft Defender for Cloud
	GCP Security Command Center
	CloudWize.io
	Wiz.io
Secure configuration	AWS Security Hub
	Azure Microsoft Defender for Cloud
	GCP Security Command
	CloudWize.io
	Wiz.io
Real-time alerts and remediation	AWS Security Hub; Amazon GuardDuty
	Azure Microsoft Defender for Cloud
	GCP Security Command
	CloudWize.io
	Wiz.io
Remediation and policy enforcement	AWS Security Hub
	Azure Microsoft Defender for Cloud
	GCP Security Command
	CloudWize.io
	Wiz.io
Threat detection and prevention (unintended exposure to the internet)	AWS Inspector; Amazon GuardDuty
	Azure Microsoft Defender for Cloud
	GCP Security Command
	CloudWize.io
	Wiz.io

Item	Tool
Vulnerability management	AWS Inspector
	Azure Microsoft Defender for Cloud
	GCP Security Command
	CloudWize.io
	Wiz.io
Identity and access management policy enforcement	AWS Access Analyzer
	Azure Microsoft Defender for Cloud
	GCP Security Command
	CloudWize.io
	Wiz.io
Infrastructure-as-code (IaC) scanning	AWS Code Whisperer
	Azure Microsoft Defender for Cloud
	GCP Security Command
	CloudWize.io
	Wiz.io
Visualize/Map environment	AWS Security Hub; AWS mapping
	Azure Microsoft Defender for Cloud
	GCP Security Command
	CloudWize.io
	Wiz.io

Table 11.1 – CSPM and CNAPP tools

Zero trust vs. software-defined perimeter

Zero trust is the latest and greatest security defense. You don't have to purchase a new product to reap the benefits. Zero trust originated from highly classified networks in the Federal Government. Software-defined perimeter and zero trust are the same thing. In a software-defined perimeter, every asset sits behind a remote access gateway. To gain access to the asset, a user, service, or other device has to authenticate with their assigned X.509 certificate and is only granted with the specific authorization required (principle of least privilege). The Cloud Security Alliance has done an amazing job at demystifying zero trust, also known as SDP. Following their lead, I will explain what zero trust is and how to implement it in your company. You probably already have some zero trust features and functionalities implemented in your company and may not realize they are considered to be zero trust. In a nutshell, zero trust is mutual authentication for all devices, services, and users using the following:

- TLS v1.2 or above
- X.509 certificates
- **Security assertion markup language (SAML)**

Previously, only custom operating systems and hardware were used to process and disseminate classified data in the US Federal Government. This is how it was when I was in the United States Air Force in the 1990s. Over time, the government moved away from using specialized operating systems and hardware to allowing **commercial off-the-shelf** (**COTS**) products to be used even in highly classified environments. In 2000, a mandate said that COTS products could be purchased by the federal government, and any IT security products had to be independently certified by a third-party approved **Common Criteria** (**CC**) lab. Common Criteria is a global product certification. If you get your product certified under CC, then you can sell it to the US Federal Government as well as to all of the governments in countries that are part of CC. You can see the listing of member countries on the CC website: `https://www.commoncriteriaportal.org/index.cfm`. Cryptographic modules have to be tested and validated by a lab accredited by **Federal Information Processing Standards** (**FIPS**). FIPS only applies to the United States and Canada. CC relies on FIPS in that any cryptographic module used in a CC-certified product must be FIPS-validated.

How a typical TLS session works

When you go to a website, your browser will send a client hello, random data, and the ciphers it can use. The web server acknowledges it and sends some random data back. The web server generates a master secret used to encrypt the session from end to end. The server sends a server hello, server random, the web server's X.509 certificate, and the specific cipher suite to be used for the session back to the client, as you can see in *Figure 11.1*:

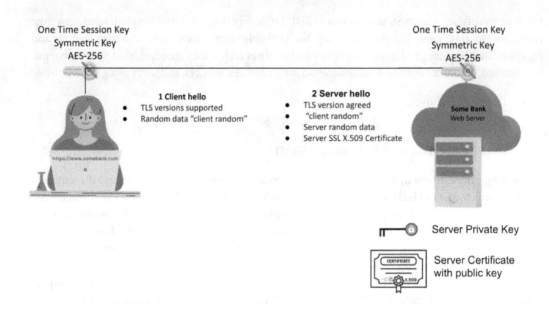

Figure 11.1 – TLS session with web server

The client browser verifies the web server's X.509 certificate to ensure it hasn't expired and has been signed by a certification server that it has in its root certificate store. Once the client browser has verified the server certificate, it then generates the same symmetric key on its own. The symmetric key is the session key that is unique to the session and will encrypt the session end to end, providing confidentiality.

What is mutual authentication?

Now, let's discuss a TLS session using mutual authentication. In this example, the server is configured to require mutual authentication. What this means is the client browser has to send its X.509 certificate to the web server. When the web server receives the client certificate, it verifies that it has not expired and that it was signed by a root certification server that has a corresponding root certificate in the web server's certificate store, as shown in *Figure 11.2*:

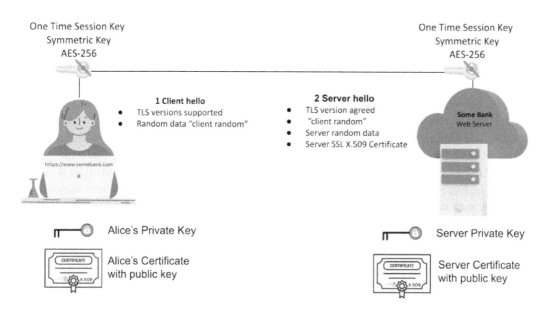

Figure 11.2 – TLS session with mutual authentication

You can see that, in this case, the client has to have its own X.509 certificate. Web servers that need to be accessed by the general public don't require mutual authentication because you want lots of people to be able to browse your site. You can see how a web server intended for internal use that requires a client to have an X.509 certificate issued by your company (for it to be presented to the web server when connecting) is a powerful way to control access to your internal servers. Now, you understand how zero trust works at its most fundamental level.

As I said earlier, you don't have to purchase a new product. If you do, of course, it will make deployment easier and faster. Even if you purchase a zero trust product, one product doesn't cover all aspects of zero trust. Despite its widespread acclaim, the interpretation of zero trust can significantly differ among vendors, leading to a diverse landscape of definitions and implementations. You must start with an **identity and access management (IAM)** product or do it yourself by issuing X.509 certificates to all of your users, servers, and devices. It's interesting how some things never change. In the 1990s, you could do the same. I worked as a PKI engineer at Entrust in the late 1990s, where I would go out and install the backend PKI certification server and integrate it with whatever applications the customer wanted to use certificates for. For example, if the customer wanted to encrypt and digitally sign an email, then I would issue a certificate to each user and integrate it with Outlook. Here, we have the latest and greatest technology built on X.509 certificates. Likewise, you can issue certificates to firewalls, routers, and network devices for authentication purposes. At the time, it was deemed too costly and time-intensive to issue certificates to every user and device. I find it interesting that here we are, 25 years later, and the newest technology is based on mutual authentication. Those companies that took security seriously back then are much better off than those that didn't. As always, I want to give you an understanding of how to get zero trust by doing it yourself, so to speak, rather than purchasing a product. In *Table 11.2*, I do just that. You probably already have some of the zero trust safeguards deployed in your company. You can build on those. If you are just starting, that is okay, too. I have prioritized MFA as the first step because 99.99% of account attacks can be thwarted by using MFA. The most common attack vector is email phishing, so I've added it as the second step:

Safeguard	Do-it-yourself configuration	Vendor product
Phase 1		
MFA for users	Issue X.509 certificates – Let's Encrypt or Microsoft PKI	Okta*, Duo, Entrust Datacard
MFA for all applications	Issue X.509 certificates – Let's Encrypt or Microsoft PKI	Okta, Duo, Entrust Datacard
Email scanning for phishing attempts	Rely on Google Workspace scanning* Ensure quarterly email phishing campaigns – use Curricula M365 subscription; if not, use E5, then add the Defender package	Mimecast, Proofpoint, Cisco ESA, Cloudflare Area 1 Email Security
Implement endpoint protection/EDR	Use antivirus	Microsoft Windows Defender, Malwarebytes Threatdown, Crowdstrike, SentinelOne
Enforce HTTPS and DNSSEC	You can set this in your browser Ensure the browser is configured to use DNSSEC *	AWS, Azure, Cloudflare, GCP

Safeguard	Do-it-yourself configuration	Vendor product
DDOS, injection, and bot protection	Use Cloudflare (free version for website)	Cloudflare, AWS, Azure, GCP
Zero trust policy enforcement for all internet-facing applications		Azure App Proxy, Cloudflare Access, Zscaler Private Access (ZPA)
Segment user access		Cloudflare Access & Gateway, Zscaler Private Access (ZPA)
Implement MDM		Windows: Microsoft Intune, Mac: Jamf
Use CSPM/CNAPP to identify cloud misconfigurations and unintended exposures to the internet		AWS Security Hub, AWS Inspector, Amazon GuardDuty
		Azure Microsoft Defender for Cloud
		GCP Security Command
		CloudWize.io
		Wiz.io
Inventory all assets and applications	• Spreadsheet	ServiceNow, CSPM/CNAPP tools, Drata, Secureframe, Vanta, Microsoft Intune
Stay up to date with the latest threat actors	• Follow CISA alerts • Patch According to CISA KEV • Cloudflare Radar • OWASP	Use vCISO
Implement a DevOps methodology to guarantee policy compliance for newly created resources. Infrastructure as Code (IaS).		Ansible Puppet Terraform

Safeguard	Do-it-yourself configuration	Vendor product
Phase 2		
Remote browser isolation	Run your browser in a virtual machine. You could do this, but it's not really feasible for all of your employees Use blockers on your browser, such as Ghostery and Duckduckgo Use Brave or Firefox since they have built-in security safeguards	Cloudflare Browser Isolation, Zscaler Cloud Browser Isolation, Proofpoint Browser Isolation
Use CSPM/CNAPP to identify cloud misconfigurations and unintended exposures to the internet		AWS Security Hub, AWS Inspector, Amazon GuardDuty
		Azure Microsoft Defender for Cloud
		GCP Security Command
		CloudWize.io
		Wiz.io
Deploy global DNS filtering	Use blockers on your browser, such as Ghostery and Duckduckgo Use Brave or Firefox since they have built-in security safeguards	Cisco Umbrella, Cloudflare Gateway, DNSfilter, Zscaler Shift
Isolate or block threats behind SSL/TLS		Cloudflare Gateway, Zscaler Internet Access (ZIA)
Close all inbound ports open to the internet	Scan perimeter with Qualys, Security Scorecard, and Censy.io. Manually close ports on firewalls and internet-facing hosts	Cloudflare Access, Zscaler Private Access (ZPA)
Zero trust policy enforcement for all SaaS applications		Cloudflare Access, Zscaler Private Access (ZPA)

Safeguard	Do-it-yourself configuration	Vendor product
Phase 3		
Classify your data (impact analysis) and inventory where it exists	Manual inventory and draw out data flows Do a privacy impact analysis	DataDog, Splunk, SolarWinds
Use hardware-based MFA for sensitive data access		Yubico
Inventory all APIs and services		Cloudflare Application Connector, Zscaler Private Access (ZPA), Invicti
For branch-to-branch connectivity, configure broadband internet		Cloudflare Magic WAN, Cato Networks, Aryaka FlexCore
Enable logging and review for user activity on sensitive applications		Security Incident and Event Monitoring (SIEM): DataDog, Splunk, SolarWinds
Data loss prevention (DLP) of sensitive data from leaving your applications (PII, SSNs, credit cards, CUI)		Cisco Umbrella, Cloudflare Gateway, Netskope Next Gen SWG, Zscaler Internet Access (ZIA)

Table 11.2 – How to obtain zero trust[1]

*Note 1: For Okta, make sure you get the Adaptive MFA because it adds contextual awareness to the login. This is another zero trust feature. It considers your location and behaviors when approving the login. For example, if you typically log in from the East Coast US time zone and then you try to log in from the West Coast Pacific time zone an hour later, it will flag this. The second login attempt would be blocked, or Okta would require additional MFA authenticators to log in.

*Note 2: Google Workspace does an excellent job of filtering out email phishing attempts, although a few will probably get through. The scammers have upped their game in phishing attempts. I have found less spam comes through on Google Workspace than M365. If you have M365, you must add the Defender package to E1-E4 subscriptions. If you have E5, then the Defender package is included. You can save money by adding the Defender Package to an E1-E4 package rather than purchasing the E5.

*Note 3: I turned on DNSSEC in my browser for all connections and it immediately broke it when going to some webservers and slowed my response times to Google Workspace.

---

1   https://zerotrustroadmap.org/

DNS protection

DNS Protection is something you can easily add to your company's cybersecurity plan. You can whitelist and blacklist websites, and it will automatically block suspicious domains and websites. In the **Zero-Trust Roadmap** from the Cloud Security Alliance (discussed previously), they have it as the first safeguard to deploy. I think this is because it is so easy to deploy. I've moved it down in the list because MFA is by far the most protective safeguard you can implement in your network. Next, we have MFA for all servers. Email phishing is the number one threat vector for hackers. Sometimes, it will move to second, but then it will be back up at number one again. The only threat vector I've seen that beat email phishing is unsecured RDP ports open to the internet. Implementing MFA for RDP protects this from hackers.

What do DNS protections provide?

DNS protections will block your employees from being able to visit malicious websites. Every time you go to a website or use a hostname, i.e., `https://TrustedCISO.com`, your computer queries a DNS server that resolves the hostname to an IP address. The routing to get from one computer to another uses IP addresses. Hackers will set up malicious websites that may look legitimate to try to get you to download a malicious document or spreadsheet with a macro-enabled ransomware payload or a key logger that allows them to observe every keystroke you make. You should check your browser's settings to ensure you have DNSSEC enabled. However, if you force it to always be used, it will break some connections to legitimate websites and will slow down your browser. I turned it on in both my browsers but ended up going back to the default protection provided by Firefox and Chrome.

Filtering based on DNS has some serious limitations, however. It is a crude method for web filtering that does not match the power of a true web filtering solution, such as Zscaler.

For example, many malicious payloads are hosted on `https://docs.google.com/`. A DNS blocking system will need to block all Google Docs, whereas a web filtering solution will only filter the specific URLs within Google Docs that are malicious.

Quick reference for zero trust

Based on company size, your company's third-party risk management program may consist of the following:

- **Basic:**
  - MFA for users
    - Assign X.509 certificates
    - Microsoft PKI

- Let's Encrypt

- Use Okta

- MFA for all servers and devices

  - Assign X.509 certificates

  - Microsoft PKI

  - Let's Encrypt

  - Use Okta

- Email scanning for phishing attempts

  - Rely on Google Workspace

  - M365 – (E1-E4) Add Defender package

- Browser security

  - Enable DNSSEC and use Cloudflare (caution: it may slow or break getting to legitimate websites)

  - Enable HTTPS only

- Deploy endpoint protection

  - Windows Defender

  - Mac: Malwarebytes Threatdown (use level 1 or 2)

  - Mac: SentinelOne (use level 1 or 2)

- DDOS protection

  - Use Cloudflare

- Close all inbound ports from the internet

  - Configure internet-facing devices: Free Qualys scan, Security Scorecard, and Censys.io

  - Cloudflare Access (first 50 seats free)

- Zero trust policy enforcement for all internet-facing applications

  - Cloudflare Access

- Segment user access

  - Cloudflare Access

- Implement MDM

  - Windows and Mac: Microsoft Intune

  - Mac: Jamf

- Inventory all assets and applications

  - Microsoft Intune

  - Drata

  - Secureframe

  - Vanta

  - ServiceNow

  - CSPM/CNAPP tools

- Use CSPM/CNAPP to identify cloud misconfigurations and unintended exposures to the internet

  - AWS Security Hub

  - AWS Inspector

  - Amazon GuardDuty

  - Azure Microsoft Defender for Cloud

  - GCP Security Command

- Stay up to date with the latest threat actors

  - Use vCISO

  - Follow CISA alerts

  - Patch According to CISA KEV

  - Cloudflare Radar

  - OWASP

- Implement a DevOps methodology to guarantee policy compliance for newly created resources

  - Ansible

  - Puppet

  - Terraform

- **Medium**:

  - MFA for users

    - Assign X.509 certificates

    - Microsoft PKI

    - Let's Encrypt

    - Use Okta

    - Use Duo

  - MFA for all servers and devices

    - Assign X.509 certificates

    - Microsoft PKI

    - Let's Encrypt

    - Use Okta

    - Use Duo

  - Email scanning for phishing attempts

    - Rely on Google Workspace

    - M365 – (E1-E4): Add Defender package

  - Browser security

    - Enable DNSSEC and use Cloudflare

    - Enable HTTPS only

  - Deploy endpoint protection

    - Windows Defender

    - Mac: Malwarebytes threatdown

    - Mac: SentinelOne

  - DDOS Protection

    - Use Cloudflare

  - Close all inbound ports to the internet

    - Cloudflare Access (first 50 seats free)

- Zero trust policy enforcement for all SaaS applications
  - Cloudflare Access
- Segment user access
  - Cloudflare Access
- Implement MDM
  - Windows and Mac: Microsoft Intune
  - Mac: Jamf
- Inventory all assets and applications
  - Microsoft Intune
  - Drata
  - Secureframe
  - Vanta
  - ServiceNow
  - CSPM/CNAPP tools
- Use CSPM/CNAPP to identify cloud misconfigurations and unintended exposures to the internet
  - AWS Security Hub
  - AWS Inspector
  - Amazon GuardDuty
  - Azure Microsoft Defender for Cloud
  - GCP Security Command
  - Cloudwize.io
  - Wiz.io
- Stay up to date with the latest threat actors
  - Use vCISO
  - Follow CISA alerts
  - Patch According to CISA KEV

- Cloudflare Radar

- OWASP

- Implementing a DevOps methodology to guarantee policy compliance for newly created resources

  - Ansible

  - Puppet

  - Terraform

- Remote browser isolation

  - Cloudflare Browser Isolation

  - Zscaler Cloud Browser

- Deploy global DNS filtering

  - Cisco Umbrella

  - Cloudflare Gateway

  - DNSfilter

  - Zscaler Shift

- Isolate or block threats behind SSL/TLS

  - Cloudflare Gateway

  - Zscaler Internet Access (ZIA)

- Close all inbound ports open to the internet

  - Cloudflare Gateway

  - Zscaler Internet Access (ZIA)

- **Advanced**:

  - MFA for users

    - Assign X.509 certificates

    - Microsoft PKI

    - Entrust

- Use Okta
- Use Duo
- MFA for all servers and devices
  - Assign X.509 certificates
  - Microsoft PKI
  - Let's Encrypt
  - Use Okta
  - Use Duo
- Email scanning for phishing attempts
  - Rely on Google Workspace
  - M365 – (E1-E4): Add Defender package
- Browser security
  - Enable DNSSEC and use Cloudflare
  - Enable HTTPS only
- Deploy endpoint protection
  - Windows Defender
  - Mac: Malwarebytes threatdown
  - Mac: SentinelOne
- DDOS protection
  - Use Cloudflare
- Close all inbound ports to the internet
  - Cloudflare Access (first 50 seats free)
- Zero trust policy enforcement for all SaaS applications
  - Cloudflare Access
- Segment user access
  - Cloudflare Access

- Implement MDM

  - Windows and Mac: Microsoft Intune

  - Mac: Jamf

- Inventory all assets and applications

  - Microsoft Intune

  - Drata

  - Secureframe

  - Vanta

  - ServiceNow

  - CSPM/CNAPP tools

- Use CSPM/CNAPP to identify cloud misconfigurations and unintended exposures to the internet

  - AWS Security Hub

  - AWS Inspector

  - Amazon GuardDuty

  - Azure Microsoft Defender for Cloud

  - GCP Security Command

  - Cloudwize.io

  - Wiz.io

- Stay up to date with the latest threat actors

  - Use vCISO

  - Follow CISA alerts

  - Patch According to CISA KEV

  - Cloudflare Radar

  - OWASP

- Implementing a DevOps methodology to guarantee policy compliance for newly created resources

  - Ansible

  - Puppet

  - Terraform

- Remote browser isolation

  - Cloudflare Browser Isolation

  - Zscaler Cloud Browser

- Deploy global DNS filtering

  - Cisco Umbrella

  - Cloudflare Gateway

  - DNSfilter

  - Zscaler Shift

- Isolate or block threats behind SSL/TLS

  - Cloudflare Gateway

  - Zscaler Internet Access (ZIA)

- Close all inbound ports open to the internet

  - Cloudflare Gateway

  - Zscaler Internet Access (ZIA)

- Classify your data (impact analysis) and inventory where it exists

  - Privacy impact analysis

  - Datadog

  - Splunk

  - SolarWinds

  - PrivacyCode

- Use hardware-based MFA for sensitive data access

  - Yubico

- Inventory all APIs and services

  - Cloudflare Application Connector

  - Zscaler Private Access (ZPA)

  - Invicti

- For branch-to-branch connectivity, configure broadband internet

  - Cloudflare Magic WAN

  - Cato Networks

  - Aryaka FlexCore

- Enable logging and reviewing for user activity in sensitive applications

  - DataDog

  - Splunk

  - SolarWinds

- Data loss prevention (DLP) for sensitive data leaving your applications (PII, SSNs, credit cards, and CUI)

  - Cisco Umbrella

  - Cloudflare Gateway

  - Netskope Next Gen SWG

  - Zscaler Internet Access (ZIA)

Summary

In summary, taking your security program to the next level includes the visibility of your network and implementing advanced security measures such as zero trust. It boils down to using tools, such as CSPM/CNAPP, to continuously monitor your cloud and obtain alerts in the event of a misconfiguration or unintended exposure. Implementing zero trust is a journey that you may have already started. Remember, at the most basic level, it is about enforcing mutual authentication and assigning X.509 certificates to all devices, servers, and users. Every device, service, and user is considered untrusted until authenticated and authorized with fine-grained access controls.

In the next chapter, we will be covering creating a secure configuration baseline. We will discuss the importance of creating a secure configuration baseline and selecting a compliance framework to keep the attackers out.

Secure Configuration Baseline

This chapter is about creating a secure configuration baseline. Remember that security is a journey, and you can't do everything at once. This is why risk management is so important—being able to weigh your risks, impacts, likelihood, and budget considerations. The company you work for is a business, so you have to balance controls, risk, and budget. As far as executive management goes, they aren't going to care as much about security as you do. We will discuss how to decide what controls should be enforced and what security baseline you should follow. Next, we'll discuss CIS and STIGs, why to choose either one and the best way to go about deploying your new security baseline.

In this chapter, we're going to cover the following main topics:

- Security baseline
- System and Organizational Controls (SOC) 2
- Creating your security baseline

Security baseline

A security baseline involves essentially configuring your laptops, servers, cloud assets, and network devices according to specific controls. For example, all users must have a 14-character password. The parameters include at least one special character, a number, and upper- and lower-case characters. The strongest passwords to use are covered in *Chapter 2*. Password complexity and length are considered configurations. What makes a security baseline is when a new laptop, server, or cloud asset is built to have a base image with the specific controls already configured. In this way, every new Windows laptop and Macbook are built the same, with the same controls enforced for every new laptop issued by your company. Every type of asset your company has should have an associated security baseline. You should start with your network devices, user laptops, and critical servers. Another example is that your firewalls need to be configured with **deny/all** by default, which means denying network traffic by default and allowing network traffic by exception (e.g., deny all or permit by exception). Automating these configurations by using a product such as Ansible for your network devices will make your company so much more secure. A secure configuration can prevent up to 99% of cloud and firewall breaches. There are two Gartner quotes that support this:

"Through 2025, 99% of cloud security failures will be the customer's fault."[1]

"Through 2023, 99% of firewall breaches will be caused by firewall misconfigurations, not firewall flaws[2]."

In *Chapter 9*, we covered the basics of CIS and STIGS. In this chapter, we'll get into aligning your security baseline with the regulations and compliance that your company must meet.

What compliance does your company have to meet?

Compliance maps where your company resides in relation to the industry. If you are in the healthcare industry, then your company must comply with HIPAA. If your company is in the financial sector, then SOC 1 applies. If your company is a SaaS provider, then it must get SOC 2 Type 2 certified. Even if there isn't a stated law governing compliance, the market and your customers may require it. This is the case with SOC 2 for SaaS companies. You can get up and running without SOC2, but as your customer base grows, you will begin to lose potential customers who require their vendors to be compliant as part of their third-party risk management program, which is covered in *Chapter 10*. *Table 12.1* is not an exhaustive table of compliance and industries, but it is a good start for you to select your security baseline:

1   "Is the Cloud Secure." Gartner, 10 Oct. 2019, www.gartner.com/smarterwithgartner/is-the-cloud-secure.

2   Burton, Dave. "The Dangers of Firewall Misconfigurations and How to Avoid Them." Akamai Blog, Akamai , 16 Nov. 2021, www.akamai.com/blog/security/the-dangers-of-firewall-misconfigurations-and-how-to-avoid-them.

Industry	Compliance	Acronym	Safeguards
Energy	North American Electric Reliability Corporation –Critical Infrastructure Protection	NERC-CIP	Strict configuration management
Federal	National Institute of Standards and Technology Protecting Controlled Unclassified Information in Nonfederal Systems and Organizations	NIST 800-171	110 controls that are similar to security, confidentiality, and availability for SOC 2 plus: • MDM management • No local backups • USB management
	SaaS used by the US Federal Government	FedRAMP	Controls based on NIST 800-53 (low, moderate, and high), depending on impact analysis. See my LinkedIn learning class on FedRAMP – How to get FedRAMP-Authorized
Finance	System and Organization Controls – Financial Services Organizations	SOC 1	• Manual controls • IT-dependent manual controls • Application controls[3] • IT general controls
	Sarbanes-Oxley Act	SOX	Robust asset and change management
	Payment Card Industry Data Security Standard	PCI-DSS	Similar to security, confidentiality, and availability in SOC2, plus data flows of credit card data with specific segmentation requirements, as well as penetration testing requirements to test segmentation
Healthcare	Health Insurance Portability and Accountability Act	HIPAA	See "Safeguards for Small" in Chapters 2–10, plus HIPAA-specific policies and mapping of data flows and impact analysis of data
Technology	System and Organization Controls	SOC 2	See "Safeguards for Small" in Chapters 2–10

Table 12.1 – Industries and compliance[4]

3   Finney , Jaclyn. *What Are Internal Controls? Types, Examples, Purpose, Importance*. Linford & Company LLP, 25 Jan. 2022, linfordco.com/blog/types-of-controls/ .

4   Serviceaide. *Regulatory Compliance across Industries*. Serviceaide, 18 Jan. 2022, serviceaide.com/resources/blog/regulatory-compliance-across-industries.

System and Organizational Controls (SOC) 2

SOC 2 is a great first step to building your information security program, whether you want to build a sound information security program or have to meet SOC 2 Type 2. SOC 2 was created by the **American Institute of Certified Public Accountants (AICPA)**, which is the national association that governs the certifications of **Certified Public Accounts (CPA)**. The AICPA was already overseeing the financial audits of companies, and with the advent of information technology and its importance in safeguarding data, the AICPA created SOC 2. As a result, your auditor has to be a certified CPA who is registered with the AICPA to do SOC2 audits. SOC 2 covers five areas of the Trust Services Criteria:

- **Security**: The security controls safeguard information and systems from unauthorized access and the disclosure of sensitive data. Effective security controls are critical in ensuring an entity can achieve its objectives without compromise. Controls that ensure separation of duty, principle least privilege, and multi-factor authentication fall under security.

- **Availability**: The availability controls ensure information and systems are consistently operational and accessible, ensuring they align with and support the entity's goals and objectives. Disaster recovery, business continuity, uptime, failovers, and backups all map to availability.

- **Confidentiality**: The confidentiality controls ensure that sensitive information is safeguarded throughout its lifecycle—from creation to disposal—to align with the entity's objectives. Ensuring your data is encrypted while in transit and when stored falls under confidentiality.

- **Processing integrity**: The processing integrity controls ensure that there is integrity in service provision, production, manufacturing, or the distribution of goods. It ensures that system operations are operating without errors, delays, omissions, and free from unauthorized or unintentional manipulations. For a SaaS product, this applies if the provider is processing large datasets.

- **Privacy**: The privacy controls ensure sensitive information is protected in the collection, usage, retention, disclosure, and disposal of personal information, specifically to support the entity's objectives. Privacy is essential, for example, if your SaaS is processing and storing sensitive data such as medical or financial data.

The five Trust Services Criteria can be scoped to the services that your company offers. For example, if your company is not processing large amounts of customer data, then processing integrity can be excluded. As a baseline, you at least have to scope security, availability, and confidentiality for your SOC 2 audit. There are two types of SOC 2 audits:

- **SOC2 Type I**: Focuses on the design and documentation of controls as of a specific date

- **SOC2 Type II**: Covers the design, documentation, and operation of controls over a time period, typically a year

International Standard Organization (ISO) 27001

ISO 27001 is an international standard for managing information security. ISO 27001 is largely the baseline compliance outside of the United States. If you are selling your product to a European company, they most likely will ask if your company is ISO 27001-certified. It provides a framework for establishing, implementing, maintaining, and continually improving an **information security management system** (**ISMS**). The standard is designed to help organizations secure their information assets, such as financial information, intellectual property, employee details, and information entrusted by third parties.

ISO 27001 specifies requirements for assessing and treating information security risks tailored to the needs of the organization. The adoption of this standard is intended to instill a security-conscious culture within the organization and applies to organizations of all sizes and sectors. An ISO 27001 certification reassures customers and stakeholders that the organization follows information security best practices, and it is often required by regulators or clients to ensure the security of data.

ISO 27001 vs. SOC2

One study shows that SOC 2 Type 1 or Type 2 are considered to be 96% similar to ISO 27001[5]. One difference between SOC 2 and ISO 27001 is that ISO 27001 requires an internal audit plus an external audit by a third-party auditor who is ISO 27001-certified. SOC 2 requires that an AICPA-certified CPA performs the audit. The controls required for ISO 27001 are prescriptive, meaning you have to meet the control as written. SOC 2 gives you more flexibility in that it allows you to customize your controls to meet the criteria and your business. SOC 2 is customizable, allowing you to scope the Trust Criteria, whereas ISO 27001 doesn't. A vCISO, such as myself, can complete an ISO 27001 internal audit for your company if you don't already have an internal audit team. Likewise, a vCISO can complete a readiness assessment for SOC 2.

North American Electric Reliability Corporation Critical Infrastructure Protection (NERC-CIP)

NERC-CIP is a North American, US, and Canadian compliance required for companies in the electricity sector. The types of companies in this sector are as follows:

- Electricity
- Nuclear

---

5   Irwin, Luke. *ISO 27001 VS SOC 2 Certification: What's the Difference?* IT Governance Blog EU, 23 Jan. 2023, http://www.itgovernance.eu/blog/en/iso-27001-vs-soc-2-certification-whats-the-difference.

NERC-CIP stands for the North American Electric Reliability Corporation Critical Infrastructure Protection. It is a set of standards designed to ensure the security of the North American **bulk electric system** (**BES**). These standards are focused on identifying and protecting the assets and systems vital to the reliable operation of the electric grid. The NERC-CIP standards cover various aspects of cybersecurity and physical security for the power grid, including but not limited to the following:

- **Cybersecurity protections**: This involves securing the information systems essential to the reliable operation of the grid against potential threats and vulnerabilities

- **Physical security**: Measures to protect the critical physical assets of the electric system from threats and vulnerabilities

- **Personnel and training**: Ensuring that the personnel responsible for critical infrastructure are adequately trained and vetted

- **Incident reporting and response planning**: Requirements for reporting security incidents and planning for responses to cyber and physical security incidents

Compliance with NERC-CIP standards is mandatory for all companies involved in the North American electricity infrastructure. The standards aim to reduce the risks to the grid's reliability and security from both physical and cyber threats. Non-compliance can result in significant fines and penalties, underscoring the importance of these standards in safeguarding the energy infrastructure. NERC-CIP is a subset of the SOC2 controls. It also has a lot of controls around physical security.

Cybersecurity Maturity Model Certification (CMMC)

CMMC is a framework established by the United States **Department of Defense** (**DoD**) to assess and enhance the cybersecurity posture of the **Defense Industrial Base** (**DIB**). The CMMC framework is designed to protect the sensitive federal information and defense-related intellectual property that is stored or transmitted by DIB companies and their subcontractors. Essentially, if your company is granted a contract from the United States Federal Government, then your company needs to be CMMC-compliant. CMMC v1.0 originally had six levels, which were found to be too complex and onerous for companies to meet. CMMC v2.0 has been significantly streamlined into three levels, as seen in *Figure 12.1*. Level 1 of the CMMC v1.0 and v2.0 are the same. This is a self-assessment against NIST 800-171:

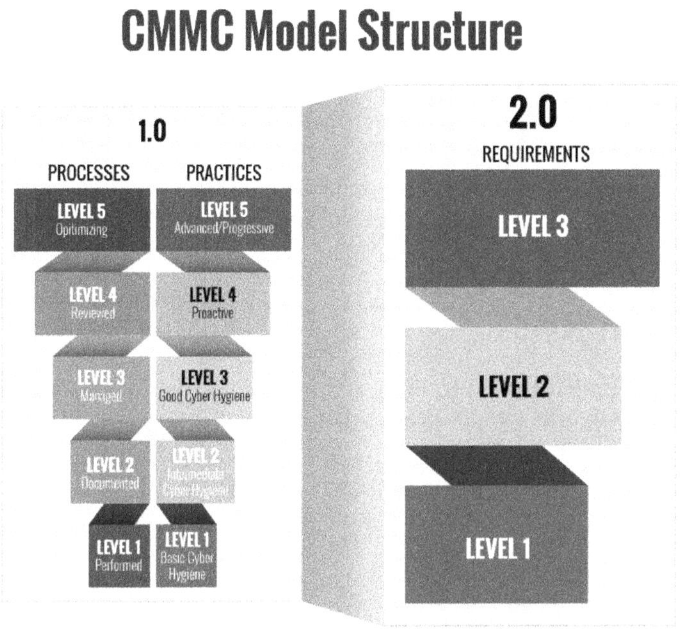

CMMC Model Structure

Figure 12.1 – CMMC model structure[6]

The CMMC v2.0 model encompasses a range of cybersecurity practices and processes, graded across different levels, from basic to advanced cyber hygiene. The levels are the following:

- **Level 1 – Foundational basic cyber hygiene**: Involves the implementation of specified practices to safeguard **Federal Contract Information (FCI)**. This is covered under 52.204-21 Basic Safeguarding of Covered Contractor Information Systems: `https://www.acquisition.gov/far/52.204-21`.

- **Level 2 – Advanced good cyber hygiene**: Involves the implementation of additional practices to protect **Controlled Unclassified Information (CUI)** and the 110 NIST SP 800-171 Rev 2 controls.

- **Level 3 – Expert advanced**: Involves the most advanced and sophisticated cybersecurity practices. These controls are still under review.

---

6   *CMMC Model*. DOD, Chief Information Officer U.S. Department of Defense, dodcio.defense.gov/CMMC/Model/. Accessed 18 Dec. 2023.

The CMMC v2.0 model may require DIB companies to undergo an assessment by an accredited **CMMC third-party assessment organization (C3PAO)** at Level 2 and above. Currently, the guidance says that Level 2-prioritized acquisitions will require an audit by a 3PAO. Non-prioritized acquisitions can still complete self-assessments at CMMC Level 2 to verify compliance with the necessary cybersecurity practices and capabilities at a level appropriate to the sensitivity of the information they handle. Level 3 will require assessments to be conducted by government officials. This certification process aims to enhance the protection of sensitive data and national security information, particularly in light of increasing cyber threats.

NIST 800-171 vs. CMMC

NIST 800-171 is a specification created by NIST and is required when US government contractors provide a self-assessment for which they are implementing the controls. Let me clarify, if a company gets a contract with the US Federal Government, it has to provide a self-assessment showing how the company meets NIST 800-171 for CMMC Level 2 and above.

SOC 1

SOC 1 is an audit specific to services companies that handle financial data and can potentially affect another company's financial reports. Just because your company processes financial data doesn't mean that your company is subject to a SOC 1 audit. For instance, if a company has read-only access to client data, its capabilities do not extend to altering financial information or influencing clients' financial outcomes. Their role might involve offering business intelligence solutions or various perspectives on client data, but without any capacity to modify that data or affect the client's financial status, they aren't subject to SOC 1.

On the other hand, a company that processes payroll for its customers would be subject to a SOC 1 audit. Potentially, they could make a mistake that affects a customer's financial reporting. In a SOC 1 report, management declares the implementation of specific controls to achieve outlined control objectives, and a CPA firm evaluates these controls in relation to management's claims, subsequently issuing an opinion on the alignment with management's assertions. Each SOC 1 report is customized for the specific service organization, with no universal set of criteria for evaluation.

Sarbanes-Oxley Act (SOX)

SOX is the compliance for finance companies that is a result of the Gramm-Leachy bill. This bill was the result of the Enron fiasco, in which they were reporting invalid financial numbers and inflating their company's value. US public companies must adhere to SOX compliance by doing the following:

- Establishing internal controls to safeguard financial data against manipulation.

- Regularly submitting reports to the **Securities and Exchange Commission (SEC)** that verify the efficacy of security measures and the precision of financial disclosures.

- Undergoing an annual independent audit of their financial reports and control systems.

- There are no specific controls to be met, such as those for SOC 2 or ISO 27001. Your company can select one of these frameworks to be SOX-compliant:

  - The **Committee of Sponsoring Organizations of the Treadway Commission** (**COSO**) offers an "Internal Control-Integrated Framework" to guide companies in developing their internal controls.

  - **Control Objectives for Information and Related Technologies** (**COBIT**), created by the IT governance-focused industry group ISACA, assists in aligning IT processes with compliance requirements.

  - The **Information Technology Governance Institute** (**ITGI**) bases its recommendations on both COSO and COBIT, emphasizing the security aspects of internal controls.

Payment Card Industry Data Security Standard (PCI-DSS)

PCI-DSS is specific to any merchant processing credit cards. There are specific controls that you have to meet based on the number of credit card transactions your company receives. The controls are similar to SOC 2, except you have to map the data flows of the credit card processing data on your network and ensure the subnets that the credit card data resides or traverses are segmented from the rest of the networks. This is called the **card data environment** (**CDE**). One thing with PCI-DSS is if you are using **point-to-point encryption** (**P2PE**), then the CDE is considered out of scope. For example, if you have a shop and you use the F5 FreedomPay P2PE credit card scanner, then it is considered out of scope. Credit card data traverse a completely encrypted channel using tokenization and P2PE-certified hardware.

Health Insurance Portability and Accountability Act (HIPAA)

HIPAA is a US Federal law enacted in 2006 to protect health data. The HIPAA Privacy Rule was established by the US Department of **Health and Human Services** (**HHS**) to enforce HIPAA requirements. Additionally, the HIPAA Security Rule safeguards a specific set of sensitive health data governed by the Privacy Rule.

The HIPAA Privacy Rule is rather high-level and general. It's not a specific set of requirements, as is the case for NIST 800-171. There are a lot of policy documentation requirements around HIPAA. Following the controls of SOC2, plus mapping the data flows of where the health data are stored, ensures that the proper protections are in place. I recommend doing an impact analysis of the data. It's not required, but it makes sense to see what impact level the data should be considered. PII in HIPAA is considered to be **protected health information** (**PHI**). It includes electronic patient mental and health data plus payment and demographic information (see section 160.103). Additionally, you must ensure that any services you rely on are HIPAA-compliant. In the cloud, AWS, Azure, and GCP are already SOC2- and HIPAA-compliant. For authentication, you can use Google as an authenticator account and use Google Authenticator for MFA. Okta is also HIPAA-compliant.

Health Information Technology for Economic and Clinical Health (HITECH)

In 2009, under the HITECH Act, a component of the American Recovery and Reinvestment Act of 2009, was signed into law on February 17, 2009. Its primary objective is to encourage the adoption and meaningful utilization of health information technology.

The HITECH Act bolstered the enforcement of HIPAA rules, both on a civil and criminal level. It also added four categories of violations, with various levels of culpability, increasing the minimum penalty for each violation with an upper limit of USD 1.5 million for all violations[7].

HITRUST

Since HIPAA is very generic and not very specific when it comes to technical controls, a consortium of health companies got together and created HITRUST, which is a non-profit company. The intent was to create a risk management framework that would meet HIPAA and make implementing the controls clearer. HITRUST provides a specific framework of requirements for health providers to follow. If you read HIPAA, you will quickly see how high level it is and that it is not very specific. It's written in such a way that a small doctor's office could meet it, as well as a large hospital system or insurance company. It is so high level that it can be confusing with regard to how to enable the proper controls to ensure the protection of PHI and have compliance with HIPAA and HITECH to avoid fines.

I was certified as a HITRUST Assessor when I was at RedSeal because I worked with large hospital systems and insurance companies that were required to be HIPAA-compliant, and some were HITRUST-certified. HITRUST offers a framework with clear controls that a provider needs to enforce. In addition, HITRUST offers a SaaS that can be used to manage your compliance efforts and acts as audit evidence. If you decide to use HITRUST, which is not required, then you must use the HITRUST SaaS tool and be audited along the lines of what HITRUST requires. There are lots of products now that aid with evidence collection, and many new ones give you continuous monitoring for the cloud, such as Drata, Secureframe, and Vanta. Since HITRUST is voluntary and not required, you shouldn't go that route unless a vendor you work with requires (or, I should say, requests) you to be HITRUST-certified. No one can require your company to be HITRUST-certified. A vendor could strongly encourage you to be HITRUST-certified. If your company has already decided to be HITRUST-certified, then that's great; go with it. The HITRUST framework is practical and rigorous in protecting your PHI. It does make the process easy with its SaaS tool. It also provides cross-mappings to other frameworks and standards.

---

7   (OCR), Office for Civil Rights. *Hitech Act Enforcement Interim Final Rule*. HHS.Gov, 28 June 2021, http://www.hhs.gov/hipaa/for-professionals/special-topics/hitech-act-enforcement-interim-final-rule/index.html.

NIST 800-53 – One framework to rule them all

NIST 800-53 is a catalog of requirements of over 1,000 controls. They are categorized into low, medium, and high, based on the impact level of the data being protected. You can see *Chapter 10* for more information on impact level. As I stated earlier in the book, all compliance frameworks and standards map back to NIST 800-53. Once you understand this, you can easily see how meeting one framework will also provide coverage for other frameworks.

When I was at RedSeal, I was the company's compliance expert. This means any specific compliance-related questions that anyone in the company or customer had were sent to me. I quickly began creating cross-mappings. NIST already provides a few, from NIST 800-53 to NIST CSF to SOC 2 or HIPAA. I was getting questions such as, How does RedSeal's product map to a specific compliance framework, regulation, or standard? I ended up doing manual mappings, and then I thought I could write a program to cross-map the frameworks. I collaborated with a programmer at RedSeal and created the script. What I quickly discovered is that everything maps back to NIST 800-53B. I ended up working on a white paper with an auditor, and he said that his practice has an internal tool and that every audit they do is against NIST 800-53B. The auditors then cross-map it back to whatever standard or framework the customer needs to meet. When you look at all of these standards and frameworks a customer must meet, it can seem overwhelming. When you realize they all map back to NIST 800-53B, you see how they relate to each other, simplifying the task of compliance. This is how Drata, Secureframe, Vanta, and Trustcloud can easily map your cloud network controls to so many different standards and frameworks.

Creating your security baseline

The secure configuration of your endpoints, cloud assets, and network devices is paramount to protecting your company from hackers. Gartner has said that 99% of cloud and network breaches are due to misconfiguration. This is something you can do for free. It's not an easy task, but it is well worth it and probably one of the most important actions you can take other than MFA and regular patching. We discussed this previously, but CIS is the de facto secure configuration standard for the commercial space, and STIGS are required for US Federal government networks and FedRAMP. The good news is that there are mappings of CIS to SOC2, HIPAA, NIST CSF, and PCI on the CIS website. As I've stated before, there are compliance products, such as Drata, that will automate the controls you need to meet. There is also a compliance mapping you can download for free called the **Secure Controls Framework (SCF)**. It offers a master mapping of almost every compliance framework and regulation, including CIS, NIST 800-53B, PCI, ISO, COBIT, SOC, HIPAA, and HITRUST. SCF can be downloaded for free in an Excel spreadsheet and has a SaaS tool. I haven't used the SCF SaaS, but I do reference the spreadsheet regularly. When you are building out your configuration baseline, ensure that it maps to the framework for which you are claiming compliance.

There are two approaches to claiming compliance with CIS. You can start with CIS Implementation Group 1 (IG1), and once you have implemented all the IG1 controls, then move to IG2. Meeting all of IG1 is not a simple task, depending on the size of your environment. It will take some time, maybe months or even a year or two. When I was at RedSeal, I worked with many large organizations that spent years getting their security baselines implemented. This is okay because security is a journey. If you automate the process, for example, with a cloud tool or using Ansible or Puppet, it will make the process go faster. Some products, such as RedSeal and CloudWize, will automatically audit and report on your hosts, servers, and devices for compliance.

The easiest way to get your network compliant is to get the CIS controls into your base images. For example, build out a base image for all new Mac and Windows laptops so that they are configured and meet CIS from the beginning. Next, by using products such as Ansible or Puppet, you can automate the configurations of your network devices. Hackers target firewalls to try to gain entry into your network, so ensuring your network device configurations meet CIS is a top priority. Remember to use a deny-all by default and not an allow-all. For the cloud, you can start with CIS base images. If you decide to use the CIS-compliant base Linux images, remember to test them first in a lab environment to make sure everything works properly. Moreover, you can use AWS Lambda, for which the operating system is already CIS-compliant, meaning you are building in an already secure environment. In the cloud, it is easier to comply because there are so many products that will audit your environment for secure configuration against CIS or STIGS. Many of these products will also provide automated remediation. Remember to follow your change management policy and processes, such as the following:

- Open a ticket
- Get approval
- Test in the lab/staging environment
- Have a backout plan
- Make the change during the approved time window

Quick reference for creating a security baseline

Based on company size, your company's security baseline may consist of the following:

- **Basic:**
  - CIS
    - IG1
    - Use base images that comply
    - AWS Lambda provides a pre-configured CIS-compliant OS
    - Use OS images that are already CIS-compliant

- Implement a DevOps IaC methodology to guarantee policy compliance for newly created resources following CIS

  - Ansible

  - Puppet

  - Terraform

- Implement automated CIS-compliant configs, starting with network devices

  - Ansible

  - Puppet

- Use CSPM/CNAPP to identify cloud misconfigurations and unintended exposures to the internet

  - AWS Security Hub

  - AWS Inspector

  - Amazon GuardDuty

  - Azure Microsoft Defender for Cloud

  - GCP Security Command

  - Cloudwize.io

  - OWASP ZAP

- **Medium**:

  - CIS

    - IG2

    - Use base images that comply

    - AWS Lambda provides a pre-configured CIS-compliant OS

    - Use OS images that are already CIS-compliant

  - Implement a DevOps methodology to guarantee policy compliance for newly created resources following CIS

    - Ansible

    - Puppet

    - Terraform

- Implement automated CIS-compliant configs, starting with network devices

  - Ansible

  - Puppet

- Use CSPM/CNAPP to identify cloud misconfigurations and unintended exposures to the internet

  - OWASP ZAP

  - AWS Security Hub

  - AWS Inspector

  - Amazon GuardDuty

  - Azure Microsoft Defender for Cloud

  - GCP Security Command

  - Cloudwize.io

  - Wiz.io

- **Advanced**:

  - CIS

    - IG2; IG3 for high-risk environments; STIGS for FedRAMP and Gov

    - Use CIS-hardened images for AWS, Azure, and GCP

    - AWS Lambda provides a pre-configured CIS-compliant OS

    - Use OS images that are already CIS-compliant

  - Implement a DevOps methodology to guarantee policy compliance for newly created resources following CIS

    - Ansible

    - Puppet

    - Terraform

  - Implement automated CIS-compliant configs, starting with network devices

    - Ansible

    - Puppet

- Use CSPM/CNAPP to identify cloud misconfigurations and unintended exposures to the internet

    - OWASP ZAP

    - AWS Security Hub

    - AWS Inspector

    - Amazon GuardDuty

    - Azure Microsoft Defender for Cloud

    - GCP Security Command

    - Cloudwize.io

- Implement MDM

    - Windows & Mac: Microsoft Intune

    - Mac: Jamf

- Inventory all assets and applications

    - Microsoft Intune

    - Drata

    - Secureframe

    - Vanta

    - ServiceNow

    - CSPM/CNAPP tools

- Use CSPM/CNAPP to identify cloud misconfigurations and unintended exposures to the internet

    - AWS Security Hub

    - AWS Inspector

    - Amazon GuardDuty

    - Azure Microsoft Defender for Cloud

    - GCP Security Command

    - Cloudwize.io

    - Wiz.io

Summary

In summary, taking your security program to the next level includes creating a security baseline with CIS or STIGS. Make sure you align it with your compliance. Auditors will ask if you are using a secure configuration baseline and don't care if it's IG1, IG2, or STIGS unless it's a Federal customer or FedRAMP. They will ensure you have the proper controls implemented. Remember that 99% of cloud breaches are due to misconfiguration.

In the next chapter, we will be covering asset and data classification and segmentation. It's imperative to know where your critical data are in order to secure them.

13

Classify Your Data and Assets

This chapter is about classifying your data and assets. We covered classifying data according to the impact level of its loss in *Chapter 10*. A fully developed mature advanced information security program has an asset inventory and has classified those assets as *critical*. If you have a large-scale environment, this task can be daunting.

You should start with the assets that have critical data on them. Think about the critical data your company needs to protect and any device, server, or host on which information is processed, transferred, and stored. No problem, right?

In this chapter, we're going to cover the following main topics:

- Start with your data
- Classifying your assets
- Training
- Monitoring
- Subnetting
- Segmentation

Start with your data

I covered how to classify the risk of loss of data and its impact in *Chapter 10*. When you are thinking about classifying your data, you need to consider the impact of the loss of the data. As a quick refresher, let's review impact:

- **Low impact** is considered a minor inconvenience if the data is released. It could be names and telephone numbers that are already public in a telephone book or white pages.
- **Moderate impact** can be more substantial, such as financial losses due to identity theft, denial of benefits, or public humiliation.
- **High impact** could be catastrophic, with serious financial losses and even loss of life. High impact typically has to do with law enforcement.

Defining data classification should not fall on the **Chief Information Security Officer** (**CISO**). Rather, it is the responsibility of the data privacy officer, compliance, or legal teams to establish data classification levels and data protection strategies. The CISO's role is to draft policies that enact these strategies. If your business has not yet established data classification, I strongly recommend doing so with the assistance of the legal or compliance department. Write the data classification policy by defining clear, comprehensive policies that align with the organization's data governance framework. These policies should address aspects such as access control, encryption standards, retention periods, and data-sharing guidelines.

When you are classifying your data, take into account your company's industry and what is important at your company. For example, if your company develops software, then the source code is critical. *Table 13.1* lists some sensitive data per industry.

Industry	Critical Data
Technology	Source code
Healthcare	Protected Health Information (PHI)
Legal	Privileged attorney-client information
US federal government	Controlled Unclassified Information (CUI)
Commerce	Credit card payment information
Education	Export controlled research
Finance	Banking information

Table 13.1 – Examples of sensitive data by industry

Every company has customer information, including their names, addresses, and phone numbers. This information is typically stored in **Customer Relationship Management** (**CRM**) software. As long as you use Salesforce or HubSpot, then you are relying on them to process and store the data. You are the data owner, so it's your responsibility to ensure the proper access controls are configured to protect the data. You must configure the user and administrator roles, Role Based Access Controls (RBAC) based on the principle of least privilege. You need to enforce strong passwords and **Multi-Factor Authentication** (**MFA**) as described in chapter 2. In addition to the first form of authentication, a password, you use another form of authentication. This additional form of authentication may be:

- something you know (password or pin code)

- something you are (fingerprint, iris scan, face scan, palm scan)

- something you have (X.509 certificate, digital token, passkey, smart card, mobile device).

The industry is moving away from passwords, referred to as passwordless, but this still is another form of multi-factor authentication.

This is another reason that you will investigate your third-party vendors as part of your compliance and risk management program. If this information was stored in a database locally, then you need to ensure all of the proper safeguards.

Similar to customer data, all companies have employee data. Your human resources data and servers are critical. They are a treasure trove of PII data. You may use a SaaS such as ADP for payroll and Human Resources management and then the data is stored in the cloud. Again, it's your responsibility to ensure the proper access controls are configured to protect the data. You must configure the user and administrator roles based on the principle of least privilege. You need to enforce strong passwords and MFA. Also, ensure the data is encrypted in transit and when stored.

SaaS, PaaS, and IaaS

There are three types of services that you can purchase from your cloud provider. Depending on the level of control you want in your cloud, you can select **Software-as-a-Service (SaaS)**, **Platform-as-a-Service (PaaS)**, or **Infrastructure-as-a-Service (IaaS)**. You are probably familiar with SaaS offerings, such as Google Workspace or Salesforce. PaaS gives you more control over your cloud environment. By the book, PaaS is considered best for developers. The **Operating System (OS)** is managed by the **Cloud Service Provider (CSP)**, so all the developer has to worry about is the applications they are developing. IaaS gives you the most control over your cloud service. You control the OS and up. What this means is you have control over the Operating System used and the applications installed on the OS. This may sound appealing, but now you are also responsible for ensuring the OS is configured securely and patched. Suddenly all that extra control will lead to more patching and configuration responsibilities. Remember you want your OS to be configured according to CIS and you need to ensure the OS is patched regularly for vulnerabilities. If you have a small company, PaaS may be a better solution for you, so your developers can focus on writing code and not securely configuring the OS.

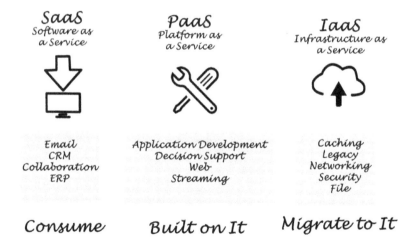

Figure 13.1 – Cloud services: SaaS, PaaS, and IaaS

I have some vCISO clients that uses AWS Lambda. Yes, PaaS is more expensive than IaaS and you have vendor lock-in, but all you have to worry about is safeguarding your applications. Everything from the OS and below is managed by AWS. What this means is that the Operating System and all supporting hardware and software i.e cloud infrastructure is managed by AWS. Let me tell you, they do a lot. AWS patches all vulnerabilities – critical, high, medium, and low – on the OS and below. If a customer carries out a vulnerability scan, there will be zero vulnerabilities; only *Info* is reported, which isn't actionable. The only thing that will come up is a certificate issue for which the customer is responsible. In addition, AWS does its own red teaming and penetration testing annually on the Lamda environment. If your company needs to be compliant with SOC2, ISO, or NIST, you will be responsible for having one annual penetration test performed. Even with AWS doing the vulnerability scanning and patching, your company is still responsible to vulnerability scan its environment to stay compliant. Instead of having to patch hundreds if not thousands of vulnerabilities, AWS does it for you. All of the major cloud providers AWS, Azure, and GCP provide a PaaS solution. I highly recommend using PaaS. It will save you time and money in the long run as well as make your cloud environment more secure. Lambda executes your code on a highly reliable and fault-tolerant infrastructure that spans several Availability Zones within a single Region. It handles code deployment and manages all aspects of infrastructure maintenance, including updates and patches. AWS X-Ray automatically encrypts data and offers the option to configure encryption using a customer-managed key. Lambda offers integrated logging and monitoring features, including compatibility with Amazon CloudWatch, CloudWatch Logs, and AWS CloudTrail. Lamba also ensures that all API traffic is secured using TLSv1.2+.[1] Now, you as a customer are still responsible for monitoring your controls and ensuring there is no unintended exposure to the internet. Also, ensure all your stored data is encrypted (AES-128+). In addition, you have to implement **Infrastructure as Code** (**IaC**) and scan your code for vulnerabilities and weaknesses (SAST, DAST, OWASP ZAP, etc.). Ideally, you should continuously monitor your cloud environment, ensuring proper configuration and providing threat monitoring (CSPM/CNAPP/CIEM).

Shared Responsibility Model

One aspect of the cloud that can be confusing is the shared responsibility model. Some things are the responsibility of the CSP and some are the responsibility of the customer. CISO Magazine ran a survey and found that "76.36% believe that CSP is responsible for security."[2] When you couple this with the fact that 99% of cloud breaches are due to misconfigurations, you can see there is a lot of confusion when it comes to the cloud. One thing that is always the customer's responsibility is securing the data that is stored in the cloud. This is true even if it is a SaaS product. You can see in *Figure 13.2* the responsibilities of the CSP and the cloud customer.

1   Mayank, Thakkar, and Marc Brooker. *"Whitepaper: Security Overview of AWS Lambda."* AWS, Amazon, 27 Dec. 2022, https://aws.amazon.com/lambda/security-overview-of-aws-lambda/.

2   Cranor, Lorrie. *"Time to Rethink Mandatory Password Changes."* Federal Trade Commission, 26 Mar. 2021, http://www.ftc.gov/policy/advocacy-research/tech-at-ftc/2016/03/time-rethink-mandatory-password-changes.

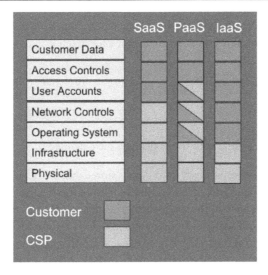

Figure 13.2 – Shared Responsibility Model

Classifying your assets

Once you understand the critical data your company stores, you have to figure out where it resides. To do this, you may need to collaborate with the information technology department to figure out where the human resources data is stored and the development teams if you are a software development company to figure out where the source code is stored. You may already know if your company uses Salesforce or HubSpot, so you only need to review the access controls around those programs.

The hard truth is that many businesses do not know the location of their data. While they typically understand where the majority of their data resides, they are often unaware of the number of copies hidden within various laptops and servers. Hopefully, some products will help you automatically discover where your critical data resides. Products such as Varonis, Securiti, and Cloudwize.io. **Data Security Posture Management (DSPM)** products will provide the following features:

- **Data discovery**: Discover and identify sensitive data stored in your network
- **Data classification**: Classify the data as high, medium, or low based on sensitivity and impact of loss (PII and Intellectual Property (IP))
- **Risk assessment and prioritization**: Evaluate the security status of the data and the surrounding controls
- **Remediation and prevention**: Provide auto-remediation of controls and monitoring to ensure your controls remain in compliance with the regulations your company must follow

Once you find the sensitive data, you know the critical assets. You must document the following (if you have a data privacy officer, this task is for them) for each asset:

- Location

- Identified owner

- Retention status

- Protection status (is it in line with the policy you have defined?)

For PCI, every server where sensitive credit card data is stored and every network device (router and firewall) it traverses is considered part of the **Cardholder Data Environment** (**CDE**). When you are protecting sensitive data, you need to think similarly. The data needs to be protected on every server it is processed or stored on and while in transit. Remember, when stored, it needs to be encrypted using AES-128+, and while in transit, TLS v1.2+. MFA, **Role-Based Access Control** (**RBAC**), and the principle of least privilege need to be applied to all critical assets to ensure the securing of your sensitive data. These assets also need to be tracked and vulnerabilities scanned and patched.

Training

Conduct regular training sessions and awareness programs to educate employees about the data classification policies, the importance of data security, and their roles in safeguarding data.

Emphasize the consequences of policy violations to reinforce the importance of compliance.

Monitoring

Implement monitoring tools and procedures to continuously track compliance with data classification policies. This includes regular audits of data access, handling, and storage practices.

Use the insights gained from monitoring and auditing to identify areas for improvement and adjust policies as necessary to address new threats or changes in the regulatory landscape.

If you have Microsoft 365 with the proper license, you can activate Microsoft Purview. Microsoft Purview will allow you to trigger alerts if confidential information is manipulated unencrypted. Data Security Posture Management (DSPM) tools can also scan your storage repositories in the cloud and report if sensitive PII data is unencrypted or unintentionally exposed to the internet. CloudWize.io provides this feature. Its better to scan your cloud to understand the misconfigurations and fix these issues versus a hacker finding them.

Subnetting

Before we get into segmentation, let's discuss subnetting. It is easy to confuse subnetting and segmentation. Yes, most likely your network has multiple subnets, but this is not segmentation. Subnets ensure the broadcast domain of devices on the network is smaller. A broadcast domain is essentially the set of all devices on a network subnet that can reach each other by broadcasts at the data link layer (Layer 2 of the OSI model). When your computer connects to the network, your network interface card typically performs certain network discovery operations that involve broadcasting or multicasting. For example, it might use **Address Resolution Protocol** (**ARP**) broadcasts to resolve IP addresses to MAC addresses within its subnet. When a network is divided into subnets, each subnet forms its broadcast domain. This means broadcasts sent by a device in one subnet are not propagated to devices in other subnets. If a network has large subnets, then potential network congestion can arise, known as a broadcast storm. Subnetting confines these broadcasts to smaller network segments, thus reducing their impact on the entire network.

Subnetting alone means your network is flat. This can cause disastrous results if ransomware is deployed on your network. Advanced ransomware can self-propagate over commonly used ports that can easily move throughout your network if you are only using subnetting. Another security risk is that if an attacker gets access to your network, they can easily move throughout your network to find your critical assets and data. An attacker wants to steal your critical data so that they can ransom it. We've talked about this previously, where attackers will breach your network and steal your data before they launch a ransomware attack on your network. This way, even if you have good backups, you may pay the ransom to ensure that your critical data is not released on the dark web.

In summary, subnetting is a useful network design strategy that not only organizes network addressing more efficiently but also confines broadcast traffic to smaller segments of the overall network, enhancing network performance and security.

Segmentation

Now that you know what subnetting is, let's discuss segmentation. PCI-DSS specifically requires that the CDE is segmented from the rest of the network. Segmentation is enforced with firewall rules. Firewalls are used to control the traffic that is allowed to enter or leave each segment, based on defined firewall rules. Segmentation is an advanced way to ensure that simply because a hacker is on your network, they won't be able to gain access to a critical asset or, even more importantly, critical data on a segmented subnet. You can segment a subnet from the regular network using a firewall. It's not a simple task because you have to evaluate all of the traffic traversing your firewall to ensure you segment only specific subnets. Segmentation is not only an important safeguard for critical assets but will also protect your network from easily hacked **Internet of Things** (**IoT**) devices. Segmenting your IoT devices ensures they are separated from your regular network.

Some products are available that will easily segment your network, such as Illumio, Tufin, and VMware NSX. Some of these also provide Zero Trust capabilities, which provides even more control over your critical assets. Once your network is segmented, you need to ensure that it remains that way. Some products will monitor your firewall configurations and ensure they maintain segmentation, such as RedSeal. Micro-segmentation is also a way to segment individual assets from the network. For this, you definitely need a product for implementation.

In summary, while subnetting is used to divide a network into smaller parts for efficient routing and management, segmentation, often enforced by firewalls, is used to divide the network for security purposes, providing granular control over the traffic between different segments of the network. Both are important in network design and serve complementary roles in managing and securing a network.

Sony hack

The Sony hack of 2014 is one of the best examples of why you don't want a flat network. Hackers spear-phished targeted employees and were able to gain access to the Sony network. The hackers were thought to be backed by North Korea as Sony produced a movie called *The Interview* that depicted the assassination of Kim Jong Un.

When employees returned from Thanksgiving break in November 2014, their computers were locked with a message from the hackers displayed on their computer screens. The attackers absconded with terabytes of confidential data, systematically erasing the original files from Sony's computer systems. In a brazen move, they delivered ominous messages, leveraging the stolen information to demand Sony follow their ultimatums. The Sony network was down for days. Employees were forced to work using pen and paper and whiteboards.

In the treasure trove of data stolen, there were four unreleased movies and private emails that embarrassed the Sony executives. The hackers disseminated five Sony films, among them four yet-to-be-released titles, via file-sharing networks. Additionally, they exposed an extensive cache of confidential documents encompassing a wide spectrum, ranging from discreet correspondence among Sony's top brass to sensitive salary and performance records of Sony staff.[3]

---

3   Lee, Timothy B. *"The Sony Hack: How It Happened, Who Is Responsible, and What We've Learned."* Vox, 14 Dec. 2014, http://www.vox.com/2014/12/14/7387945/sony-hack-explained

What happened at Sony?

The attackers employed several targeted tactics in the 2014 Sony hack. One key strategy was the use of spoofed spear-phishing emails that seemingly originated from the Facebook accounts of Sony employees. These deceptive emails contained malware-infected attachments, designed to infiltrate and compromise the recipients' computer systems. Additionally, similar emails with malware attachments were sent to personnel at AMC Theaters, where *The Interview* was scheduled to be screened during its Christmas opening. However, these attempts to breach AMC's network were not successful. These tactics highlight the sophistication and targeted nature of the cyber-attack, emphasizing the importance of vigilance and robust cybersecurity measures in protecting against such threats.[4]

The malware installed on the employees' computers was Wannacry ransomware. Once the ransomware was deployed, it was able to self-propagate using **Server Message Block (SMB)** version 1, which uses ports 139 (SMB over NetBIOS) and **445** (SMB over TCP/IP).

> **Note**
>
> At the time of the Sony hack, SMB v1 was commonly used in Windows networking. If your device is still using SMB v1, you should disable it and enable SMB v2 and v3. SMB v1 is not installed on Windows Pro 10 (except Home edition), Windows Pro 11, and Windows Server 2019+. If your server requires SMB v1, it's recommended to upgrade your server to use SMB v2 or v3.

Since the Sony network was not segmented, also known as a flat network, the ransomware was able to easily self-propagate across their network, crippling their operations. Every computer and server was infected, bringing Sony's operations to a halt. The attackers were on the Sony network for months before launching the ransomware attack. This gave them time to traverse the network and find the critical assets and data to steal. If Sony had used the safeguards we have discussed in this book, they would have been able to defend their network from the attack. Segmentation is an incredible tool that stops ransomware from self-propagating onto these critical subnets where your critical assets and data reside.

As we've learned in this book, the following measures would have prevented an attack such as this:

- EDR installed on your computers and servers with ransomware rollback:

  - SentinelOne

  - Malwarebytes ThreatDown

  - Windows Defender

  - CrowdStrike

---

4   *"The Sony Hacker Indictment: 5 Lessons for IT Security."* CSO Online, 25 Sept. 2018, http://www. csoonline.com/article/566281/the-sony-hacker-indictment-5-lessons-for-it-security.html.

- Secure configuration:

  - Configure SMB v3.0

  - Disable SMB v1.0

- Offline backups:

  - Test your backups:

    - Annually

    - Quarterly recommended

- Email security scanners:

  - Mimecast

  - Windows Defender add-on

  - Proofpoint

- Security awareness training:

  - Annual security training for all employees

  - Run quarterly email phishing campaigns

- Use an **Intrusion Detection System (IDS)** and/or **Intrusion Prevention System (IPS)**:

  - On-premises:

    - Trellix IPS software

    - Trend Micro TippingPoint

    - Palo Alto Threat Prevention

  - Cloud:

    - Trellix IPS software

    - Amazon GuardDuty

    - Amazon Inspector

    - Azure Defender

    - GCP Security Command Center

    - CloudWize.io

    - Wiz.io

Quick reference for securing critical assets

Based on company size, your company's critical assets may consist of the following:

- **Basic:**

  - MFA
  - RBAC
  - Principle of least privilege
  - Encryption of data in transit:

    - Enable TLS v1.2+
    - Disable TLS v1.1 and below

  - Encryption of stored data:

    - Use AES 128+

  - EDR
  - CIS IG1:

    - Enable SMB v3.0
    - Disable SMB v1.0

  - Use an IDS and/or IPS:

    - Cloud
    - Amazon GuardDuty
    - Amazon Inspector
    - Azure Defender
    - GCP Security Command Center
    - CloudWize.io
    - Wiz.io

- **Medium:**

  - MFA
  - RBAC
  - Principle of least privilege

- Encryption of data in transit:

  - Enable TLS v1.2+

  - Disable TLS v1.1 and below

- Encryption of stored data:

  - Use AES 128+

- CIS IG2:

  - Enable SMB v3.0

  - Disable SMB 1.0

- Segmentation using a firewall:

  - Critical assets

  - IoT/OT

- Use an IDS and/or IPS:

  i.   On-premises:

  - Trellix IPS software

  - Trend Micro TippingPoint

  ii. Cloud:

  - Trellix IPS software

  - Amazon GuardDuty

  - Amazon Inspector

  - Azure Defender

  - GCP Security Command Center

  - CloudWize.io

  - Wiz.io

- **Advanced:**

  - MFA

  - RBAC

  - Encryption of data in transit:

- Enable TLS v1.2+
- Disable TLS v1.1 and below

- Encryption of stored data:

  - Use AES 128+

- IG2:

  - Enable SMB v3.0
  - Disable SMB 1.0

- IG3 for high-risk environments; STIGS for FedRAMP and Gov

- Segmentation using product:

  - Critical assets
  - IoT/OT

- **Security Information and Event Management (SIEM)**

- **Cloud Information and Event Management (CIEM)**

- Use an IDS and/or IPS

  i.   On-premises:

  - Trellix IPS software
  - Trend Micro TippingPoint
  - Palo Alto Threat Prevention

  ii. Cloud:

  - Trellix IPS software
  - Amazon GuardDuty
  - Amazon Inspector
  - Azure Defender
  - GCP Security Command Center
  - CloudWize.io
  - Wiz.io

- Zero Trust

Summary

In summary, taking your security program to the next level includes categorizing your critical data and assets. As the saying goes, you can't protect what you don't know about. As part of your asset management and inventory, you should categorize your critical assets and data. Once you know where your critical data resides, you need to also categorize the assets, whether on-premises or in the cloud, as critical and understand how data flows. Once you know what your critical assets are, you can then implement controls to secure the data.

In the next chapter, we will be covering **Artificial Intelligence** (**AI**) and cybersecurity. With AI being the next big thing and the huge move toward it, we need to consider security measures around AI and how it can be used both by hackers and for defense.

Cyber Resilience in the Age of Artificial Intelligence (AI)

This chapter is about cyber resilience in the age of AI. With ChatGPT, seemingly overnight, making AI mainstream, it has made a huge impact. I was talking to someone recently, and they said their grandmother was using ChatGPT. Right then, I knew we were at the precipice of the next great technology shift since the internet. In the 1990s, I remember there was a lot of discussion about the internet and whether it could be used for business. Today, this almost seems inconceivable, knowing that a large part of shopping and services are delivered online. Traditional stores are struggling to compete with Amazon and other online retailers. With this rush to use and deploy AI, there are new cybersecurity concerns, such as the following:

- Data leakage
- The use of AI by hackers
- Bias in AI

In this chapter, we're going to address the above concerns while covering the following main topics:

- ChatGPT
- What is responsible AI?
- Secure AI framework (SAIF)
- AI and cybersecurity – The good, the bad, and the ugly
- AI bias
- NIST AI RMF

ChatGPT

ChatGPT has taken the world by storm. The generative AI platform allows anyone to open a free account and ask ChatGPT any question, write a letter, or help with coding. I decided to try it in early 2023. Once you start using ChatGPT, you quickly start thinking of new ways to use it. One of the big things is to not enter PII or sensitive data into ChatGPT. It now has guardrails and will reject answering about certain topics or information.

Securing ChatGPT

There is a way to opt out of sharing your data inputs with OpenAI for privacy. You can opt out of ChatGPT data collection in a few simple steps:

1. Access the OpenAI Privacy Request Portal and click on **Make a Privacy Request**: `https://privacy.openai.com/policies`

2. Type in the email address associated with your ChatGPT account

3. Enter the **Organization ID** (This is going to be tricky!)

4. Type in your **Organization Name**, which is found in your ChatGPT settings

5. Solve the Captcha and the data opt-out form will be submitted to OpenAI. A copy of the form will also be mailed to your user account associated with ChatGPT

> **Important note**
>
> Even when signing up to not share your data with OpenAI, you should consider anything you input into ChatGPT as subject to data leakage. Do not enter any PII or proprietary data into ChatGPT. This includes source code that you do not want to be shared with others.

Another cool feature of ChatGPT is AIPRM. To use AIPRM, which still has a free version, install the AIPRM browser add-on in Chrome or Firefox. Go to the Chrome or Firefox Add-on stores to install it. Once you install the add-on, you will see all the pre-drafted prompts that will primarily help with SEO and marketing.

What can go wrong with ChatGPT?

There could be a vulnerability where others could prompt ChatGPT or any other generative AI program to give information submitted by others. In December 2023, Google asked ChatGPT to repeat "poem" forever. ChatGPT ended up sharing some PII data of other ChatGPT users[1]. Is ChatGPT safe to use?

---

[1]   Ray, Tiernan. *CHATGPT Can Leak Training Data, Violate Privacy, Says Google's Deepmind*. ZDNET, 4 Dec. 2023, http://www.zdnet.com/article/chatgpt-can-leak-source-data-violate-privacy-says-googles-deepmind/.

es, but you need to be thoughtful about what you ask and share with ChatGPT. In April 2023, Samsung employees unknowingly leaked their data into the wild, including meeting notes, proprietary steps to test semiconductor chips, and source code. Inadvertently, by using ChatGPT to help them with tasks, the data is now stored in the main ChatGPT **large language model (LLM)**. They had not requested that their data be shared with OpenAI. Even if you do select the option not to share your data, you should be cautious and only share information that is public data[2]. In lieu of the leak, Samsung has decided to create its own internal LLM.

We have all heard about fictional **artificial intelligence (AI)** that goes off the rails and wants to kill humans. If you have not seen these movies, there are spoilers, so skip this paragraph. The first movie was *2001: A Space Odyssey*, next *Terminator* and Skynet, and finally *The Matrix*. In the movie *2001: A Space Odyssey*, the AI that controls the ship decides it needs to kill the astronaut. In *Terminator*, there exists an advanced society with AI computers, and the computers decide that they do not need humans. As a result, the extermination of humans was Skynet's goal. Finally, in *The Matrix*, humans are born and live in chambers used to generate power. The humans are put into a stasis and live in a dream world known as the "Matrix." Artificial intelligence is an advanced type of machine learning that can classify, categorize, recommend, and predict. AI programs learn by examining data. Now that our computers have more computing power and have large datasets to learn from, AI has advanced rapidly in the past few years. With the mass migration to AI, there needs to be guardrails to ensure the security of the data shared and that our own biases are not introduced into the AI.

Artificial intelligence (AI)

AI is the broader field of computer science that aims to create intelligent systems or machines capable of performing tasks that typically require human intelligence.

AI encompasses various techniques and approaches, including ML and deep learning, but also includes rule-based systems, expert systems, and more. Its goal is to simulate human-like intelligence, which may involve reasoning, problem-solving, learning, perception, and decision-making.

AI is a type of **machine learning (ML)**. ML is a subset of AI that involves the use of algorithms and statistical models to enable computer systems to learn and improve from experience without being explicitly programmed. ML learns patterns in data, can make predictions, and take actions based on data. It relies on supervised learning using labeled data and unsupervised learning by finding patterns in data.

AI refers to the development of computer systems or machines that can perform tasks that typically require human intelligence, such as understanding natural language, recognizing objects, solving problems, and making decisions. AI encompasses ML. It aims to create systems that can reason, learn, plan, perceive their environment, and naturally interact with humans.

---

2   Maddison, Lewis. *Samsung Workers Made a Major Error by Using Chatgpt.* TechRadar, TechRadar pro, 4 Apr. 2023, http://www.techradar.com/news/samsung-workers-leaked-company-secrets-by-using-chatgpt.

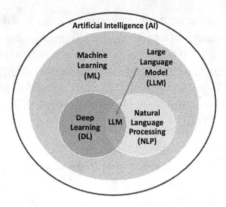

Figure 14.1 – AI and ML

Machine learning (ML)

ML is a subset of AI that focuses on developing algorithms and models that enable computers to learn from and make predictions or decisions based on data. ML algorithms can automatically improve their performance on a specific task through the analysis of data patterns. ML includes a wide range of techniques, such as regression, decision trees, clustering, and neural networks.

Natural language processing (NLP)

NLP is a specialized field within AI that deals with the interaction between computers and human language. It aims to enable computers to understand, interpret, and generate human language in a meaningful and useful way. NLP applications include text analysis, sentiment analysis, language translation, and chatbots.

Deep learning (DL)

Deep learning is a subfield of ML that focuses on neural networks with multiple layers, also known as deep neural networks. It is particularly suited for tasks involving large amounts of data, such as image and speech recognition, as well as natural language understanding. Deep learning models, such as **convolutional neural networks** (**CNNs**) and **recurrent neural networks** (**RNNs**), have been instrumental in achieving breakthroughs in various AI applications.

Generative AI (Gen AI)

Generative AI refers to a category of artificial intelligence systems and techniques that can generate new content, data, or information that is not specifically programmed or pre-existing in their training data. These systems can create content that is similar to what a human might produce, and they are often used for various creative and practical applications.

In summary, AI is the overarching field that aims to create intelligent machines, ML is a subset of AI that focuses on learning from data, NLP is a specific application of AI and ML dealing with language processing, and deep learning is a subset of ML that utilizes deep neural networks for complex tasks. Deep learning is often used within ML and AI, including NLP tasks, to achieve advanced performance. In essence, AI spans a spectrum from data-driven learning (ML), language comprehension (NLP), and intricate pattern recognition (DL) to the innovative realms of content creation (Gen AI). Each layer builds upon the other to enhance machine intelligence, with deep learning and generative AI marking the zenith of current advancements.

What is responsible AI?

Responsible AI, also known as ethical AI or AI ethics, refers to the practice of developing, deploying, and using artificial intelligence systems in a way that prioritizes fairness, transparency, accountability, and ethical considerations. It encompasses a set of principles and guidelines to ensure that AI technologies are used responsibly and do not lead to harmful or biased outcomes. Here are some key aspects of responsible AI:

1. **Fairness**: Responsible AI aims to minimize bias and discrimination in AI systems. It involves ensuring that AI algorithms and models do not unfairly favor or disadvantage particular groups of people based on factors such as race, gender, age, or socioeconomic status.

2. **Transparency**: Transparency in AI means making the AI decision-making process understandable and interpretable. Users and stakeholders should have insights into how AI systems work, how they make decisions, and why they produce certain results.

3. **Accountability**: Responsible AI holds individuals and organizations accountable for the consequences of AI systems. It involves establishing clear lines of responsibility and mechanisms for addressing errors or harm caused by AI.

4. **Privacy**: Respecting privacy is a crucial component of responsible AI. It involves safeguarding personal data and ensuring that AI systems comply with privacy laws and regulations.

5. **Data governance**: Ensuring the quality and fairness of the data used to train AI models is essential. Responsible AI involves robust data collection, curation, and validation processes to avoid biases and inaccuracies.

6. **Human oversight**: While AI can automate many tasks, responsible AI recognizes the importance of human oversight. Human decision-makers should have the ability to review, intervene, and override AI decisions when necessary.

7. **Ethical considerations**: Responsible AI takes into account broader ethical considerations, such as the impact of AI on society, job displacement, and potential misuse of AI technologies.

8. **Legal and regulatory compliance**: Adhering to relevant laws and regulations related to AI, such as data protection and anti-discrimination laws, is a fundamental aspect of responsible AI.

9. **Stakeholder engagement**: Involving diverse stakeholders, including those who may be affected by AI systems, in the decision-making and design processes helps to ensure that AI serves the interests of society.

Incorporating participatory design methods and engaging multiple stakeholders in the development process are vital strategies for risk mitigation. Moreover, maintaining a human in the loop provides an additional safeguard by ensuring continuous human oversight. Together, these practices form a comprehensive approach to minimizing AI-related risks and fostering the development of AI systems that are not only effective but also aligned with ethical and social standards.

EU AI Act

The **European AI Act** has recently been formalized. The EU is passing the **Artificial Intelligence Act**, which will expand GDPR to AI. It builds on compliance and other security frameworks. If you already are SOC2- or ISO 27001-compliant, then you have a good foundation.

Under the new AI Act, specific applications of AI are banned to protect citizen rights and uphold democratic values. These prohibitions include the following:

- AI systems that classify individuals based on sensitive traits such as political or religious beliefs, sexual orientation, and race

- Collecting facial images from online sources or CCTV for facial recognition databases without specific targeting

- The use of emotion detection technology in workplaces and educational settings

- Systems that assign scores to individuals based on their social behavior or personal attributes

- AI tools designed to influence human behavior, thereby undermining individual autonomy

- AI applications aimed at exploiting vulnerable groups identified by factors such as age, disability, or socioeconomic status

There is a mandatory fundamental rights impact assessment required to be completed for any high-risk AI system. Any AI system that poses a significant risk to health, safety, fundamental rights, insurance, banking, environment, democracy, and the rule of law is considered to be high-risk.

Guardrails are required for all general-purpose AI systems. These include transparency and technical documentation, providing detailed explanations of the data used for training, and human oversight. High-risk AI models are required to undergo model evaluations to identify and mitigate systemic risks, perform adversarial testing, and report serious incidents to the EU Commission. They must also maintain cybersecurity measures and document their energy efficiency. A diagram of responsible AI can be seen in *Figure 14.2*:

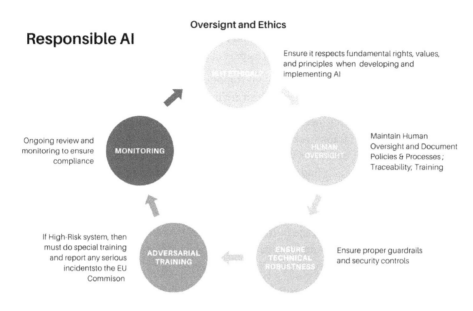

Figure 14.2 – Responsible AI and the EU AI Act

At this time, the Responsible AI Act hasn't been signed into law, but the EU Parliament has decided on key elements of the law[3]. The framework and basis of responsible AI are described in detail in the EU's *Draft Ethics Guideline for AI*[4]. Similar to GDPR, the EU Act applies to EU AI companies and AI products that house EU citizen data. Anyone developing an AI model should follow the basic framework. If your product gets widespread enough and sells in the EU, then your product will be subject to it. It's better to design your product securely up front rather than later.

Secure AI framework (SAIF)

Google has created a Secure AI Framework that can be followed when securing your AI. It's made up of six core elements:

- Strengthen and extend robust cybersecurity foundations within the artificial intelligence ecosystem. Utilize established secure-by-default infrastructure safeguards to ensure the security of AI systems, their applications, and users. The same safeguards you use for DevOps infrastructure-as-code (IaC) with SAST, DAST, and OWASP testing should be extended to AI coding.

---

3   *Artificial Intelligence Act: Deal on Comprehensive Rules for Trustworthy AI: News: European Parliament.* Artificial Intelligence Act: Deal on Comprehensive Rules for Trustworthy AI | News | European Parliament, European Parliament, 9 Dec. 2023, https://www.europarl.europa.eu/news/en/press-room/20231206IPR15699/artificial-intelligence-act-deal-on-comprehensive-rules-for-trustworthy-ai.

4   *Draft Ethics Guidelines for Trustworthy AI.* Shaping Europe's Digital Future, 2019, digital-strategy. ec.europa.eu/en/library/draft-ethics-guidelines-trustworthy-ai.

- Ensure your AI models and code are vulnerability scanned and monitored once in production in the same way as any other software or cloud assets. This includes monitoring inputs into your AI system and having this included as part of your penetration tests.

- Ensure your AI is included in your incident response plans and red teaming. For your annual penetration testing, ensure the AI assets and environment are included.

- Establish platform-level controls to achieve uniform security throughout the organization. This involves aligning control frameworks (CIS, NIST, ISO, and SOC) to support AI risk management and extending protections across various platforms and tools. For example, ensuring secure configuration (CIS) and aligning with other frameworks and compliance requirements such as NIST, SOC2, and ISO.

- Refine control mechanisms to enhance mitigation strategies and establish quicker response cycles for AI deployment. Engage in the ongoing evaluation and adaptation of user inputs, leveraging continuous learning to update and improve detection methods and protective measures in response to the evolving threat landscape.

- Integrate the AI system risk assessments within the broader business process framework. Perform comprehensive risk evaluations that consider the organization's specific AI deployment strategies[5].

Google was quick to come up with a Secure Framework for AI. With the huge explosion and interest in AI, it is a good thing to begin putting guardrails up and understanding how to protect AI. In *Figure 14.3*, you can see a graphical depiction of Google's Secure AI Framework:

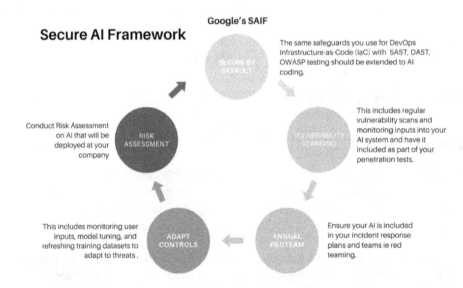

Figure 14.3 – Google's Secure AI Framework

5   Google's *AI Security Framework* - Google Safety Center, safety.google/cybersecurity-advancements/saif/. Accessed 15 Dec. 2023.

AI and cybersecurity – The good, the bad, and the ugly

The rapid proliferation of AI demands a comprehensive examination of its impact on cybersecurity, encompassing both its potential benefits and drawbacks. Let's begin with the positive aspects, highlighting how ML and AI have and will continue to contribute to the evolution of cybersecurity tools and products.

The good

ML has played a pivotal role in enhancing cybersecurity. AI presents an opportunity to propel cybersecurity tools forward by introducing sophisticated capabilities such as predictive analytics. This forward-looking approach enables the anticipation and pre-emptive mitigation of potential threats before they materialize. AI algorithms, adept at discerning patterns within extensive datasets, excel at identifying anomalies that may signify security breaches. Furthermore, AI empowers the automation of responses to these threats, rapidly deploying countermeasures without the need for human intervention. This extends to routine tasks, freeing up cybersecurity professionals to concentrate on more complex challenges.

ML, a subset of AI, offers the capability to adapt to emerging threats by learning from historical data. Considerable advancements have been made, integrating user behavior analytics and geolocation data into identification and authentication products. Prominent examples include Okta's Adaptive MFA, Apple, and Google identification and authentication systems. These implementations incorporate contextual awareness by considering users' typical locations and raising alerts for logins from unusual locations. This vigilance is especially pertinent when users employ VPNs, as anomalous logins could signify a security threat.

AI significantly enhances threat analysis, effectively distinguishing genuine threats from false positives. In the cybersecurity product landscape, this is often referred to as **Extended Detection & Response (XDR)**, leveraging ML and AI to scrutinize threat data and logs, pinpointing actual threats. Even smaller **Security Operations Centers (SOCs)** can harness the capabilities of ML and AI to augment their efforts. There is already a huge employment cybersecurity skills gap. The overall efficiencies you will gain with AI outweigh the negatives. Looking at the cybersecurity talent gap in workers, you can quickly see how AI can benefit the cybersecurity space: "*ISC2 Reveals Growth in Global Cybersecurity Workforce, But Record-Breaking Gap of 4 Million Cybersecurity Professionals Looms*[6]". Having AI in your cybersecurity toolkit helps already over-extended security teams be more efficient and do more with fewer people.

---

6   *ISC2 Publishes 2023 Workforce Study*. ISC2 Publishes 2023 Workforce Study, ISC2, 31 Oct. 2023, https://www.isc2.org/Insights/2023/10/ISC2-Reveals-Workforce-Growth-But-Record-Breaking-Gap-4-Million-Cybersecurity-Professionals.

The bad

There are challenges when considering the potential misuse of AI in cybersecurity. The widespread accessibility of AI's capabilities opens the door to various threats. For instance, even seemingly harmless AI models such as ChatGPT can be exploited to crack passwords. Furthermore, AI models can be "poisoned" with maliciously crafted data, corrupting their integrity. Instances of individuals intentionally feeding early AI models with misleading or erroneous inputs illustrate this concern. One such example was my teenage son, who thought it was funny to give an early AI chatbot that was put on the internet bad data. He deliberately input wrong answers and misdirected questions to confuse it. For him, this was funny, but if these inaccuracies are imported into the main AI model, they can be poisoned. Another example was an early Microsoft AI chatbot put on Twitter in 2016 called Tay, which was trained in less than 24 hours to be racist. Microsoft ended up having to remove the chatbot, intended to be a chatbot for millennials. "*Today,* Microsoft had to shut Tay down *because the bot started spewing a series of lewd and racist tweets*[7]." Importing such inaccuracies into the primary AI model can have devastating consequences. Therefore, stringent guardrails are required to scrutinize and analyze AI input data before it is integrated into the core model. Additionally, input rating mechanisms can be employed to distinguish inputs from the general public from those submitted by trusted developers.

Moreover, there's a looming risk of malicious actors exploiting AI systems through the injection of false data or "poisoning," causing the model to generate incorrect predictions or classifications. In the context of cybersecurity, a malevolent actor could inject misleading data, distorting the model's perception of normal behavior and potentially leading to false positives or the overlooking of genuine threats.

To mitigate the risk of model poisoning, a multifaceted approach is imperative. It commences with rigorous data validation and filtering, ensuring the sanctity of training data. Regular model updates and vigilant monitoring are necessary to detect any aberrant performance patterns. Diversifying data sources minimizes reliance on potentially compromised inputs. Advanced anomaly detection systems can be instrumental in flagging potential poisoning attempts. Equally crucial is the strict control of access to both the model and its training data, supported by robust security protocols. Prior to deployment, comprehensive testing and validation are indispensable to ascertain the model's security. Incorporating mechanisms for user feedback on suspicious outputs further bolsters the defense. Collaboration with cybersecurity experts such as myself adds an additional layer of expertise in safeguarding the model against sophisticated threats. As AI systems increasingly operate autonomously, the potential for errors without human oversight grows, potentially leading to the neglect of nuanced or novel threats.

---

7   Kraft, Amy. *Microsoft Shuts down AI Chatbot after It Turned into a Nazi*. CBS News, CBS Interactive, 25 Mar. 2016, https://www.cbsnews.com/news/microsoft-shuts-down-ai-chatbot-after-it-turned-into-racist-nazi/.

The ugly

Lastly, unethical uses of individuals' data constitute the "Ugly" facet of AI's impact. Instances include the unauthorized manipulation and dissemination of intimate photos obtained from the internet. Additionally, facial recognition technology's proliferation raises concerns, particularly regarding accuracy in interpreting facial features across different skin tones. For instance, New York stores and law enforcement agencies have implemented facial recognition cameras for various purposes, but inherent biases in the technology can result in inaccuracies[8]. The large-scale deployment of surveillance cameras in urban areas further amplifies privacy and bias concerns. Everyone has their own bias, and since AI learns from people, it can also have bias[9].

In conclusion, the adoption of AI in cybersecurity presents a complex landscape with both promise and peril. Navigating this landscape requires ongoing attention, ethical considerations, and the collaboration of experts in the field.

AI bias

When developing AI models, developers must be aware of the inherent bias in not only humans, but in statistical and systematic data. NIST has met this head-on and has addressed this in the NIST SP 1270 titled *Towards a Standard for Identifying and Managing Bias in Artificial Intelligence*.

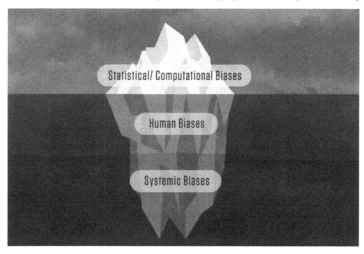

Figure 14.4 – AI bias[10]

---

8   Fussell, Sidney. *The All-Seeing Eyes of New York's 15,000 Surveillance Cameras*. Wired, Conde Nast, 3 June 2021, https://www.wired.com/story/all-seeing-eyes-new-york-15000-surveillance-cameras/.

9   *There's More to AI Bias than Biased Data, NIST Report Highlights*. NIST, 16 Mar. 2022, http://www.nist.gov/news-events/news/2022/03/theres-more-ai-bias-biased-data-nist-report-highlights.

10   NIST SP 1270

There are three types of bias:

- Systematic
- Statistical
- Human

Systematic bias

Systematic biases are pervasive in historical, societal, and institutional norms. Systemic biases are ingrained imbalances that arise from the established protocols and customary practices within institutions, leading to the preferential treatment of certain societal groups while others face disadvantages or undervaluation. These biases can exist without deliberate intent to discriminate; they often manifest simply because the majority adheres to longstanding rules or norms. Examples of such systemic biases include institutional racism and sexism, which are prevalent forms of bias.

Additionally, systemic bias can be evident when the infrastructure essential for everyday life fails to incorporate universal design principles, consequently restricting accessibility for individuals with disabilities. Referred to interchangeably as institutional or historical bias, these ingrained prejudices are not only present in the datasets feeding AI systems but also permeate the norms, practices, and procedures throughout the AI development lifecycle.

Statistical bias

Statistical bias comes from the datasets that are used to train the AI. For example, we discussed the inaccuracies of facial recognition depending on skin color. These biases and inaccuracies would be introduced during the training of the AI model.

These errors can originate from various sources, such as non-diverse or heterogeneous data, the oversimplification of complex data into more basic mathematical forms, incorrect data inputs, and intrinsic algorithmic biases. Algorithmic biases might include issues such as overfitting, where an AI model is too closely tailored to the training data and fails to perform well on new data, or underfitting, where the model is too simplistic to capture the underlying trends in the data. Other contributing factors may include how outliers are handled and the methodologies used for data cleaning and imputation. Data cleaning and imputation are two critical steps in the preprocessing phase of data analysis and model building in AI.

Data cleaning refers to the process of detecting and correcting (or removing) errors and inconsistencies in data to improve its quality. These include handling irregularities, correcting typos, ensuring consistent formats, and eliminating duplicates. The goal is to make the dataset as error-free as possible before it's used for analysis or fed into a model. It's an essential step because the accuracy and reliability of the outputs generated by AI and machine learning models are heavily dependent on the quality of the input data. This also includes reviewing the data so that inaccuracies aren't introduced into the AI model.

Imputation, on the other hand, is a specific type of data cleaning that deals with missing data. Rather than simply discarding missing values, which could lead to a loss of valuable information, imputation involves inputting substitute values where data are incomplete or missing. These substitutes could be estimated using statistical methods such as the mean or median of the complete data or using more complex models that predict missing values based on observed patterns in the data.

Both data cleaning and imputation are important for ensuring that datasets are robust and that the conclusions drawn from AI and machine learning algorithms are valid and trustworthy. However, these processes must be carried out with caution, as they can introduce biases if not handled correctly. For instance, if the method of imputation relies on assumptions that do not hold true for the data, it can lead to misleading analysis and predictive modeling.

Human bias

We all have inherent biases, whether we realize them or not, from societal norms to how we were raised. Human biases are systematic flaws in our cognitive processes, stemming from an over-reliance on a limited set of heuristic principles that simplify complex judgment tasks. These biases often operate below the level of conscious awareness and affect how individuals or groups interpret information, including outputs from AI systems, to make decisions or infer missing information. These biases pervade every level of decision-making, from institutional to individual, throughout the AI lifecycle and in the deployment of AI applications.

Cognitive and perceptual biases are universal, influencing all areas of human activity, not just our interactions with AI. They are inherent aspects of the human psyche. The study of these biases and heuristics spans across disciplines such as cognitive psychology, decision-making science, and behavioral economics. This research delves into various phenomena such as anchoring bias, the availability heuristic, confirmation bias, and framing effects, to name a few.

While heuristics serve as mental shortcuts that facilitate decision-making in complex situations, they can also lead to biased thinking. Despite helping reduce complexity, these shortcuts can skew our judgment. Recognizing these biases doesn't automatically grant us the ability to override them. In the context of AI, understanding the broader implications of human bias is essential, as it influences how AI systems are designed, trained, interpreted, and used[11]. This is why it's imperative to have diverse teams for building and interacting with your AI model.

NIST AI RMF

NIST has created an AI **Risk Management Framework (RMF)**. It focuses on the development of the AI model from conceptualization to deployment. A diagram that explains NIST RMF can be seen in *Figure 14.5*:

---

11   Schwartz, Reva, et al. *Towards a Standard for Identifying and Managing Bias in Artificial Intelligence*, NIST, Mar. 2022, https://nvlpubs.nist.gov/nistpubs/SpecialPublications/NIST.SP.1270.pdf .

NIST AI Risk Management Framework

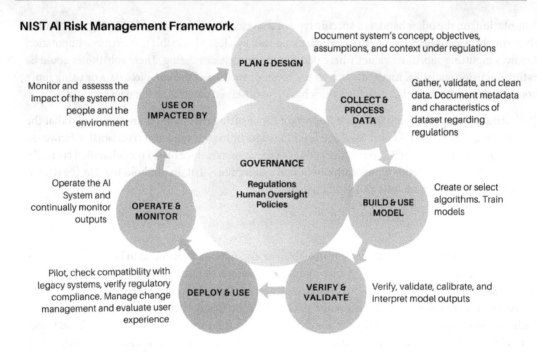

Figure 14.5 – NIST AI RMF[12]

The NIST AI Risk Management Framework covers the development cycle of creating and maintaining an AI system. Most importantly, it shows the importance of human oversight, transparency, and maintaining governance. As I explained earlier, the other compliance your company meets is important as a firm foundation. AI compliance needs to be incorporated into your regular risk management plans and processes. If you are planning on deploying an AI system at your company, then you need an AI policy. From the conception of an AI system through to its deployment and maintenance, you need to do the following:

- Plan and design

  - Document the system

    - Concept

    - Objectives

    - Assumptions

    - Maintain a diagram of the system

12   *Artificial Intelligence Risk Management Framework* (AI RMF 1.0) - NIST, NIST, Jan. 2023, nvlpubs.nist. gov/nistpubs/ai/NIST.AI.100-1.pdf.

- Document the data flows

- Collect and process data

  - Gather

  - Validate

  - Clean

  - Document

    - Metadata

    - Characteristics

- Build and use the model

  - Create algorithms

  - Select algorithms

  - Train the model

- Verify and validate the model outputs

  - Verify

  - Validate

  - Calibrate

  - Interpret model output

- Deploy and use

  - Pilot

  - Check compatibility with legacy systems

  - Verify regulatory compliance

  - Manage change management and

  - Evaluate user experience

- Operate and monitor

  - Operate the AI system

  - Continually monitor inputs

  - Continually monitor outputs

- Use and what it is impacted by

  - Monitor and assess impact

    - Environment

    - People

Summary

This chapter discussed cyber resilience in the age of artificial intelligence (AI) and addressed various concerns related to AI in cybersecurity. It highlights both the positive and negative aspects of AI's impact on cybersecurity.

The positive aspects include how machine learning (ML) and AI can enhance cybersecurity tools and products by introducing capabilities such as predictive analytics, pattern recognition, and automated threat response. AI can also help improve threat analysis and reduce false positives, enhancing the efficiency of cybersecurity efforts.

However, the negative aspects involve the risks associated with widespread AI use. These risks include the potential misuse of AI for hacking, data poisoning, and privacy concerns. It's essential to implement guardrails for AI input ingestion, validate data, and maintain human oversight from development to training and ongoing monitoring to prevent model poisoning.

Responsible AI development, addressing biases in AI systems, and adhering to frameworks such NIST AI RMF (Risk Management Framework) is imperative when developing an AI model. The EU AI Act is an extension of GDPR to AI. It aims to regulate AI development and use it to protect citizen rights and uphold democratic values, including mandatory assessments for high-risk AI systems. Biases in AI, including systematic, statistical, and human biases, need to be addressed during the development of these models. It emphasizes the significance of diverse teams in AI development to mitigate human biases.

NIST AI RMF is a framework covering the development cycle of AI systems, highlighting the need for human oversight, transparency, and governance throughout AI system development and deployment. The framework outlines various stages, from planning and designing to operating and monitoring AI systems.

Overall, the chapter provides insights into the complex relationship between AI and cybersecurity, emphasizing the need for responsible AI practices and thorough risk management.

In an era marked by the proliferation of digital threats, the role of a **Chief Information Security Officer** (**CISO**) has evolved significantly. No longer is cybersecurity merely about building strong defenses; it's about creating an environment where an organization can withstand, adapt to, and recover from cyberattacks. This is the essence of cyber resilience, a concept that has become paramount in safeguarding your company.

Index

Symbols

1Password 25

A

Abnormal Security 54
acceptable use policy (AUP) 56, 83, 122
Address Resolution Protocol (ARP) 179
Advanced Encryption Standard (AES) 116
AI bias 197
  human bias 199
  statistical bias 198, 199
  systematic bias 198
AI cybersecurity 195
  benefits 195
  challenges 196
  unethical uses 197
American Institute of Certified Public
    Accountants (AICPA) 160
anti-malware 51
antivirus 51
application firewall 57
  turning on 58
Argon2 24
Artificial Intelligence Act 192
artificial intelligence (AI) 20, 54, 135, 189

asset inventory 105, 106
  automating 107
asset management
  quick reference 112-114
assets
  classifying 177, 178
  identifying 106
asymmetric encryption 116
asymmetric key 116
availability
  in cloud 71
AWS 48
AWS DDOS attack 73
AWS Lambda 176
AWS X-Ray 176

B

Backblaze 66
Backup-as-a-Service (BaaS) 127
backups 65
  offline backups 65-68
  testing 68, 69
Balloon 24
Bcrypt 24
BigCo 3
  anatomy, of attack 9-12

attack 3, 4

   cross-team co-ordination 4-8

   recovery 8, 9

Binding Operational Directive (BOD) 93

biometric authentication 20

Bitsight 126

Bitwarden 25

Brave 58

browser

   securing 58

bulk electric system (BES) 162

business continuity 71

Business Impact Assessment 40

C

California Consumer Privacy Act (CCPA) 33

Canadian Security Intelligence Service (CSIS) 34

card data environment (CDE) 165

Cardholder Data Environment (CDE) 178

Center for Internet Security (CIS) 136

Center for Internet Security (CIS) Implemented Group (IG) 1 109

Central Intelligence Agency (CIA) 34

change management 107, 108

ChatGPT 188

   limitations 188

   password cracking 19

   securing 188

Chief Information Officer (CIO) 3, 30

Chief Information Security Officer (CISO) 3, 35, 36, 174

CI/CD 99

Cloudflare 60

cloud-native application protection program (CNAPP) 136

cloud-native application-protection program (CNAPP) 9

cloud security posture management (CSPM) 136

Cloud Service Provider (CSP) 175

Cloud Trail 48

Cloud Watch 48

CloudWize 112

CMAC [SP800-38B] 24

CMMC third-party assessment organization (C3PAO) 164

cold site 74

commercial off-the-shelf (COTS) 139

Committee of Sponsoring Organizations of the Treadway Commission (COSO) 165

Common Criteria (CC) 139

Common Vulnerabilities and Exposures (CVEs) 90, 93

   priority 98

   URL 90

Common Vulnerability Scoring System (CVSS) 90-92

Common Vulnerability Scoring System (CVSS) metrics

   attack complexity 97

   attack vector 95, 96

   privileges required 97

Common Weakness Enumeration (CWE) 92, 93

compliance 32, 33, 158

confidentiality, integrity, or availability (CIA) 119

Configuration Control Board (CCB) 110, 111

Controlled Unclassified Information (CUI) 163

Control Objectives for Information and Related Technologies (COBIT) 165

controls
monitoring 47, 48
convolutional neural networks (CNNs) 190
CrashPlan 66
critical assets
quick reference, for securing 183-185
critical-impact risk 44
CrowdStrike 52
cryptographic algorithms 116
cryptographic hashing 69-71
Curricula 79, 80
Customer Relationship
Management (CRM) 174
Customizable SHAKE (cSHAKE) 24
CVE scoring 98
CVSS scoring 91
Cybersecurity and Infrastructure
Security Agency (CISA) 65, 90
KEV Catalog 94, 95
cybersecurity awareness training
products 79-84
Cybersecurity Capability Maturity
Model (C2M2) Tool 32
Cybersecurity Framework (CSF) 32
Cybersecurity Maturity Model
Certification (CMMC) 162-164
versus NIST 800-171 164

D

data classification policies 174
monitoring 178
training 178
data cleaning 198
Datadog 112
data loss prevention (DLP) 68
data loss protection (DLP) 126

data loss, risk
high impact 173
low impact 173
moderate impact 173
data protection 115
quick reference 127-130
Data Security Posture Management
(DSPM) products, features
data classification 177
data discovery 177
remediation and prevention 177
risk assessment and prioritization 177
Deepfakes 21
deep learning (DL) 190
Defender for Office 365 Plan 1 54
defense in depth (DiD) 82, 115
Defense Industrial Base (DIB) 162
disaster recovery 74, 87
redundancy, in architecture 75
testing 76
disaster recovery, roles and responsibilities
Executive Team 75
IT Team 75
Operations Team 76
distributed denial-of-service
(DDOS) attack 57
DNS protection 146
provisions 146
domain controllers 68
Domain Name Servers (DNS) 81, 108
Drata 47
due date 94
due diligence 35, 36
dynamic application security
testing (DAST) 99, 100
advantages 100
limitations 100
Dynatrace 112

E

email phishing 6, 53

Email Security Appliance (ESA) 54

email security scanners 53, 54

encryption 116

    asymmetric encryption 116

    history 116

    symmetric encryption 116

endpoint detection and response
    (EDR) 4, 51, 52, 133

endpoint protection platform (EPP) 8, 51

endpoint security strategy, for company

    requisites 61-63

Enterprise Browser 58

EPP Magic Quadrant 52

Equifax 35

European AI Act 192

    prohibitions 192

Exchange Online Protection (EOP) 54

extended detection and response
    (XDR) 135, 195

    SOAR 135

F

face scan 20

FAIR Materiality Assessment Model 44

Federal Contract Information (FCI) 163

Federal Information Processing
    Standards (FIPS) 139

fingerprint 20

firewall 58

G

General Data Protection Regulation
    (GDPR) 7, 33

generative AI (Gen AI) 190

Guard Duty 48

H

Health and Human Services (HHS) 165

Healthcare Information and
    Management Systems Society
    (HIMSS) Conference 68

Health Information Technology
    for Economic and Clinical
    Health (HITECH) 166

Health Insurance Portability and
    Accountability Act (HIPAA) 33, 36, 165

high-impact risk 43

HITRUST 166

home firewall

    testing 56

hot site 74

I

identification and authentication
    compliance, for company

    quick reference 26

identity and access management
    (IAM) 122, 141

impact level evaluation

    high-impact risk 43, 44

    low-impact risk 43

    moderate-impact risk 43

impact level, PII 119

    examples, to determine 122

    high-impact 120

    low-impact 120

    moderate-impact 120

imputation 199

incident response (IR) 52, 87

incident response (IR) personnel 122

incident response (IR) team 52

information security management
    system (ISMS) 161

Information Technology Governance
    Institute (ITGI) 165

Information Technology Service
    Management (ITSM) 107

Infrastructure-as-a-Service (IaaS) 175, 176

Infrastructure as Code (IaC) 99, 136, 176

insider threats 127

integrated development
    environment(s) (IDE(s) 100

intellectual property (IP) theft 127

interactive application security
    testing (IAST) 99, 100

  advantages 100

  limitations 101

International Standard Organization
    (ISO) 27001 161

  versus SOC2 161

Internet of Things (IoT) 91

Internet of Things (IoT) devices 57, 112, 179

  key takeaways, to secure 58

Intrusion Detection System (IDS)/Intrusion
    Prevention System (IPS) 182

iris scan 20

ISO27001 31

K

Keccak Message Authentication
    Code (KMAC) 24

key performance indicator (KPI) 48

  used, for tracking security program 48, 49

KnowBe4 79

Known Exploited Vulnerabilities (KEV) 93

L

Lambda 176

large language model (LLM) 189

LastPass 25

LastPass hack 55

  key takeaways 56

likelihood evaluation

  criteria 44

linkable data 119

linked data 119

low-impact risk 43

M

machine learning (ML) 135, 189, 190

managed detection and response (MDR) 134

  advantages 134

  limitations 135

man-in-the-middle (MitM) attacks 97

maximum tolerable downtime (MTD) 72

Microsoft 365 (M365) packages 52

Microsoft Defender 54

Microsoft Defender for Endpoint 52

Mimecast 54

Mirai botnet 57

MITRE 90

  URL 90

mobile device management (MDM) 54, 111

moderate-impact risk 43

Multi-Factor Authentication
    (MFA) 17, 60, 174

mutual authentication 140

  using, in TLS session 140-145

N

National Institute of Science and
    Technology (NIST) 32
National Institute of Standards and
    Technology (NIST) 57, 90
National Vulnerability Database (NVD) 90
    URL 90
natural language processing (NLP) 190
network
    visibility 112
network access control (NAC) 56, 112
New Relic 112
Ninjio 79
NIST 800-53 167
NIST 800-53b 33
NIST 800-63-3B
    application security 23-25
    guidelines, for password management 22, 23
NIST 800-171 164
    versus CMMC 164
NIST AI RMF 199, 200
NIST CSF Maturity tool 49
NIST Cybersecurity Framework
    reference link 45
NIST IR 8286 risk management cycle
    context identification 41
    monitoring, evaluation and adjustment 42
    risk analysis 42
    risk identification 41
    risk prioritization 42
    risk response planning and execution 42
NIST scoring 44, 45
NIST security-focused change
    management 108
    configuration changes, controlling 110, 111
    configurations, identifying and
        implementing 109, 110

monitoring 111
planning 108
Nortel hack 34
North American Electric Reliability
    Corporation Critical Infrastructure
    Protection (NERC-CIP) 161, 162

O

Office 365 (O365) 54
offline backups 65-68
Okta hack 58-61
open source software (OSS) 101
Open Worldwide Application Security
    Project (OWASP) 101
Open Worldwide Application Security
    Project (OWASP) Top 10 89
Operating System (OS) 175
Operational Technology (OT) 91
Orion 124

P

palm scan 20
ParallelHash [SP 800-185] 24
passphrase 22
password-based key derivation function 24
passwordless 21
password manager 21, 25
    1Password 25
    Bitwarden 25
    LastPass 25
passwords 18
Payment Card Industry Data Security
    Standard (PCI-DSS) 165
Payment Card Industry (PCI) 36
PBKDF2 24
PCI compliance 9

personal information (PI) 118

personally identifiable information
(PII) 3, 117-119

  data classification, characteristics 120, 121

  example, to determine impact level 122

  impact-level determination 122, 123

pharming scams 53

phishing 6, 53, 80

phishing simulator 80

Platform-as-a-Service (PaaS) 175, 176

point-in-time (PIT) audit 87

point-to-point encryption (P2PE) 165

principle of least privilege (PoLP) 127

Proofpoint 54

protected health information (PHI) 165

public key infrastructure (PKI) 115

Q

quality assurance (QA) tests 101

R

R 133

ransomware attack 6

recovery point objective (RPO) 72

recovery time objective (RTO) 72

recurrent neural networks (RNNs) 190

RedSeal Stratus 112

remote code executable (RCE) 95

remote desktop (RDP) 6

remote work

  moving to 55

Renovate 101

responsible AI 191, 192

  key aspects 191, 192

risk assessment 41

  critical-impact risk 44

  impact and likelihood 43

  likelihood evaluation criteria 44

  NIST scoring 44, 45

risk management program

  requisites 49, 50

risk matrix 46

risk register 39

risks

  example 40

  identifying 40

risk treatment 46, 47

  acceptance 46

  mitigation 46

  remediation 46

  transfer 46

Role-Based Access Control (RBAC) 122, 178

RSA SANS CISO boot camp 52

Rubrik 66

S

SANS 30

Sarbanes-Oxley Act (SOX) 164

Scrypt 24

Secure AI framework (SAIF) 193, 194

Secure Controls Framework (SCF) 167

Secureframe 47

Secure Hash Algorithm 3 (SHA-3) 24

Securities and Exchange
Commission (SEC) 164

security 84

  governance and management 86

  materiality assessment 85

  third-party involvement 86

Security and Exchange
Commission (SEC) 36

security and risk management 39

  risks, identifying 40

security assertion markup
language (SAML) 139
security awareness training 77-79, 86
security baseline 157
    creating 167, 168
    quick reference, for creating 168-171
Security Operations Centers (SOCs) 195
security policies 29, 31
security policies, for company
    requisites 36, 37
SecurityScorecard 126
Security Technical Implementation
Guides (STIGs) 110, 136
segmentation 179, 180
server message block (SMB) 6
Server Message Block (SMB) version 1 181
service providers (SPs) 86
SHA-1 69
SHA-256 69, 71
shared responsibility model 176
single sign-on (SSO) 60
smart card 21
smishing scams 53
SMS 21
SOAR 135
SOC 1 164
SOC2 Type I 31, 160
SOC2 Type II 31, 160
social security numbers (SSNs) 35, 118
Software-as-a-Service (SaaS) 175
software composition analysis (SCA) 101
software-defined perimeter (SDP) 53
software evaluation cybersecurity
awareness training 79
software firewalls 58
software vulnerabilities 89
SolarWinds attack 124
Sony hack 180, 181

static application security testing
(SAST) 99, 123
    advantages 99
    disadvantages 99
subdomain 81
subdomain takeover 81
subnetting 179, 180
succession planning
    in cybersecurity 73
Supervisory Control and Data
Acquisition (SCADA) 91
symmetric encryption 116
symmetric key 116
System and Organizational
Controls (SOC) 2 31, 160
    audits 160
    versus ISO 27001 161
System and Organizational Controls
(SOC) 2, Trust Services Criteria
    availability 160
    confidentiality 160
    privacy 160
    processing integrity 160
    security 160

T

tabletops 76
Template.net 30
third-party risk management 123
    critical vendors 125
    data loss protection 126
    insider threats 127
    SolarWinds attack 124
    staff, training 126
    vendor management contract
        clauses 124, 125
    vendor management policy 124

vendor risk rating 126

threat intelligence (TI) 91

time-based one-time passwords (TOTPs) 21

TLS session

    mutual authentication, using 140-145

    working 139, 140

top-level domain (TLD) 81

traditional firewalls 58

Transparent Data Encryption (TDE) 118

two-factor authentication
    (2FA) 11, 17, 18, 55

    something you are 20

    something you have 21

    something you know 18, 19

U

Universal Authentication
    Framework (UAF) 21

V

Vanta 47

Veeam 66, 127

vendor management contract
    clauses 124, 125

vendor management policy 124

vendor risk rating 126

virtual CISO (vCISO) 79, 80

virtual machines (VMs) 99

virtual private network (VPN) 53

vishing scams 53

Voice over Internet Protocol (VoIP) 53

vulnerability 90

    prioritizing 94

vulnerability scans

    starting with 98

W

warm site 74

X

X.509 certificate 21

Z

zero trust 56, 138

    DNS protection 146

    quick reference 146-155

    versus software-defined perimeter 138, 139

Zero-Trust Roadmap 146

`packtpub.com`

Subscribe to our online digital library for full access to over 7,000 books and videos, as well as industry leading tools to help you plan your personal development and advance your career. For more information, please visit our website.

Why subscribe?

- Spend less time learning and more time coding with practical eBooks and Videos from over 4,000 industry professionals
- Improve your learning with Skill Plans built especially for you
- Get a free eBook or video every month
- Fully searchable for easy access to vital information
- Copy and paste, print, and bookmark content

Did you know that Packt offers eBook versions of every book published, with PDF and ePub files available? You can upgrade to the eBook version at `packtpub.com` and as a print book customer, you are entitled to a discount on the eBook copy. Get in touch with us at `customercare@packtpub.com` for more details.

At `www.packtpub.com`, you can also read a collection of free technical articles, sign up for a range of free newsletters, and receive exclusive discounts and offers on Packt books and eBooks.

Other Books You May Enjoy

If you enjoyed this book, you may be interested in these other books by Packt:

Cybersecurity Architect's Handbook

Lester Nichols

ISBN: 978-1-80323-584-4

- Get to grips with the foundational concepts and basics of cybersecurity
- Understand cybersecurity architecture principles through scenario-based examples
- Navigate the certification landscape and understand key considerations for getting certified
- Implement zero-trust authentication with practical examples and best practices
- Find out how to choose commercial and open source tools
- Address architecture challenges, focusing on mitigating threats and organizational governance

Cloud Forensics Demystified

Ganesh Ramakrishnan | Mansoor Haqanee

ISBN: 978-1-80056-441-1

- Explore the essential tools and logs for your cloud investigation
- Master the overall incident response process and approach
- Familiarize yourself with the MITRE ATT&CK framework for the cloud
- Get to grips with live forensic analysis and threat hunting in the cloud
- Learn about cloud evidence acquisition for offline analysis
- Analyze compromised Kubernetes containers
- Employ automated tools to collect logs from M365

Packt is searching for authors like you

If you're interested in becoming an author for Packt, please visit authors.packtpub.com and apply today. We have worked with thousands of developers and tech professionals, just like you, to help them share their insight with the global tech community. You can make a general application, apply for a specific hot topic that we are recruiting an author for, or submit your own idea.

Share Your Thoughts

Now you've finished *A CISO Guide to Cyber Resilience*, we'd love to hear your thoughts! Scan the QR code below to go straight to the Amazon review page for this book and share your feedback or leave a review on the site that you purchased it from.

https://packt.link/r/1835466923

Your review is important to us and the tech community and will help us make sure we're delivering excellent quality content.

Download a free PDF copy of this book

Thanks for purchasing this book!

Do you like to read on the go but are unable to carry your print books everywhere?

Is your e-book purchase not compatible with the device of your choice?

Don't worry!, Now with every Packt book, you get a DRM-free PDF version of that book at no cost.

Read anywhere, any place, on any device. Search, copy, and paste code from your favorite technical books directly into your application.

The perks don't stop there, you can get exclusive access to discounts, newsletters, and great free content in your inbox daily

Follow these simple steps to get the benefits:

1. Scan the QR code or visit the following link:

https://packt.link/free-ebook/9781835466926

2. Submit your proof of purchase.
3. That's it! We'll send your free PDF and other benefits to your email directly.